⭐ The Confederate General ⭐

Volume 1

⋆ *The Confederate General* ⋆

Volume 1

Adams, Daniel W. to Cobb, Howell

William C. Davis, Editor

Julie Hoffman, Assistant Editor

A Publication of the
National Historical Society

Library of Congress Cataloging-in-Publication Data
The Confederate General / William C. Davis,
   editor; Julie Hoffman, assistant editor.
     p. cm.
   Contents: v. 1. Adams, Daniel W. to Cobb, Howell
   ISBN 0-918678-63-3 (v. 1) : $29.95
     1. United States—History—Civil War, 1861-1865—
Biography. 2. Confederate States of America. Army—Biography. 3. Generals—Confederate States of America—Biography. 4. Generals—Southern States—Biography. 5. Generals—United States —Biography.
I. Davis, William C., 1946-   .   II. Hoffman, Julie.
   E467.C76   1991
   973.7' 42' 0922—dc20   91-8508
   (B)   CIP

Editorial Assistant, Eleanor Mauck
Designed by Art Unlimited
Printed in the United States of America

✮ Contents ✮

✷ *Introduction* ✷

They are without a doubt the most romantic characters in American military history, and certainly the ones most studied in the story of the Civil War. The general officers of the Confederate States of America have so captured the imagination of Americans—and of hosts around the world—that their legend and lore have far overshadowed the careers and achievements of almost all other military leaders of all other American conflicts.

No doubt in part this is due to the irresistable romance of the Civil War itself, and especially the lure of the "Lost Cause." Then too, these generals—those that survived the war—left behind a mammoth legacy of papers and memoirs that tell, and often exaggerate and romanticize, their story. Indeed, having lost the war, the old Confederates largely won the postwar battle of the books, virtually overwhelming their old Northern foes by capturing and holding the public imagination. The picture that most Americans have today of what happened in 1861–1865 is based heavily on the literary legacy of these old warriors.

Given this fact, it is all the more surprising how little we really know about many of them. After more than a century, there is still discussion even as to who really was and was not a general. Lee, Stuart, Stonewall Jackson, are almost household words. But who knows anything of Danville Leadbetter, or Camille Armand Jules Marie de Polignac? Who other than a few historians and buffs can name the senior ranking general of the Confederate Army, Samuel Cooper? Who knows that General Frank Armstrong actually fought in both Union and Confederate Armies during the war?

An important step in redressing this great dearth of information about these men was taken back in 1959 with the publication of Ezra Warner's landmark *Generals in Grey*. In brief 200-word essays, he presented sketches of each of the 425 men he accepted as having been generals for the South. Better yet, each sketch was accompanied by a portrait. The biographies were

necessarily brief; nevertheless Warner's book quickly became a standard reference, and still is today, as it remains the most easily used desktop quick reference on these men.

Yet it has its weaknesses, some inherent, and others only revealed by the passage of time. Given the constraints of space, Warner could hardly include more than a few bare facts and dates in his brief sketches, leaving most students anxious for more. Unfortunately, Warner also based most of his essays on unreliable old secondary sources, which meant that he incorporated erroneous dates and other material into many of his profiles. As for the portraits, actual photographs for many of the generals were not located when he published his book, requiring the use of lithographs and other artworks, while in a few cases, he misidentified the individuals in the portraits. Though these shortcomings have increasingly limited the usefulness of *Generals in Gray*, they still have not reduced the stature of the work as a whole.

But scholars and students do want and need more, hence *The Confederate General*. The editorial rationale is simple. In a six-volume series, it presents 1,000–1,500 word biographies of each general. A team of more than twenty of the nation's leading Civil War historians, after meticulous research in a wide range of sources, present not just facts and dates, but also interpretive evaluations of their subjects where justified. To support their work, an exhaustive search has been conducted through an often ignored resource, the compiled service records of each general in the records of the National Archives in Washington, D.C. Mitchell Yockelson and Bryce L. Suderow have checked each general's original records to establish definitively his dates of appointment to rank, senatorial confirmation if received, and the effective date of rank, the dates so often in error in Warner. And finally, a brief bibliography of useful sources for further study is provided.

Then come the photographs. Most generals sat for

at least one while in uniform, and some like P. G. T. Beauregard seemingly spent much of the war in front of a camera. Where Warner published but a single portrait, regardless of its composition, *The Confederate General* presents every known photographic portrait in uniform that can be located. Thus, while for some officers it shows nothing new, for others it offers a virtual gallery, revealing that general's progression through the ranks and in some cases showing the effects of the war up on him.

Many of these portraits are previously unpublished, and come from public and private collections all across the country. Each is credited to its source. Furthermore, careful study has been applied to make certain that age-old misidentifications are corrected, while equal attention has been expended to try to avoid creating new errors. In cases where an unidentified photograph "looks like " a general, but there is no supporting evidence to help corroborate such an identification, only the most patently obvious examples have been included, and on these the captions make it clear that the identification is conditional. In many cases where the general sat for several portraits at the same time, the reader will detect only slight variations in pose. Nevertheless, every pose has been included, for each image has something to teach us.

Also evident to the observer will be the wide variation of insignia. Confederate regulations specifically prescribed what a general officer should wear. On his collar he should have three stars, the center one slightly larger than those on either side, and all three to be within a wreath. Furthermore, on his tunic or blouse there should be two rows of eight buttons, placed in two's. On his sleeves he should wear coiled braid in gold needlework, four rows or wales in width. Further regulations covered kepi decorations and trouser stripes, but these seldom show in any portraits.

It does not take long looking at these portraits to see just how idiosyncratic generals were in their observance of these regulations. A few generals never wore uniforms at all. Others, when promoted to generalship, continued to wear the button or collar arrangement of their previous rank. Some even continued wearing their old prewar United States Army of state militia uniforms, including even shoulder straps or epaulettes. Even high ranking men like Robert E. Lee and Joseph E. Johnston habitually wore three stars with no wreath, the insignia for a colonel, but a rank

they never even held in the Confederate Army. Meanwhile, though regulations never provided for any uniform distinction in the four grades of general—brigadier, major, lieutenant, and full general—many officers adopted the Union military regulation for major generals by changing their coat buttons to two rows of nine, arranged in three's.

What all this means is that these men, from a variety of causes, were remarkably informal about their uniforms and regulations. Part of this may stem from wartime scarcity and the fact that they were often too busy to take time to find a qualified seamstress or tailor to adjust uniforms for changes in rank. A result is that it is very difficult to pinpoint the time a photo was taken from the apparent rank displayed on the officer's uniform, a difficulty compounded by the fact that some colonels put wreaths around their collar stars when they were assigned to brigade command—a brigadier general's customary position—even though they were never actually promoted to generalship. As much as possible, attempts have been made to offer an approximate idea of when an image was made, especially if several photos are available for an officer. At the same time, the location of the sitting and the name of the photographer is given when known, though for most images this information is long lost, and even many surviving portraits are in fact postwar copies. Thus while they carry photographers' backmarks on the prints, these are not the original artists.

Speaking of artists, it will also be observed that a number of portraits have been retouched sometime in the past, even to the point of painting uniforms over civilian clothing. Most of this was done prior to 1911, probably by artists working for the Review of Reviews Company when it published its monumental *Photographic History of the Civil War*, edited by Francis T. Miller. Much of this work is sufficiently clumsy that it is obvious. Nevertheless, where there is any doubt, suspicions of retouching are mentioned in the captions.

Of course, for all of the wonderful new portraits brought to light, others remain either unfound as yet, or else lost forever. There are some generals like Addley Gladden and Ben McCulloch who almost certainly never even wore a uniform prior to their early deaths. There are other officers whose service was so short, or in such a remote area, that they never had a chance to sit for a photographer in uniform. And for others, housefires and the ravages of time have destroyed forever images that were taken. Thus, for some of the men in these volumes, the civilian portraits are all that we will ever find. And for those for whom uniformed poses survive, certainly there are others out there that were not located, and that may come to light after publication. Thus these books are designed in such a fashion that future editions will allow substitution of uniformed poses when they come to light, or to add additional poses as discovered. Furthermore, the sixth and final volume will contain an addenda including anything new that appears right up to the last moment before publication.

Inevitably some will question the criteria used for deciding those men to include and those to exclude. Basically the same qualifications used by Warner will be used in *The Confederate General*. All officers appointed for generalship by President Jefferson Davis and nominated/confirmed and by the Senate qualify. So do officers appointed by Davis while the Senate was not in session, even though the Senate might later reject the nomination, or Davis himself might have chosen not to nominate after the fact. There are also cases of officers nominated or appointed by Davis, but upon whose nominations the Senate never acted at all. Also some men were killed in battle after their appointment, but before the Senate convened for Davis to nominate them.

All of the above criteria allow 425 men to fill the pages that follow. Yet there were others known in their own time and later as "generals," even wearing the uniform of that rank and exercising commensurate command. In the Trans-Mississippi Department, General E. Kirby Smith needed generals badly, yet it took far too long for communications with Richmond to get the men promoted. Consequently, he appointed several men to brigadiership on his own, later asking Davis to nominate or appoint them, but Davis did not so act. A special section in the final volume will cover these men who, though not regular Confederate generals by common definition, still deserve recognition. And in that same volume will appear a few other officers who somehow defy neat description, men who wore the uniform of a general but who seem not to have been nominated or appointed to such rank by any official authority. State militia generals, however, will not be included, nor will those officers who apparently "promoted" themselves after the war in

their memoirs and recollections, or who held general rank and wore a general's uniform as officers in the postwar United Confederate Veterans. In this last volume will also appear a selection of photographs of men in general's uniform who cannot be identified.

With regard to the sources used by the historians preparing the essays, only those that provide special help or information on an individual are listed in the brief bibliographies. Standard works such as the *Dictionary of American Biography*, the U.S. War Department's *War of the Rebellion: Official Records of the Union and Confederate Armies*, and John Wakelyn's *Biographical Dictionary of the Confederacy*, are not listed, and the reader may simply take it for granted that these may have been consulted, especially the last three. Neither are the individual compiled service records in the National Archives specifically cited. It is sufficient to say that each and every one has been consulted, and of course they all contain vital information.

Much more could be said about these extraordinary men. But having said this much, now it is time to let their faces and their deeds speak for themselves.

William C. Davis

✳ *Daniel Weisiger Adams* ✳

To date, no photograph of Adams has come to light. This portrait dates from the 1850s. (Warner, *Generals in Gray*)

Daniel W. Adams was born in Frankfort, Kentucky, on May 1, 1821, and both he and his older brother, William Wirt Adams, were destined to become Confederate generals. The family moved to Natchez, Mississippi, in 1825, where Adams' father became a prominent politician. His younger son attended the University of Virginia from 1838 to 1842, then returned to Mississippi, where he read law and gained admission to the state bar. He killed James Hagan in a duel in 1843, after the Vicksburg editor wrote critically of Adams' father. A jury later acquitted Adams of charges for murder. He served later in the Mississippi legislature as senator from Jackson until 1852, then moved to New Orleans to enter that state's bar.

In early 1861, Governor Thomas O. Moore appointed Adams as one of three members of a military board to get the state on a war footing. Then upon the formation of the 1st Louisiana Regular Infantry on February 5, Adams became the unit's lieutenant colonel. The regiment transferred to Confederate service on March 13 and received orders in April to report for duty at Pensacola, Florida. When its Colonel Adley H. Gladden was promoted to brigadier general on September 30, Adams became the regiment's commander, with promotion to full colonel on October 30, 1861. The 1st Louisiana went to Corinth, Mississippi, in late February 1862, and Adams and his men served in Gladden's Brigade during the Battle of Shiloh. When Gladden received a mortal wound on the morning of April 6, Adams succeeded to brigade command

and led his men in pushing back the Union troops on his front, who came from Benjamin M. Prentiss' Division. That afternoon, while directing a charge on the Hornet's Nest, Adams received a wound in the head that resulted in the loss of his right eye. Adams was promoted to brigadier general on May 23, 1862, to rank from that date, and accepted his commission on June 14. In August, he was given command of a brigade of Louisiana troops in J. Patton Anderson's Division of the Army of Mississippi, leading it in the Battle of Perryville, Kentucky, on October 8 where he received praise for his gallantry from Major General William J. Hardee.

Anderson's Division was broken up in mid-December, and Adams' brigade joined John C. Breckinridge's division. On the afternoon of December 31, at the Battle of Stones River, Adams and his men made an unsupported attack on Union troops holding an area known as the Round Forest. He received a second wound during this unsuccessful assault, and severe enemy artillery and musketry fire drove his troops back. He had returned to duty by June 1863 and commanded his brigade during operations in central Mississippi in June and July. On September 20, at the Battle of Chickamauga, the brigade formed the extreme right of the army as it attacked Union General George H. Thomas' corps. At first the Louisianians drove the enemy back, but Federal reinforcements forced them to retreat. In the fighting, Adams received a third wound and fell into enemy hands. His corps commander, Daniel Harvey Hill, wrote of Adams' conduct during the battle: "It was difficult for me to decide which the most to admire, his courage in the field or his unparalleled cheerfulness under suffering." Adams was given command of a cavalry brigade in northern Alabama in 1864 after his exchange and recovery. On May 23, he received command of the District of North Alabama in the Department of Alabama, Mississippi, and East Louisiana. The District of Central Alabama was added to Adams' command after September 24. His main duties consisted of gathering supplies, chasing deserters, and putting down pockets of Unionist sympathizers. Adams' men, mostly Alabama state troops, occasionally helped repel enemy advances in northern Alabama, and cooperated with the Army of Tennessee in its campaign through the area as John Bell Hood prepared to send his forces into Tennessee. Adams was offered command of a division under Nathan Bedford Forrest in January

1865 but declined the appointment because he anticipated receiving orders to report for duty in the Trans-Mississippi Department. However, when the District of Alabama was created on March 11, 1865, Adams became its commander. Consisting of all of the state not included in the District of the Gulf, he led a command of Alabama state troops under Forrest in opposing Union General James H. Wilson's raid into Alabama in March and April, and his men fought in the Battle of Selma on April 2 and in an engagement in Columbus, Georgia, on April 16, shortly after he supervised the evacuation of Montgomery on the night of April 11. Adams received his parole at Meridian, Mississippi, on May 9, 1865. After a brief visit to England, he returned to New Orleans and again began practicing law. There he died on June 13, 1872, and was buried near his brother in Jackson, Mississippi. Though he had no military training or experience prior to the war, Adams performed capably as a brigade commander in the Army of Tennessee. His three wounds testify as well as any words to his bravery and willingness to lead his men in battle.

Arthur W. Bergeron, Jr.

✶ John Adams ✶

John Adams was born in Nashville, Tennessee, on July 1, 1825, to an Irish immigrant father who came to the United States in 1814. Little is known of Adams' early life. He entered West Point in 1841 and graduated twenty-fifth in the class of 1846. Commissioned a 2d lieutenant in the 1st Dragoons, Adams served in the Mexican War under Capt. Philip Kearny and was a brevet 1st lieutenant for gallantry at the Battle of Santa Cruz de Rosalea.

From 1850–51 Adams served at various outposts in New Mexico and skirmished with Indians. Promoted to 1st lieutenant, he transferred in 1852 to Minnesota, where he married Georgia McDougal, the daughter of a prominent army physician. In 1853 Adams served as aide-de-camp to the Minnesota governor with the rank of lieutenant colonel in the state militia. This duty proved short-lived, however, and 1854–56 saw him back on active duty in Kansas, New Mexico, and Colorado. In 1856 he was promoted to captain and spent the next two years on recruiting duty.

The 1861 secession crisis found Adams with Company F, 1st Dragoons, serving as commandant of Fort Crook, California. He resigned his commission on May 27 and traveled east to offer his services to the Confederacy. General Winfield Scott was determined to stop such treasonous activity, and on August 5, 1861, Scott wrote Secretary of State William Seward that Adams was arriving in New York City and "I think it desireable that [he]...be arrested and held a political prisoner, as I do not doubt that he designs to take service in the rebel army against us" Fortunately Adams heard of Scott's intentions and slipped into the South safely. Quickly gaining a commission as a captain of Confederate cavalry, Adams was placed in command of Memphis, Tennessee.

Among Adams' duties in Memphis were the housing, transferring, and exchanging of Union prisoners. Records do not document a failure on Adams' part to carry out his duties, but Major General Leonidas Polk complained to Albert S. Johnston on November 28 that Adams was lacking in ability. Polk wrote, "His habits, I fear, are bad, and this leads to other things not in keeping with the best interests of the service." The general recommended that Adams

---

The uniform on this photograph of Adams is quite clearly an artist's addition. No genuine uniformed portrait has surfaced. (Museum of the Confederacy, Richmond)

be promoted to regimental commander and put into the field. It is unclear to what shortcomings Polk was referring, but in April 1862 Adams was promoted to colonel and was given a brigade of cavalry operating in north Alabama and middle Tennessee. During the rest of 1862 he served as acting brigadier general.

Throughout May 1862 Adams' Brigade skirmished with Union patrols and in one clash it captured eight black prisoners. In his report Adams noted, "The negroes I shall have tried by a military commission, and, if it is found that any were taken with arms in their hands, it may be necessary to inflict summary punishment" Despite this ominous threat, there is no record of what happened to the prisoners.

On June 4, 1862, a Union force surprised Adams' men at Sweeden Cove, twelve miles northwest of Jasper, Tennessee. Adams' pickets were captured, his men routed, and wagons seized. One Union officer declared, "They fled in the wildest disorder, strewing the ground for miles with guns, pistols, and swords." The Yankees claimed Adams escaped "without sword, hat or horse," and that his command fled the forty-three miles to Chattanooga without stopping. Adams never wrote a report of the affair, but his superior, Major General E. Kirby Smith, acknowledged that "General Adams" lost about one hundred men.

By August 1862 Adams was in command of Columbus, Mississippi, site of a valuable Confederate arsenal. He kept this position until January 1863, when he oversaw the dismantling and removal of the arsenal, and then went to command the Fourth Military District, headquartered at Jackson, Mississippi. There he again supervised the exchanging of prisoners and aided in the chase of Union raider Benjamin Grierson in April. In May he watched over the removal of valuable railroad stock when Grant's army approached the city.

Adams' commission as brigadier general dated from December 29, 1862, but sources conflict over the date of his appointment. In May 1863 Joseph E. Johnston wired Adjutant General Samuel Cooper concerning the promotion, stating Adams was worried that it may not have been confirmed. "I hope," Johnston added, "the apprehension is groundless. He is very valuable."

Apparently he was first appointed on January 9, 1863, but the Senate failed to confirm him. His reappointment on May 23 was confirmed, however, and Adams took command of Lloyd Tilghman's Mississippi infantry brigade that same month when the officer died. Sometimes serving as mounted infantry, Adams' Brigade was part of Johnston's force that operated between Vicksburg and Jackson throughout the Vicksburg Campaign. For the next year, Adams shifted his headquarters between Vicksburg and Meridian. In the spring of 1864, Adams' brigade, as part of William Loring's Division in Polk's Corps, joined Johnston at Resaca, Georgia, for the beginning phase of the Atlanta Campaign. His brigade is mentioned in several reports of skirmishing, but apparently Adams was not present with the brigade through parts of the campaign, and his absence is not explained.

When John Bell Hood invaded Tennessee to try and draw Sherman out of Georgia, Adams' brigade led the advance and captured a large number of Union prisoners at Dalton, Georgia. At Franklin on November 30, 1864, he fought his last fight. Early in the battle Adams was severely wounded in the right arm but refused to leave the field. "No," he replied when urged to go to the rear, "I am going to see my men through." Personally leading a desperate charge against the Union line, Adams galloped up to the enemy breastworks. A Union officer who witnessed the attack wrote a letter to Adams' widow after the war describing his death. "General Adams," he said, "rode up to our works and, cheering his men, made an attempt to leap his horse over them. The horse fell upon top of the embankment and the general was caught under him, pierced with bullets." Shot nine times, Adams lay dying as the Confederate assault was beaten back. His shattered brigade had lost 450 men. Immediately a number of Union soldiers came to his aid and dragged him from beneath the dead horse. Conscious and lucid, Adams asked for water. One Yankee handed him a canteen while another made a pillow from an armful of cotton retrieved from a nearby gin. Adams thanked them for their kindness and when the soldiers expressed their sorrow at his wounding, he exclaimed, "It is the fate of a soldier to die for his country." He soon died and was buried in Pulaski, Tennessee.

Terry Jones

William W. Adams, photographed probably in 1864 by a Mobile artist, and taken from a group photograph now lost. (Alabama Department of Archives and History, Montgomery)

⋆ *William Wirt Adams* ⋆

William Wirt Adams was born on March 22, 1819, in Frankfort, Kentucky, but when he was six the family moved to Natchez, Mississippi. After attending college in Bardstown, Kentucky, William returned to Mississippi in 1839 and enlisted as a private in a regiment bound for Texas. Adams served as adjutant of the unit and briefly fought against the Indians in northeast Texas before returning to Mississippi that fall, following the death of his father. In 1846 he was a sugar planter in Iberville, Louisiana, but upon his marriage to Sallie Huger Mayrant of Jackson, Mississippi, in 1850, he returned to Mississippi once more. Between 1850 and 1861 he was a successful planter and banker in the Vicksburg-Jackson area, and won election to the state legislature in 1858 and 1860.

When his adopted state seceded, Adams served as a commissioner to Louisiana whose purpose was to secure the secession of that state. In February 1861, President Jefferson Davis offered him the position of postmaster general, but Adams declined because of business interests. In June he began organizing a unit initially known as the 1st Mississippi Cavalry but which was officially redesignated by the secretary of war on December 24 as "Wirt Adams Regiment of Cavalry."

Mustered into Confederate service in Memphis, Tennessee, in August, the regiment was ordered to Columbus, Kentucky, in September, and to Bowling Green in October. In February 1862, the regiment covered the Confederate withdrawal from Kentucky to Corinth, Mississippi. Adams' regiment fought with the infantry on the extreme right at the Battle of Shiloh and remained in the vicinity to observe the enemy when the Confederate army withdrew to Corinth. During the Union investment of that town, the regiment served on outpost duty, participated in a raid on the Nashville and Chattanooga Railroad, and engaged in several skirmishes.

In late July and again in late August–early September, Adams participated in a raid into West Tennessee. He fought at Bolivar on August 30 and on September 1, at Britton's Lane, near Denmark, his regiment charged down a narrow lane and captured an enemy battery posted on a hill after three other regiments had failed. With his own and an Arkansas regiment, Adams covered the withdrawal following the Battle of Iuka and, on September 17 near Burnsville, captured a train loaded with Union reinforcements. During the unsuccessful Corinth campaign, Adams' charge at the Hatchie bridge on October 4 probably saved Major General Earl Van Dorn's only line of retreat, which he desperately needed and used the following day.

The regiment next served along the Mississippi River in Washington County, Mississippi, where Adams labored to prevent enemy raids and to warn of any movement down river against Vicksburg. In February 1863 the regiment patrolled the river between Warrenton and Grand Gulf. In March in contested Acting Rear Admiral David D. Porter's attempts to reach Yazoo City by way of Deer Creek. During Union Colonel Benjamin Grierson's raid in late April and early May, Adams commanded all the cavalry south of Jackson. Although he failed to capture Grierson, the stubborn resistance by part of his old regiment at Union Church on April 28 forced Grierson to abandon his plan of linking up with Union forces at Natchez and to attempt to reach Baton Rouge.

Adams' forces were quickly redirected to the Union landing at Grand Gulf in an effort to block any movement toward Jackson. His first encounter with the enemy occurred at Fourteen Mile Creek on May 12, where he delayed their advance for three hours. Adams kept Lieutenant General John C. Pemberton correctly informed of enemy movements prior to the Battle of Baker's Creek on May 16. When Pemberton withdrew to Vicksburg, he left Adams to harass the enemy's rear, which the latter did, particularly at Bear Creek and Mechanicsburg. During late June and early July, Adams opposed Major General William T. Sherman's advance against Jackson.

On September 28, 1863, Adams was commissioned a brigadier general for his services during the Vicksburg Campaign, to rank from September 25, though the Senate only confirmed it the following January 25. That same day Union Major General Ulysses S. Grant reported that Adams' men "infest the country from about Rodney [Mississippi] to Port Hudson [Louisiana]." Adams' cavalrymen appeared to be everywhere, skirmishing with Union expeditions, disrupting Union shipping on the Mississippi, destroying cotton, and transporting small arms across the Mississippi to Lieutenant General Edmund Kirby Smith. In December Adams received orders to threaten southeastern Louisiana if Major General Richard Taylor wished to advance in southwestern Louisiana. Adams promptly occupied Bayou Sara on the Mississippi and skirmished before Port Hudson on January 8, 1864. After threatening Baton Rouge, Adams' men hurried to Mississippi and were engaged near Natchez on the twenty-fourth.

In February, Adams was ordered to contest Sherman's movement toward Meridian. Much of the Confederate success in thwarting Sherman's advance was due to Adams, whom Major General Stephen O. Lee reported deserved his thanks for his "distinguished gallantry on the field and the able management" of his command. During the Union expedition up the Yazoo River in mid-April, Adams' men engaged the enemy at and near Mechanicsburg and captured the U. S. gunboat *Petrel* near Yazoo City. Adams managed to remove eight 24-pounder cannon before burning the vessel. During the next few months his command would engage in numerous skirmishes throughout Mississippi.

Late in 1864 his brigade formed part of Lieutenant General Nathan Bedford Forrest's command and it remained under Forrest until the end of the war. He defeated a Union brigade near Eutaw on April 5, 1865, one of the last Confederate victories. Adams surrendered his command near Ramsey Station, Sumpter County, Alabama, on May 4, 1865, delivered his farewell address on the 6th, and received his parole on the 12th at Gainesville. Despite numerous encounters with the enemy, he was never wounded.

After the war Adams retired to Vicksburg and labored for that city's economic recovery. In 1880 he received an appointment as state revenue agent but resigned three years later to accept an appointment by President Grover Cleveland to become postmaster of Jackson. On May 1, 1888, Adams encountered John Martin, a local editor, walking along a street. Martin had criticized Adams in his paper and the two faced each other with weapons now. When the smoke cleared, both men had been killed. Adams is buried in Jackson. His brother, Daniel Weisiger Adams, also served as a brigadier general in the Confederate army.

Lawrence L. Hewitt

Evans, Clement A., ed. *Confederate Military History*. Atlanta, 1899.

Rowland, Dunbar, ed. *Mississippi: Comprising Sketches of Counties, Towns, Events, Institutions, and Persons, Arranged in Cyclopedic Form*. 1907. Spartanburg, S.C. 1976.

Wakelyn, Jon L. *Biographical Dictionary of the Confederacy*. Westport, Conn., and London, England, 1977.

A slightly variant view of Adams, again circa 1864-1865. (Museum of
the Confederacy, Richmond)

E.P. Alexander's insignia in this portrait indicate a colonel's rank, though it is quite possible that, like several other generals, he was informal in observing regulations requiring a wreath around his stars. The arrangement of his tunic buttons also indicates a colonel. Thus this image probably dates from 1863 or earlier. (George H. and Katherine M. Davis Collection, Tulane University Library, New Orleans)

✴ *Edward Porter Alexander* ✴

Edward Porter Alexander, whose remarkably varied Confederate career extended literally from Manassas to Appomattox, was born in Washington, Georgia, on May 26, 1835. Afforded all the advantages available to members of Georgia's wealthy planting elite, Alexander received excellent instruction from private tutors before entering West Point in 1853. He graduated third in the class of 1857, took a commission as brevet 2d lieutenant of engineers, and immediately joined the faculty at the Academy. Marked from the beginning as an officer of great promise, he interrupted his teaching duties in the spring of 1858 to accompany an expedition to reinforce Albert Sidney Johnston's column sent against the Mormons in Utah the previous year. He returned to West Point in October 1858, received promotion to 2d lieutenant on the tenth of that month, and in the fall and winter of 1859–60 assisted Surgeon Albert J. Myer in developing the "wig-wag" system of motion telegraphy. Ordered to the west coast in the summer of 1860, he spent several pleasant months at Fort Steilacoom, Washington Territory. "I had a position for life," he later wrote of his time at Steilacoom, "and an assured support in the profession I loved, and I had only to get the most pleasure that I could out of my surroundings."

Sectional tensions soon intruded in Alexander's world. Although not a secessionist, he was determined to follow Georgia's lead. He learned in February 1861 that his home state had left the Union on January 19; shortly thereafter, he sailed to San Francisco, where his friend Lieutenant James B. McPherson attempted to talk him out of resigning. Alexander replied that he had to go with his own people; "If I don't come and bear my part, they will believe me to be a coward." He resigned from the U.S. Army and traveled to Richmond, Virginia; arriving on June 1, 1861, he found waiting for him a commission as captain of engineers in the Confederate service dated March 16 (the day of his resignation).

Alexander joined P. G. T. Beauregard's army near Manassas Junction at the end of June. As chief signal officer on the general's staff, he rapidly erected a series of observation towers in the area, from one of which he detected the approach of the Union flanking column during the battle of First Manassas. Beauregard praised Alexander in his report and, recognizing his versatility and skill at organization, made him chief of ordnance for the army. From the summer of 1861 until the end of the 1862 Maryland Campaign, Alexander served successively on the staffs of Beauregard, Joseph E. Johnston, and R. E. Lee as chief of ordnance and chief signal officer. He brought great efficiency to the daunting task of supplying arms and ammunition to the army during the Peninsula Campaign, the Seven Days, Second Manassas, and the raid into Maryland. Numerous other projects also came his way; he drilled various artillery units and recommended reorganizing the Southern "Long arm" into battalions; coordinated extensive secret service work; carried out engineering and reconnaissance assignments for a number of general officers; oversaw the use of a balloon that Lee acquired during the Seven Days (Alexander himself was aloft in the balloon during the battle of Gaines' Mill), and participated in the testing of various new weapons. In the course of these activities, Alexander was promoted to major of artillery on April 18, 1862, and to lieutenant colonel of artillery on July 17, 1862.

Lee recognized Alexander's manifold gifts, especially his theoretical and practical skill as an artillerist. When Stephen D. Lee, who commanded a battalion of artillery in James Longstreet's wing, was promoted and sent west in November 1862, the commanding general selected Alexander to replace him. Lee and Artillery Chief William Nelson Pendleton reorganized the army's artillery in twelve battalions during the winter of 1863, placing six in each of Longstreet's and Jackson's corps. "We have no more accomplished officer," stated

Pendleton in recommending Alexander for promotion to colonel and command of one of Longstreet's battalions. The colonelcy came through on March 3, 1863, and Alexander could take pride in the army's adoption of many organizational changes he had advocated in 1861.

Alexander vindicated Lee's confidence in him during the campaigns of 1862–63. At Fredericksburg he deployed Longstreet's artillery so that it could fire into attacking Federals, rather than in positions to duel with Union guns across the Rappahannock. Lee disagreed with Alexander's disposition but did not insist on a change. When Ambrose E. Burnside launched his assaults against Longstreet's corps on December 13, Alexander's guns wreaked havoc among the attackers. After the battle, Alexander commented within earshot of Lee that "it was a mighty good thing those guns…were located on the brows of the hills when the Yankees charged them!" Lee overlooked this impertinent remark (if, indeed, he heard it) in light of the excellent results. At Chancellorsville on May 3, 1863, Alexander discerned that high ground at Hazel Grove dominated the battlefield, hurried artillery to that plateau, and directed the fire that drove Union defenders away from Fairview Cemetery and enabled Lee's wings to reunite.

Gettysburg offered Alexander his most famous stage. On July 2, his guns ably supported Longstreet's powerful offensive against the Federal left, while on July 3 he orchestrated the massive bombardment that preceded the Pickett-Pettigrew-Trimble assault. In all of these battles Alexander functioned as tactical chief of artillery in the Ist Corps, despite the fact that Colonel John B. Walton officially held that post. Longstreet clearly considered Alexander his best gunner and wanted him in control on the battlefield. This awkward arrangement sometimes upset Walton, as when he watched helplessly at Gettysburg while his subordinate carried out tasks logically reserved for the corps chief of artillery.

Alexander and his battalion accompanied Longstreet's Corps to north Georgia in September 1863, arriving too late for Chickamauga but taking part in the siege of Chattanooga and the bitterly disappointing Knoxville Campaign. With Walton on detached duty, Alexander again functioned as corps chief of artillery. Returning to Virginia in the spring of 1864, he learned that Joseph E. Johnston had requested that he be made brigadier general and chief of artillery in the Army of Tennessee. Lee refused to let

him go, however, and Jefferson Davis commented that Alexander was "one of a very few whom Gen. Lee would not give to anybody." Lee arranged Alexander's promotion to brigadier general on March 1, 1864 (to rank from February 26) and his elevation to chief of artillery in the 1st Corps on March 19.

During the Overland Campaign of 1864, the Siege of Petersburg, and the retreat to Appomattox, Alexander continued his distinguished service. He helped design significant portions of the defensive works around Richmond; eventually commanded all the artillery between the James and Appomattox rivers, and drew the Army of Northern Virginia's last line of battle at Appomattox on April 9, 1865. He surrendered with the rest of Lee's army, closing a remarkable military career as the South's premier artillerist and one of the most versatile soldiers in American history.

Alexander's postwar life was varied and successful. He taught for a time at the University of South Carolina, invested in cottonseed production, and ultimately entered the railroad business. Within a decade, he compiled a record that prompted one contemporary to call him "the young Napoleon of the Railways." Retiring from railroading in 1892, he acted, at the request of his friend President Grover Cleveland, as arbitrator of a boundary dispute between Costa Rica and Nicaragua during 1897–1900. He wrote a long personal memoir for his family while in Nicaragua (published eighty years after his death as *Fighting for the Confederacy*), revising it extensively over the next six years into *Military Memoirs of a Confederate*. His writings, like his career as a soldier, set him apart from his contemporaries. Brilliantly analytical, impartial, and filled with telling anecdotes, they rank among the best sources on the war in Virginia. Alexander died on April 28, 1910, in Savannah, and was buried at the City Cemetery in Augusta, Georgia.

Gary W. Gallagher

A better known, and probably somewhat earlier, portrait of Alexander, shows him once again with colonel's insignia. It is unusual that in both portraits, his stars are not embroidered or sewn on, but are of metal mounted on studs. (Cook Collection, Valentine Museum, Richmond)

⋆ *Henry Watkins Allen* ⋆

Henry Watkins Allen was born on April 29, 1820, near Farmville, Virginia. After the death of his mother, his father moved with his children to Ray County, Missouri, and Allen later attended Marion College in Philadelphia, Missouri. He then worked as a store clerk in Lexington before moving to Grand Gulf, Mississippi, in 1837, and there he tutored on a nearby plantation before opening his own school. Meanwhile, after studying law with local attorneys, Allen received a license to practice in May 1841. The next year, he became captain of a volunteer company that offered its services to President Sam Houston of Texas, and in the six months they spent in Texas, Allen and his men saw some minor skirmishing with Mexican troops near Patricio.

Allen involved himself in politics after his return to Mississippi, served one term in the state legislature in 1846, and then moved to West Baton Rouge Parish, Louisiana, in 1852 to operate a sugar plantation. The next year he travelled through the South and sent accounts of his journey to the Baton Rouge *Daily Comet* for publication under the name "Guy Mannering." He attended Harvard University briefly in 1854; joined the American, or Know-Nothing, Party in 1855, and won a seat in the Louisiana state senate, but in 1859 he became a Democrat.

Because of poor health, Allen travelled to Europe in the summer of 1859; a series of letters he wrote to the

Baton Rouge *Weekly Advocate* were eventually published in book form as *The Travels of a Sugar Planter, or, Six Months in Europe.* In February 1861, he became president of the Louisiana Historical Society.

Allen enlisted in a volunteer company as a private in December 1860, then after the outbreak of the War, he helped recruit several companies, and on May 25, 1861, was elected lieutenant colonel of the 4th Louisiana Infantry. The regiment received orders to report to the Mississippi Gulf Coast, where Allen commanded four companies stationed on Ship Island. Ordered to abandon the island in September, Allen took his men to Mississippi City, and from there, the regiment proceeded to Brashear (now Morgan) City and Berwick on the Louisiana coast. In February 1862, the 4th Louisiana received orders to report to General Pierre G. T. Beauregard in western Tennessee. The resignation of the regiment's colonel on March 21 resulted in Allen's promotion to that rank. At the Battle of Shiloh, Tennessee, April 6–7, 1862, Allen's regiment served in Colonel Randall Lee Gibson's brigade of Daniel Ruggles' division, II Corps. An enemy bullet passed through his mouth and tore away part of his cheek

Henry Allen's brigadier's buttons and collar insignia (above) date this portrait to some time after August 1863, and most likely 1864 prior to his taking office as governor of Louisiana. (Department of Archives and Manuscripts, Louisiana State University, Baton Rouge)

during the first day's fighting. Despite the wound, he continued to lead his regiment. One of Beauregard's staff officers remembered, "the last I saw of him he was off with them like a whirlwind into the thick of the battle." On April 7, Allen left the hospital and received orders from Braxton Bragg to gather several regiments and some artillery and to hold back the advancing enemy. This he did successfully, retiring only when ordered.

After several weeks in the trenches at Corinth, Allen received orders on May 2 to take his regiment to Vicksburg, Mississippi, and assist in fortifying and defending the town. Allen's men constructed one river battery after their arrival and performed picket duty during the intermittent Union bombardment of the town in June and July. The 4th Louisiana accompanied John C. Breckinridge's force that left Vicksburg in July to attempt to recapture Baton Rouge, Louisiana, and for the battle, fought on August 5, Allen's troops formed the extreme left of the army and slowly drove back the Federals on their front. While leading an attack on an enemy battery, Allen rode to within fifty feet of a cannon before its crew fired a round of canister or grapeshot. The shot killed Allen's horse and crippled his legs so badly that he walked on crutches for the rest of his life. Governor Thomas O. Moore of Louisiana appointed Allen a major general in the state militia, and Allen took his oath of office on February 28, 1863. Though still trying to recuperate from his wounds, Allen received a commission as brigadier general in the Confederate Army on August 19, 1863, to rank from that date. The War Department ordered him to western Louisiana to collect and reorganize paroled prisoners and recruit their regiments back to full strength. In late 1863, Allen was elected governor of Louisiana and resigned his commission on January 10, 1864, prior to being inaugurated on January 25. By every account, Allen virtually performed miracles in securing supplies for his war-ravaged state and its people and in establishing some fledgling industries to aid the war effort. Douglas Southall Freeman pronounced Allen "the single great administrator produced by the Confederacy." After the surrender of the Trans-Mississippi Department on June 2, 1865, Allen chose to go into exile in Mexico rather than risk arrest by Federal authorities. He began publishing the *Mexican Times*, an English-language newspaper, in the City of Mexico in September, but died on April 22, 1866, from a stomach disorder. In 1885, Allen's remains

were buried on the grounds of the old state capitol in Baton Rouge. One of his biographers has written, "As a military leader Allen was spectacular." It is difficult to evaluate him as a brigade commander since he fell so early in his one engagement in that position. Certainly, Allen exhibited great personal bravery in battle, and he did perform competently at Shiloh. Given the skills as an administrator he demonstrated as governor, Allen might well have proven an above average general had he continued in field command.

Arthur W. Bergeron, Jr.

Though never promoted to major general, Allen wears his tunic buttons in rows of three's, commensurate with that rank, in this 1864 portrait. (Department of Archives and Manuscripts, Louisiana State University, Baton Rouge)

✷ William Wirt Allen ✷

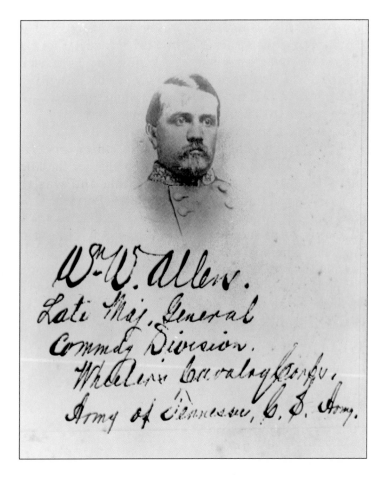

Although William Wirt Allen was born in New York City on September 11, 1835, he was reared in the South because his family relocated to Montgomery, Alabama while he was still a child. He attended schools in Montgomery and then entered the College of New Jersey (now Princeton). After graduating in 1854 he studied law but never practiced the profession. Instead, in 1861 he became a farmer. He acquired the polish of a Southern gentleman, "cordial in manner, and of ardent public spirit," his tall, stout frame presenting a stalwart figure.

Despite his lack of enthusiasm for the war, Allen entered the Confederate Army as 1st lieutenant of the Montgomery Mounted Rifles in April 1861, and served under Captain (later Major General) Henry D. Clayton at Pensacola prior to the company's transfer to Tennessee. On March 18, 1862, Allen was elected major of the 1st Alabama Cavalry. He engaged in his first serious action at Shiloh, where he had a horse shot from under him. Promoted to colonel later that summer, he led his regiment in General Braxton Bragg's invasion of Kentucky, distinguishing himself in skirmishes at Bear Wallow, Horse Cave, and Green River.

During a charge at Perryville, Allen sustained a slight wound that disabled him for a few days. His immediate superior, Brigadier General Joseph Wheeler, gave the following description of the attack: "The charge, one of the most brilliant of the campaign, was made in column; detachments of the 1st and 3d Alabama Cavalry with the gallant Cols. W. W. Allen and James Hagan being in advance.

Fully recuperated, Allen joined Lieutenant General William J. Hardee's wing of Bragg's army to command the cavalry during Wheeler's tenure as Bragg's chief of cavalry. Allen led Wheeler's brigade on a raid near Murfreesboro, Tennessee, which circumvented the Union Army and won praise both from Bragg and Wheeler for his actions on November 27 at La Vergne. Engaged on a daily basis between December 26 and 31, Allen saw action at Stewart's Creek Bridge on the twenty-sixth and he received a serious gunshot wound at Overall's Creek on the thirty-first. The latter action earned him another commendation from Wheeler for "gallantry and good soldierly conduct," but the loss of part of his right hand resulted in a lengthy recuperation at home.

Allen's uniform shows evidence of retouching in this image, which raises the possibility that it is not a wartime photo, or that originally it did not show him in uniform. If genuine, however, it dates from 1864-65. (Manuscripts Section, Tulane University Library)

Described as being "cool amid danger, and faithful and tireless in the discharge of his duty," Allen, after recovering from his wound, was commissioned a brigadier general on March 1, 1864, to rank from February 26, 1864, and was given command of a brigade stationed at Dalton, Georgia. Comprised of units from several states, this brigade was one of two in Brigadier General John H. Kelly's division of Wheeler's corps. At that time Allen commanded the only full-strength brigade of cavalry in the Army of Tennessee. And as spring approached, Wheeler called upon him to probe Major General William T. Sherman's front and guard against any sudden advance by Sherman's forces toward Atlanta. The Confederate Army of Tennessee was soon in retreat, and when it reached Marietta, Allen was reassigned to an all-Alabama brigade formerly commanded by Wheeler, a brigade comprised of the 1st, 3d, 4th, 9th, 12th, and 51st cavalry regiments. Allen led the brigade during the Atlanta Campaign until August 1864 when, during a raid through Tennessee, he succeeded Major General William T. Martin as commander of the division that contained Colonel Charles C. Crew's Georgia brigade as well as his own. Prior to the fall of Atlanta, Allen further distinguished himself in Georgia with his actions at Cassville, Pickett's Mill, and Decatur, and in the capture of the raiding column under Major General George Stoneman on July 29 near Macon.

Allen's original brigade, now led by Brigadier General Robert H. Anderson, was added to his command in the fall of 1864, and Allen distinguished himself at the head of his enlarged division at Waynesboro, Georgia, on November 28. During that engagement, he sustained a painful wound and had two horses shot from under him; still, he remained on the field throughout the battle. At the head of his division he entered South Carolina and doggedly snapped at Sherman's relentlessly advancing army. His defense of Aiken prevented that town from being occupied by the enemy, and his performance there was lauded by Governor Andrew G. Magrath and by the ladies of Aiken. The latter presented him with a beautiful silk flag that bore the inscription: "Your valor cheers our hearts."

On March 4, 1865, he was promoted major general with temporary rank, the last such appointment by President Jefferson Davis. Allen's nomination was dated the thirteenth, and when it was received by the Senate on the fourteenth for confirmation, it was referred to the Committee on Military Affairs. In an autobiographical sketch written after the war, Allen claimed that he was confirmed by the Senate, but there is no record that the Senate acted upon his nomination prior to its final adjournment on March 18. In either case, he was paroled at Salisbury, North Carolina, as a brigadier general on May 3, 1865. During the war, he had been wounded three times and had ten horses shot from under him.

After the war, he resumed operating his plantation, became involved with a railroad based in New Orleans, and served as a city official of Montgomery. He began several years of service as adjutant general of Alabama in 1870. During President Grover Cleveland's first administration, he served as a United States marshal for the Middle and Southern districts of Alabama and was the first president of the Confederate Survivor's Association at Montgomery. His bullet-riddled coat is sealed in the cornerstone of the Confederate monument in that city. He moved to Sheffield, Alabama, in 1893 and died there November 21, 1894. Apparently, his initial burial was in Florence prior to his reinterment in Birmingham.

Lawrence L. Hewitt

✶ *George Burgwyn Anderson* ✶

No photograph of Anderson has come to light to date. This rough engraving shows him during the last four months of his life, in the summer of 1862. (Miller, *Photographic History*)

George Burgwyn Anderson was born just outside Hillsboro, Orange County, North Carolina, on April 12, 1831—thirty years to the day before the Civil War's opening shot at Fort Sumter. After schooling at two North Carolina preparatory schools, young Anderson matriculated at the state university at Chapel Hill in 1847. The following year he entered the United States Military Academy, where he immediately demonstrated scholastic excellence. A Northern contemporary at the Academy wrote that Anderson "was not only one of the brightest intellects, but the *very superior* mind of his class." At the end of his first year at West Point, the brilliant Carolinian stood second among fifty-six cadets. Although Anderson continued to shine scholastically through his four years at the Academy, his standing faded somewhat because drawing classes counted in the grade average and evidently he just could not draw. Grades near the bottom of the class in that subject offset Anderson's other success to such a degree that he stood tenth among forty-three graduates in the class of 1852. Most of the relatively few 1852 graduates who later became prominent during the Civil War came from the North, including Phil Sheridan, who was suspended from the Academy out of this class. During his last year at West Point, George B. Anderson ranked 194th in conduct among 224 cadets at the institution.

Anderson put in nearly two years as brevet 2d lieutenant in the 2d United States Dragoons before he received Regular rank of 2d lieutenant in the same regiment. His only other promotion came during the 1850s came in December 1855, to the rank of 1st lieutenant. For portions of 1857, 1858, and 1859, Anderson held the post of regimental adjutant of the 2d Dragoons. Despite suffering under the stagnation of rank in the prewar army, Lieutenant Anderson benefitted from a wide range of experiences. He attended the cavalry school at Carlisle Barracks, assisted an engineer detachment surveying routes to California, and served with his regiment in Texas. In the fall of 1855 the 2d Dragoons marched overland from Texas to a new post at Fort Riley, Kansas, and in that troubled place Anderson and his comrades had a first-hand view of the unrest that prestaged the Civil War. Anderson participated in the Utah expedition in 1858, and the following year he went to Kentucky, where he married a Louisville woman. His final prewar posting with the United States Army was on recruiting duty in his wife's hometown.

Lieutenant Anderson moved promptly to leave United States service when his native state seceded. One source insists that he was "the first officer of the old army, then in service, who proffered his sword and his life to North Carolina." Anderson's resignation took effect on April 25, 1861, and he was commissioned colonel commanding the 4th North Carolina Infantry on May 16. One of the eager volunteers joining the new unit described his colonel as "a splendid specimen…tall, erect, brown-bearded, deep-chested, round-limbed, with a musical voice." Even after discounting the inevitable contemporary hyperbole about leaders of that era, it remains clear from several sources that Colonel Anderson's personal style was uncommonly cheerful and amiable.

The 4th North Carolina followed George B. Anderson to Virginia in July 1861 and arrived at Manassas just a few days after the war's first major engagement. Beginning soon after his arrival, Colonel Anderson exercised the tedious responsibilities of post commandant at busy Manassas Junction through the winter. In March 1862 the regiment moved to Orange County, and in April on to the Peninsula.

Although several secondary accounts insist that Anderson won his general's wreath for gallantry at the Battle of Williamsburg, he was not engaged there. Both the 4th North Carolina and its colonel faced their baptism of fire at Seven Pines on May 31, 1862. Anderson commanded W. S. Featherston's Brigade in that action because the general was absent sick. He led the brigade into fighting so desperate that it suffered nearly 900 casualties—about one-half of its strength. In the process, George B. Anderson impressed Division Commander D. H. Hill of his worth. In a letter dated June 6, Hill complained to the secretary of war about three subordinate generals and various other units and officers, but lauded Anderson: "I most earnestly request that Col. G. B. Anderson be appointed a Brigadier and assigned to my command." Anderson's commission at that rank came three days later, to date from that same day.

As part of the June 1862 reorganization of the army under its new commander, R. E. Lee, and in keeping with President Davis' enthusiasm for brigading regiments by state, Anderson's new brigade would consist of all North Carolina units. In addition to his old 4th Infantry, Anderson would command the 2d, 14th, and 30th. The brigade that he molded from those pieces went on after Anderson's death to perform splendid service under others, notably Stephen Dodson Ramseur. Just two weeks after his promotion, the new general and his new brigade plunged into violent action in the Seven Days Campaign. They fought on the Confederate left under D. H. Hill at Gaines' Mill, and participated in the vain folly of Malvern Hill. At the latter place Anderson suffered a wound in the hand serious enough to take him out of action. During the Seven Days the brigade lost nearly 900 men, the second loss at that level within one month in brigades led by Anderson.

Anderson's Brigade moved near the rear of the army as it pressed northward from Richmond, and as a result the unit missed any involvement in the Second Battle of Manassas. As though to make up for that hiatus, the brigade fought desperately at critical points in both of the army's September battles in Maryland. On September 14, Anderson sealed the line near Fox's Gap on the chaotic battlefield of South Mountain. Near Sharpsburg three days later his brigade, together with Robert E. Rodes' Alabamians, fought so ferociously from shelter in a sunken road that their bodies turned into the ghastly and famous Bloody Lane. General Anderson's blood was among that which christened the lane. While the general encouraged his men from a slightly elevated position just behind the lane, a rifle ball struck his ankle near the joint. The wound caused him intense suffering, but it did not seem to be dangerous. Anderson insisted on returning home to convalesce, making the trip to Raleigh in nine days by way of Shepherdstown, Staunton, and Richmond. Infection in the wound caused increasing concern and eventually forced the amputation of the leg. General Anderson succumbed to the combined effects of the wound, its infection, and the operation on the morning of October 16, 1862. His pregnant wife gave birth to their daughter the next day. He is buried in the Old City Cemetery in Raleigh.

Robert K. Krick

✴ *George Thomas Anderson* ✴

Anderson appears post-1862 in this handsome glass plate image. (Cook Collection, Valentine Museum, Richmond)

This Georgian, born in Covington, February 3, 1824, was described by prewar contemporaries as "a man of considerable property." Nevertheless, he not only served as a 2d lieutenant in a Georgia Mounted Volunteer Company during the Mexican War but also entered the new 1st U.S. Cavalry Regiment in 1855 as a captain, one of many civilians to receive direct commissions in the big force expansion then. Three years later, he resigned and returned to Georgia.

When the Civil War began, he offered to serve the Confederacy as captain or major of Regular cavalry. There was, however, no Regular cavalry, so he raised Company H of the 11th Georgia Infantry among his neighbors in Walton County. His military experience and social standing led to his being elected colonel of the 11th as of July 2, 1861. He took his regiment to Virginia, where it served briefly in Richmond and then became part of Colonel Francis S. Bartow's brigade of Joseph E. Johnston's Army of the Shenandoah on July 17. The following day, Johnston headed for Manassas, but due to a railroad accident, over half the brigade, including Anderson and the 11th, arrived too late to fight at First Bull Run.

Because Bartow was killed in that combat, primarily Brigadier General Samuel Jones and briefly Brigadier Generals W. H. T. Walker and David R. Jones were assigned command of the brigade in the latter half of 1861 and early in 1862. For part of that time, however, Anderson as senior colonel had charge of the brigade. From March 24, 1862, onward, except for brief intervals of absence, he led it for the rest of the war.

It originally consisted of the 7th, 8th, 9th, and 11th Georgia and 1st Kentucky Infantry Regiments. In mid-May 1862, the "Blue Grass" unit mustered out, and the 1st Georgia Regular Infantry joined the brigade. After Fredericksburg, the Regulars in turn departed; in the spring of 1863 they were replaced by the 59th Georgia Infantry Regiment. Those five outfits—7th, 8th, 9th, 11th, and 59th—thereafter composed the brigade. Initially part of the division led successively by G. W. Smith, Robert Toombs, and D. R. Jones, the brigade (and the rest of Jones' Division) was incorporated into John B. Hood's Division in October 1862. It thenceforth fought in that division, first under Hood and then under Charles W. Field.

Anderson saw much action during the Siege of Yorktown, the Seven Days' Battles (especially at Garnett's Farm, Savage's Station, and Malvern Hill), Thoroughfare Gap, Second Manassas, South Mountain, and Antietam. His superiors' reports of those battles recorded Anderson's operations but did not particularly compliment him—except for effusive John B. Magruder's laudation that "Colonel Anderson, commanding his brigade...deserve great praise for the promptness with which they rushed to the conflict and repelled this serious attempt of the enemy" to storm Lee's Mill on April 16.

The Georgian, however, was loved by his soldiers. "Anderson is the most fearful man I ever saw, the most watchful," wrote one of his privates on May 13, 1862; "he stands up to us like a father." The officers of his brigade also respected him. As early as April 24 and again on October 3, 1862, they petitioned the War Department that he be promoted to brigadier general. The latter document stated that "He has led the Brigade in eight or ten hard-fought battles and in the midst of the greatest peril has always been cool, deliberate, and self possessed and on every occasion has borne himself with marked ability and gallantry. He is always at his post."

More importantly, the colonel had earned the respect of R. E. Lee. The senior officer's overall proposal of October 27 for refining the command structure of the Army of Northern Virginia recommended Anderson for brigadier general, to receive permanent command of the brigade he had led for so long. Ten days later, the Georgian assumed that command; ever afterwards, the unit was known as "Anderson's Brigade." His commission as brigadier general on November 1 ranked from that same date.

Although present at Fredericksburg and Suffolk, he did not see major action again until Gettysburg, where he was severely wounded in the thigh on July 2. This wound forced him to go on furlough for over two months. Neither he nor his Georgians accompanied their corps to Chickamauga in September. By the time the brigade rejoined James Longstreet in early October, Anderson had resumed command. He then led his troops at Campbell's Station, Fort Sanders, and Mossy Creek.

On returning to Virginia in the spring of 1864, he fought at the Wilderness (including Longstreet's great counterattack on May 6), Spotsylvania, North Anna, and Cold Harbor. As the armies neared Petersburg, Anderson's Brigade participated in the Clay's Farm fight, which restored the Butternut hold on Bermuda Hundred neck. Criticized by some for the Hare's Hill fiasco a week later, he and the rest of Field's Division were held blameless by General Lee himself. After shifting to the Peninsula in late July, his Georgians fought in all the battles there from August through October, particularly Second Deep Bottom, Chaffin's Bluff, and First Darbytown Road. His premature attack contributed significantly to Southern failure to recapture Fort Harrison on September 30.

With the rest of the division, he returned to Petersburg on April 2 for a final stand in the city's inner works. Then on the ensuing retreat, he successfully counterattacked at Cumberland Church and served with Longstreet's rear guard at Appomattox. At the subsequent surrender, Anderson and 1,000 of his men were still with the colors, Lee's third largest brigade.

Postwar, he returned to Georgia, served as Atlanta police chief, then moved to Alabama in the 1880s. On April 4, 1901, he died in Anniston and is buried there. Nicknamed "Tige" or "Tiger" but also just called "Tom" by his original regiment, Anderson served through the war competently but not brilliantly—one of many mediocre brigadiers who added experience and solidity to command but who rarely proved the margin of victory. Significantly, in his last battle as in his first, he held brigade command: a good enough officer to retain that position but never good enough to be promoted.

Richard J. Sommers

Taken after February 1862, and probably prior to February 1864, this portrait of "Patton" Anderson reveals unusual detail in his collar insignia. (U.S. Army Military History Institute, Carlisle, Pa.)

✶ *James Patton Anderson* ✶

James Patton Anderson was born on February 16, 1822, in Franklin County, Tennessee. Reared by his grandfather after the death of his father in 1831, Anderson attended country schools before studying at Jefferson College in Canonsburg, Pennsylvania, from 1836 to 1840. After working several odd jobs, he moved to Hernando County, Mississippi, in 1843, where he studied medicine and began his practice. From 1843 to 1846 he served as sheriff of DeSoto County except for the summers of 1844 and 1845, when he studied at the Montrose Law School. He became a practicing attorney in 1847. During the Mexican War he raised and served as lieutenant colonel of the 1st Battalion Mississippi Rifles. Because the unit organized after the fall of Mexico City, it only performed garrison duty, primarily at Tampico.

After his return to the United States, Anderson's interest turned to politics. Elected to the Mississippi legislature in 1850, Anderson was an ally of Jefferson Davis. His opposition to the Compromise of 1850 prevented his reelection in 1851. Two years later, President Franklin Pierce appointed him U.S. marshal for Washington territory, and in 1855 he became the first person to hold the position of territorial delegate to Congress.

His interest in the northwest waned in 1857 because he thought that secession was imminent. He moved to Florida to manage his aunt's plantation, "Casablanca," in Monticello, and by 1860 he had established himself sufficiently to be elected as a delegate to that state's secession convention. A member of the provisional Confederate Congress, he served on the Military Affairs and Public Lands Committees before resigning to organize the Jefferson County Volunteers.

Anderson's company became part of the 1st Florida Infantry and he became the regiment's first colonel. Nicknamed the "Magnolia Regiment", the unit served at Pensacola throughout 1861, where, before daylight on October 9, it participated in an assault against a Federal camp on Santa Rosa Island. J. Patton Anderson succeeded to command Brigadier General Richard H. Anderson's brigade three days later and on January 1, 1862, Major General Braxton Bragg urged the War Department to promote J. Patton Anderson to brigadier general. Secretary of War Judah P. Benjamin notified Bragg on February 8, "The President and myself have both a very high opinion of the merits and soldierly qualities of Colonel Anderson."

Anderson was commissioned a brigadier general on February 10, 1862, to rank immediately, and soon found himself transferred to Corinth, Mississippi, where his brigade formed part of Brigadier General Daniel Ruggles' Division of Bragg's corps. Of Anderson's performance at Shiloh, Bragg wrote:

"Brigadier General Patton Anderson was among the foremost where the fighting was hardest, and never failed to overcome what resistance was opposed to him. With a brigade composed almost entirely of raw troops, his personal gallantry and soldierly bearing supplied the place of instruction and discipline."

Anderson fought at Farmington, Mississippi, on May 9, and when Bragg succeeded to army command, he availed himself of the first opportunity to assign Anderson to a division.

During the invasion of Kentucky he led his new command in the Battle of Perryville, but on December 20, Bragg disbanded his division. Anderson was assigned to command Brigadier General Edward C. Walthall's Brigade of Major General Jones M. Witner's Division on the evening of December 27, four days before the Battle of Murfreesboro. In that engagement, Anderson distinguished himself on the first day by his desperate charge which captured three Union batteries. On the final day of the conflict he covered the retreat of Major General John C. Breckinridge's Division. Regarding the latter, Bragg reported:

"Brigadier General J. Patton Anderson for the coolness, judgment, and courage with which he interposed his brigade between our retreating forces and the enemy, largely superior to him...and saved our artillery, is justly entitled to special mention."

Following the wounding of Major General Thomas C. Hindman during the early stages of the Battle of Chickamauga, Anderson assumed command of his division. Anderson remained in divisional command during the Chattanooga Campaign, where he held the center of the Confederate line on Missionary Ridge; the first unit to break along the seemingly impregnable line was his old brigade.

On February 17, 1864, Anderson finally received his well-earned promotion to major general. Almost simultaneously with his promotion, a Union expedition landed at Jacksonville, Florida, and Anderson was placed in charge of the District of Florida despite General Joseph E. Johnston's request that President Jefferson David allow Anderson to remain with his division. Anderson assumed command of the district on March 4 and concentrated his efforts toward containing the enemy near Jacksonville, which involved the use of torpedoes and the construction of several small naval vessels.

After General John Bell Hood failed to defeat Major General William T. Sherman at Peachtree Creek, Bragg, now serving as general in chief, notified Adjutant General Samuel Cooper: "After learning the result of yesterday's operations at Atlanta, I have ordered Major General Patton Anderson to report to General Hood. It is important that he should go immediately." Upon his arrival on July 29, Anderson reassumed command of Hindman's Division, at the head of which he fought at Ezra Church and Utoy Creek. At Jonesboro, Anderson sustained a wound that forced him to abstain from field service. Nevertheless, when Sherman had pushed the Confederates into North Carolina, Anderson disregarded his surgeon's instructions and returned to active duty. Anderson had only 890 infantrymen present for duty on April 24, 1865, the weakest division in Johnston's army. Anderson surrendered with that army and took his parole at Greensboro, North Carolina.

Anderson's military leadership consisted of recklessness, sincerity, and sternness, a combination that secured the loyalty of his men, even when his command was only temporary. Bragg held him in high esteem, probably because he was as quick to execute a deserter as was Bragg. He resided in Memphis after the war, where he sold insurance, published a paper

devoted to agriculture, and served as state tax collector for Shelby County. He died in Memphis on September 20, 1872, and is buried there.

Lawrence L. Hewitt

Anderson, James Patton. "Autobiography of Gen. Patton Anderson, C.S.A." *Southern Historical Society Papers.* XXIV (1896)

Hoffman, John. *The Confederate Collapse at the Battle of Missionary Ridge.* Dayton, Ohio: 1985

A very slight variant of the previous portrait, and obviously made at the same sitting, this one shows Anderson's head turned slightly more to the right. (*Confederate Veteran*, IX, p. 341)

✶ *Joseph Reid Anderson* ✶

This portrait of Anderson must have been made between September 1861 and his resignation in July 1862, and was almost certainly taken in Richmond. (Museum of the Confederacy, Richmond)

He was born in Botetourt County, Virginia, February 6, 1813. Though fourth in the West Point Class of 1836 (and cadet captain), he remained in the Army only fifteen months. The next four years saw him constructing the Staunton-Winchester portion of the Shenandoah Valley Turnpike—which became the most famous wayfare of warfare during the Civil War. In 1848, he purchased the Tredegar Iron Company of Richmond. By 1861, it ranked as the South's principal iron works, one of the foremost such firms in America.

A secessionist, he promoted defense preparedness in Virginia and the South, especially following John Brown's Harpers Ferry raid. The preceding month he raised the Richmond Light Dragoon Company (subsequently called the "Governor's Mounted Guard") and served as its captain until 1860. In May 1861, the Tredegar employees formed the 8th Virginia Infantry Battalion (later the 6th Virginia Local Defense Battalion) to protect the vital factory against sabotage and raids; he became the 8th's commanding major.

That summer, Anderson went to war for eleven months. Chafing at news that West Point classmates were becoming Union generals and that the Confederacy "finds it necessary to confer military command on civilians who have not had the advantage of military education," he notified the War Department on August 21, that "I think it is time now for me to claim some exemption from purely business occupations and to ask for a command in the field." He was commissioned brigadier general on September 3, to rank from that same date.

Earlier that week, Federal victory at Hatteras Inlet threatened calamity to the Carolina coast. Anderson, who helped build Fort Pulaski while in the U.S. Army, was accordingly made responsible for North Carolina's coast defense, as principal subordinate to department commander Richard C. Gatlin. His superior, however, realized the logistical impossibility of expecting one man to oversee the entire coast, so at month's end Gatlin divided his department into two sectors. Anderson received charge of the more southerly District of Cape Fear. There he rendered important service in fortifying the approaches to Wilmington, subsequently the Confederacy's principal port.

Despite fears of Federal forays, the Virginian was never attacked. Instead, he repeatedly transferred troops to more threatened sectors, first to Port Royal and then to New Berne. The latter defeat caused the ill Gatlin to summon Anderson himself to the threatened front and then to send him to Richmond to request reinforcements and a new department commander. On March 15, however, the Secretary of War replaced Gatlin with Anderson. On March 19, the junior officer took charge of the burgeoning force at Kinston, expanding from a bruised brigade to a strong division. His tenure proved temporary, though, for Theophilus Holmes succeeded him on March 25. Rather than return to Wilmington, Anderson took over the new Third Brigade of Holmes' command, containing the 2d Georgia and 3d Louisiana Infantry Battalions and the 45th and 49th Georgia, 34th and 38th North Carolina, and 1st South Carolina (Provisional Army) Infantry Regiments.

This concentration proved excessive for a quieting front, once campaigning resumed in Virginia. Anderson's Brigade was, therefore, transferred to the Fredericksburg front, and on April 25 he was assigned Holmes' former responsibility for that sector. His little "Army of the Rappahannock" contained his own brigade under Daniel H. Hamilton and Charles W. Field's and Maxcy Gregg's Brigades. The least active of the five Confederate commands on the strategic chessboard of northern Virginia that spring, his division nonetheless was an important corps of observation confronting Irvin McDowell. In late May, just as McDowell prepared to attack Anderson, events elsewhere drew them apart—the Unionists westward after "Stonewall" Jackson, the Secessionists southward to avoid Fitz John Porter's push up the Pamunkey. Again arriving too late to fight at Hanover Court House, Anderson could only help succor L. O'Bryan Branch's buffeted Butternuts (the same brigade beaten at New Byrne).

This withdrawal brought Anderson into the immediate orbit of the Army of Northern Virginia. On May 27, his and Branch's commands were combined to form the Light Division under A. P. Hill. Anderson then resumed commanding his own brigade. Its North Carolina regiments had already been transferred to Gregg's Brigade; the Provisionals now went there, too; and the 2d Georgia Battalion had not accompanied him from North Carolina. To replace these units, two veteran outfits joined him. His brigade thereafter contained the 3d Louisiana Infantry Battalion and the 14th, 35th, 45th, and 49th Georgia Infantry Regiments. He fought at Mechanicsville, Gaines' Mill, and Frayser's Farm, always bravely but never successfully. Perhaps significantly, his brigade lost less than half the average casualties for Hill's other five brigades during the Seven Days' Battle. Anderson was hit in the head by a spent ball on June 30. It disabled him for several days, but by July 13 he was back on duty and temporarily commanded the Light Division.

The following day, Anderson himself resigned. His resignation was accepted on July 19, and by month's end he was back in civilian life. he was hardly out of the war, however, for he left service to resume charge of his business. The principal Confederate manufactory of cannons, munitions, gun carriages, and armor plating, Tredegar proved crucial to the Southern war effort. Anderson's greatest contribution came as head of that plant.

The Confederacy, nevertheless, eventually collapsed. Anderson, who always served his company as well as his country, continued safeguarding his business even then. He did not allow the Tredegar Battalion to accompany Clement Sullivane's Brigade to Danville but kept it protecting the plant from looters. He met President Lincoln in Richmond on April 4 and played a major part in the short-lived effort to take Virginia out of the Confederacy. Postwar, he regained control of Tredegar. Death came on September 7, 1892; he is buried in Richmond. (His son, Colonel Archer Anderson, also served the Confederacy prominently as Chief of Staff to Holmes, D. H. Hill, and Braxton Bragg, and his postwar second wife was John Pegram's sister.)

Joseph Anderson had little opportunity to display military talents as a strategist, tactician, or engineer. But as logistician—arms manufacturer—he served the Confederacy well, that work he performed not as a Confederate commander but as a Confederate capitalist.

Richard J. Sommers

✶ *Richard Heron Anderson* ✶

Born near Statesburg, South Carolina, on October 7, 1821, he graduated fortieth in the 1842 West Point class, then served in the 1st and 2d U.S. Dragoon Regiments in the Mexican, Mormon, and Comanche Wars and "Bleeding Kansas." He resigned on February 15, 1861, effective March 3. (His wife's uncle, George Gibson, remained Union commissary general).

Commissioned Confederate cavalry major on March 16, and prospectively appointed colonel of the 1st South Carolina Regular Infantry on January 28, Anderson helped capture Fort Sumter. P. G. T. Beauregard's departure on May 27 left him commanding South Carolina. Promoted brigadier general on July 19, to rank from that date, Anderson transferred to the Army of Pensacola on August 21. The 1st Florida, 5th Georgia, 1st Louisiana Regular, and 5th and 8th Mississippi Infantry Regiments and a Marine Battalion eventually composed his brigade there. He led the Santa Rosa Raid (where he was wounded in the left arm) and participated in two bombardments. Army commander Braxton Bragg charged him as drunk in the January 1 action. Before the court met, however, Anderson was ordered to the Army of Northern Virginia on January 31.

On February 15, he was assigned command of D. R. Jones' original brigade, containing the 4th, 5th, 6th, and 9th South Carolina Infantry Regiments (later also the Palmetto Sharpshooter and 2d South Carolina Rifle Regiments). With these troops, "Fighting Dick" Anderson at Williamsburg, Seven Pines, Gaines' Mill, and Frayser's Farm proved one of the South's best battle brigadiers.

He led James Longstreet's Division as senior brigadier on May 5, June 30, and briefly on May 31. Promoted to major general on July 14, he took over Benjamin Huger's Division, containing Lewis A. Armistead's, William Mahone's, and Ambrose R. Wright's Brigades on July 16. In early September, Cadmus M. Wilcox's, Winfield S. Featherston's, and Roger A. Pryor's Brigades of Longstreet's Division joined Anderson. Armistead's Virginians transferred elsewhere in October. The remaining brigades composed Anderson's (later Mahone's) Division until Appomattox.

Unlike Huger's poor performance at Seven Pines and Glendale, Anderson started well with his telling counterattack at Second Manassas. His troops also fought at Crampton's Gap and Antietam. He personally played a little role on September 17, because a thigh wound soon disabled him. By mid-November,

---

The only known image of Anderson in uniform, this portrait shows him as a major general, dating it after the summer of 1862. (Cook Collection, Valentine Museum, Richmond)

he was back on duty but saw little action at Fredericksburg. Chancellorsville proved different. His contributions delaying the Yankees on May 1, attacking them on May 3, and pursuing John Sedwick on May 4 earned Anderson R. E. Lee's accolade of "noble old soldier."

In all these operations, except Harpers Ferry, Anderson's Division belonged to the corps of his West Point classmate and former division commander, Longstreet. The reorganization of May 30, 1863, however, transferred his division to A. P. Hill's III Corps. There it fared less successfully at Gettysburg and Second Bristoe Station. In the Wilderness, Anderson arrived from far away only in time to join Longstreet's counterattack on May 6, 1864.

On May 7, Anderson succeeded the wounded Longstreet in commanding the I Corps, containing E. Porter Alexander's Artillery Brigade and Charles W. Field's, Joseph B. Kershaw's, and (after May 27) George E. Pickett's Divisions. On June 1, Anderson received the temporary grade of lieutenant general, to rank from May 31.

His first combat as corps commander proved his best, when his hard-marching and hard-fighting on May 8 saved Spotsylvania. There and at North Anna he fought heavily. At Second Cold Harbor he repulsed onslaughts on June 1 and 3, but ominously his offensive on June 1 proved disastrous. His one successful attack came June 16–17 in recovering the Howlett Line. But at First Deep Bottom, Chaffin's Bluff, and First Darbytown Road, his uncoordinated assaults repeatedly met defeat. Nor did his strategic operations along the Blue Ridge in late summer secure significant success. Only on the defensive, as at Second Darbytown Road, did he gain victory.

Six days later, Longstreet resumed command. Anderson then took over Beauregard's old corps, containing Bushrod R. Johnson's and Robert F. Hoke's Divisions, Hilary P. Jones' Artillery Brigade, and Edward L. Thomas' Infantry Brigade. Hoke, however, remained with Longstreet, and Thomas rejoined Hill in December, so Anderson's IV Corps really consisted of barely one division.

Guarding the eastern approaches to Petersburg, where Federal lines were closest, he constantly endured bombardment, sharpshooting, and raids; on October 27, raiders actually penetrated his main works before being repelled.

When such affrays escalated to assaults, though, Anderson's corps were transferred to the quiet area

west of Hatcher's Run, and another command (including two of his brigades) was entrusted with attacking Fort Stedman. The westerly sector did not remain quiet long, and Anderson with part of his own corps and two other brigades fought at Gravelly Run and White Oak Road. However, he did virtually nothing on April 1–2 except retreat. He was not that fortunate at Sayler's Creek, where his corps (Johnson's and Pickett's Divisions) was destroyed. No command remained for them; Lee relieved all three generals on April 8.

Postwar years proved even unkinder, as Anderson lived in near poverty. Dying on June 26, 1879, he is buried in Beaufort, South Carolina.

Alexander called Anderson "as pleasant a commander to serve under as could be wished [and]…a sturdy [and] reliable fighter…[He] won both the love [and] confidence of all, for the brave, simple minded [and] earnest soldier that he was." That corps' adjutant agreed that Anderson "had showed commendable prudence and an intelligent comprehension of the work in hand [at Spotsylvania]. He was a very brave man, but of a rather inert, indolent manner for commanding troops in the field, and by no means pushing or aggressive…He seemed to leave the corps much to his staff, while his own meditative disposition was constantly soothed by whiffs from a noble, cherished meerschaum pipe." The Carolinian's confidence and comfort collapsed in the war's waning weeks, however. "A head he could see the ruin of the Southern cause," wrote Douglas Southall Freeman, concerning 1865; "he knew that his men had no faith in the future of the Confederacy and little spirit for the [coming] conflict." And Mahone called Anderson, just escaped from Sayler's Creek, "the picture, the sad picture, of a man who was whipped."

These contentions are not contradictory. As battle leader, Anderson was one of the best brigadiers in the Confederate Army. At division level, too, he proved sound, often outstanding. But like many generals, Southern and Northern, he failed to rise to corps responsibility, which required not just inspirational leadership but grand-tactical competence. Such failure produced defeat, which led to defeatism. Among the brightest glories of mid-level generals in 1862, Anderson by war's end epitomized the deterioration of Lee's high command.

Richard J. Sommers

Though showing signs of retouching, this is apparently a genuine image of Anderson in uniform, and is the only one known to exist from wartime. (Museum of the Confederacy, Richmond)

⋆ Robert Houstoun Anderson ⋆

Robert Houstoun Anderson was born October 1, 1835, in Savannah, Georgia. After attending schools in Georgia, he received an appointment to the United States Military Academy at West Point and graduated in 1857 thirty-fifth out of a class of thirty-eight. For about a year he was on duty at Fort Columbus, New York, with the 9th Infantry, then from 1858 until just before he left the army in 1861 Anderson was stationed at Fort Walla Walla, Washington. He resigned his commission on the day he learned that Georgia had seceded, and returned to Savannah to take a commission as a 1st lieutenant of artillery on March 16. Anderson joined General W. H. T. Walker's staff on the Georgia coast as a major and adjutant on September 4, 1861, and remained in that position until Walker resigned. Major Anderson then organized and took command of the 1st Battalion of Georgia Sharpshooters on June 20, 1862, and held that office until transferred to the 5th Georgia Cavalry.

On January 20, 1863, he was promoted to colonel, and placed in command of all the forces on the Ogeechee River, with headquarters at Fort McAllister near Savannah. In February the Confederate battery at Genesis Point was attacked by an ironclad, three wooden gunboats, and a mortar boat. The Confederates withstood the assault, and Anderson won high praise for the defense. This clash demonstrated that sand embankments were more than a match for the new revolving-turret ironclads. In April he wrote Robert E. Lee requesting that the 5th Georgia Cavalry be transferred to Virginia to join J. E. B. Stuart. He told Lee that if he could not come to Virginia he would apply for a transfer to the Army of Tennessee. Instead, in September he was ordered to report to Brigadier General R. S. Ripley in Charleston, South Carolina, for assignment as commander of the outposts on Sullivan's Island.

In October, Anderson asked P. G. T. Beauregard to brigade the Georgia cavalry which consisted of thirty-one companies of 2,500 men. Anderson pointed out

that all of the regiments were poorly organized and drilled except his own, the 5th Georgia. Although this did not happen, in February 1864 the Charleston cavalry was placed under Anderson. He did not remain long in South Carolina; in February his regiment left for temporary service in Florida. Early in the month Federal forces had landed at Jacksonville and marched inland, fighting the battle of Olustee on February 20. The Confederates wanted to reinforce their troops in northern Florida; Anderson arrived at Tallahassee in March. Anderson soon observed that he needed more men if he was to scout effectively, reporting that he had only 948 privates to patrol a line nine miles long. He remained in Florida throughout April, but was transferred back to South Carolina by May. Hoping for active service, Anderson wrote personally to General Braxton Bragg, saying that he wanted to join General Joseph Wheeler because his regiment was "doing nothing but unimportant picket duty on the coast." He appealed to a fellow graduate of West Point and pleaded: "I know General that an officer of your cultivation and eminent military character will appreciate my professional anxiety to get into active service, and will wait patiently, having an abiding faith that you will soon give me an opportunity of drawing my sabre in an active field, for our holy cause."

As a result, by June Anderson took over a brigade in John H. Kelly's Division of Wheeler's Corps. His command included the 3d, 8th, 10th, and 12th Confederate cavalry along with the 5th Georgia. On June 21 Anderson took part in Wheeler's attack on Kenner Garrard's division, driving it from the field. During Edward McCook's raid in late June, Anderson was wounded and replaced by Colonel Edward Bird. Wheeler censured the actions of the cavalry under Bird, claiming: "It was full daylight before I heard from him at all, and then I learned that he had fallen asleep and allowed the demoralized mass to escape to the river." Although criticizing Bird's actions, Wheeler gave special thanks to Anderson, and as a result, on July 26, Anderson was promoted to brigadier general, to rank from that same day.

In November, Anderson's Brigade was ordered to report to Major General Howell Cobb to observe the Federals approaching Macon on the east side of the Ocmulgee River. Anderson remained with Wheeler as Sherman marched toward Savannah, and in December held a line on the South Carolina side of the Savannah River. He reported that with five hundred men, "I have a river front to guard of thirty miles, every foot of which is accessible to the enemy in the rice flats that they are using upon the river. The consequences is that nearly every man is upon picket duty every day, and no force is left to reinforce the pickets when they are driven in." Anderson requested that the men of his brigade in the trenches around Savannah be returned to him.

By Christmas, his situation was grave and he reported that horses were dying for lack of corn. In January his cavalry was stationed near Hardeeville, South Carolina. The following month, Anderson was one of three that Wheeler recommended for promotion to major general. In his request Wheeler praised Anderson's actions during Sherman's march through Georgia. But no promotion was forthcoming, and when Sherman's soldiers evacuated Savannah, Anderson's cavalry waited for them in South Carolina. For the next several weeks, his cavalrymen skirmished with the Union troops frequently. On March 11, Anderson skirmished with the Federals at Fayetteville, and then crossed the Cape Fear River and burned the bridge. During this fight, he was again wounded. By early May his command was camped forty-four miles from Sherman's army at Greensboro; Anderson reported 723 men with him, and a few more with his wagon train. He was paroled at Hillsboro on May 3. When his men were given their final papers at Greensboro, however, the Federals counted 1,800 in Anderson's cavalry.

At the conclusion of the war Anderson returned to Savannah where from 1867 until his death he was chief of police. In 1879 and again in 1887 he was a member of the board of visitors to the United States Military Academy. He died in February 8, 1888, and is buried at Bonaventure Cemetery in Savannah.

Anne Bailey

A certain image of Anderson in uniform is this 1857 West Point class portrait made four years prior to the war. (United States Military Academy Archives, West Point)

✶ *Samuel Read Anderson* ✶

Samuel Anderson posed for this portrait either between July 1861 and the following spring, or else after November 1864. His apparent age argues for the later date. (Virginia Historical Society)

Born in Bedford County, Virginia, on February 17, 1804, he moved to Kentucky and then relocated to Tennessee at a young age. In 1846, Anderson volunteered for the Mexican War and was appointed lieutenant colonel of the 1st Tennessee Infantry. Between the end of that conflict and the beginning of the Civil War, Anderson served as cashier of the Bank of Tennessee and as postmaster of Nashville.

When Tennessee seceded after the firing on Fort Sumter, Governor Isham Harris appointed Anderson major general of Tennessee volunteers. He assisted in the organization and training of the troops before Confederate authorities ordered him and three regiments into southwestern Virginia in July. At the same time he received his commission as brigadier general in the Confederate Army, to rank from July 7, and took command of a brigade in William W. Loring's Division of the Army of the Northwest. His command consisted of the 1st, 7th, and 14th Tennessee regiments.

Loring's Division was dispatched into western Virginia under the command of Robert E. Lee. Earlier in the summer the Federals had won a pair of key victories in the region, securing much of the pro-Union section of the state. Lee decided on an offensive against Federal positions on Cheat Mountain in central western Virginia.

The Confederate attack began on September 11. While part of Loring's command advanced against the main Federal position, Anderson led his 3,000-man brigade beyond the enemy lines, striking for a wagon road in the Federal rear. Anderson succeeded the next day and, with Loring pressing along the front, the Yankees withdrew. The Confederates might have enjoyed more success if not for the failure of another brigade commander.

Anderson remained in the region until late in the year when the division was assigned to the Valley District, commanded by Stonewall Jackson. The Tennesseeans participated in the miserable Romney Campaign in January 1862. Two months later, Anderson's brigade was transferred to Joseph E. Johnston's army in northern Virginia, and was assigned to the divisions of W. H. C. Whiting.

On May 7, 1862, Anderson led two regiments of his brigade in a minor engagement at Eltham's Landing on the Virginia peninsula. In the action, Anderson moved his men forward and supported the left flank of John B. Hood's attacking troops. Whiting praised Anderson in his official report, writing: "I take occasion to make my acknowledgements to Brigadier General Anderson, of Tennessee, who, arriving on the field at a critical moment to the support of General Hood, and placing two of his regiments in the fire of the enemy, courteously waived the command, although senior to us all."

The 58-year-old Anderson resigned his commission because of ill health within days of the fight at Eltham's Landing. Although the nature of the disability was unspecified, Anderson remained out of Confederate service for over two years. On November 19, 1864, Anderson was reappointed to his previous rank, to date from November 7, and placed in charge of the Bureau of Conscription for Tennessee. But with Union forces in control of much of the Volunteer State, Anderson had his headquarters at Selma, Alabama. The success of his efforts must have been meager, but he retained his post until the war's conclusion.

Anderson returned to Nashville in 1865, and shortly thereafter entered the mercantile business in the city. He died in Nashville on January 2, 1883, and was buried in Old City Cemetery. The 78-year-old soldier had rendered faithful, if uninspired, service to both the United States and the Confederacy.

Jeffry D. Wert

Archer wears the buttons of brigadier and the collar insignia of a colonel, though most probably this portrait was taken after his June 1862 promotion to brigadier. (U.S. Army Military History Institute, Carlisle, Pa.)

✫ James Jay Archer ✫

Born in Bel Air, Maryland, on December 19, 1817, he graduated from the College of New Jersey (now Princeton University) in 1835 and then practiced law in his home state. When the Mexican War began in 1846, Archer volunteered, secured a commission as a captain of infantry and earned a citation for gallantry at Chapultepec. He mustered out of the army on August 31, 1848, returning to Maryland, where he resumed his profession.

His experiences during the Mexican War eventually induced Archer to reenlist in the army in 1855. Commissioned a captain in the 9th United States Infantry, Archer spent the next six years at various frontier posts. After the firing on Fort Sumter, Archer resigned his commission, spurred in part by his resentment over the slow promotion policy of the antebellum army. He was appointed colonel of the 5th Texas on October 2, 1861.

From the fall of 1861 until the spring of 1862, Archer's Regiment served in northern Virginia in the brigade of Louis T. Wigfall. When Wigfall resigned his commission to enter the Confederate Senate in February 1862, Archer assumed temporary command of the brigade. Within a month, however, President Jefferson Davis selected a West Pointer, Colonel John B. Hood of the 4th Texas, as commander of the brigade. Archer served under Hood during the Battle of Seven Pines, before receiving his commission as brigadier general on June 3, 1862, to rank from that day.

Eight days later, on June 11, Archer's Brigade, consisting of the 1st, 7th, and 14th Tennessee, 19th Georgia and 5th Alabama Battalion, joined A. P. Hill's Light Division. During the Seven Days Campaign, Archer demonstrated solid battlefield ability. At Mechanicsville and at Gaines' Mill he led his brigade in two bloody charges and, at Frayser's Farm, his troops counterattacked, stabilizing a section of the Confederate line. The week of fighting cost Archer's Brigade over 500 casualties.

Hill's Light Division earned enduring renown during the campaigns of the summer and fall of 1862, and Archer contributed to this record. At the Battle of Cedar Mountain, on August 9, three of Hill's Brigades, including Archer's, counterattacked and secured the left front of the Confederate line, earning a hard-fought victory for the Southerners. Three weeks later at Second Manassas, Archer had a horse shot from under him during the two-day struggle. His brigade manned Hill's front line on the 30th, repulsed Union assaults, and was in the forefront of the Confederate counterattack late in the day.

After the victory at Second Manassas, the Army of Northern Virginia crossed into Maryland. At Sharpsburg, on September 17, Hill's Division, racing to the battlefield from Harpers Ferry, saved the Confederate Army by crushing the left flank of the Federals as they drove toward the village. Archer was very ill and rode to Sharpsburg in an ambulance. But once his brigade moved into position, he mounted a horse and led it in a vicious attack that recaptured a Confederate battery. Three days later at Shepherdstown, Virginia, his men and those of William D. Pender spearheaded Hill's assault that drove Union pursuit forces into and across the Potomac River. Hill asserted in his report that his troops advanced "in the face of the most tremendous fire of artillery I ever saw."

One of the finest days of Archer's career came at the Battle of Fredericksburg on December 13, 1862. Archer's Brigade manned the front line of Hill's Division with the brigade of James H. Lane on his left. A wooded gap of 600 yards separated the two brigades, and into it the Union division of George G. Meade surged. Lane's troops broke under the assault, and Archer's veterans wavered until he shifted regiments from the right to the left flank. Other Confederate units charged, replugging the gap, and repulsed the Federals. Stonewall Jackson praised the brigadier and his command: "Notwithstanding the perilous situation in which Archer's Brigade was placed, his right, changing front, continued to struggle with undaunted firmness, materially checking the advance of the enemy until reenforcements came to its support."

The highlight of Archer's Confederate service occurred at the Battle of Chancellorsville. On the morning of May 3, 1863, Archer's 1,400 men advanced through the wooded terrain of the battlefield, moving toward a four-gun Federal battery on a hill. The Southerners charged the artillerists capturing the cannon and 100 of the enemy, and seized the high ground. The site was Hazel Grove, the key terrain of the battlefield and, when Confederate batteries rolled onto the crest, the Rebels dominated the ground. During the latter stages of the battle, Archer assumed temporary command of the division after Hill and two successors fell in the combat.

After the Battle of Chancellorsville, Robert E. Lee reorganized the army into three infantry corps. The Light Division was broken up, and Archer's brigade was assigned to the division of Henry Heth in Hill's Third Corps. Weeks later the revamped army marched northward toward Pennsylvania.

On the morning of July 1, 1863, Heth's Division led the army's march toward Gettysburg. When the unit encountered Union cavalrymen, Heth shook out a battle line with the brigades of Archer and Joseph Davis in the front. Archer's men advanced south of the Chambersburg Pike. Crossing Willoughly Run, his troops charged up the slope of McPherson's Ridge, meeting the Union Iron Brigade. The Federals had the best of the combat, shredding Archer's ranks and driving the Southerners back across the run. Archer, who had not handled the brigade skillfully, lagged behind because of exhaustion and was captured. He was the first brigade commander in the Confederate Army captured by the enemy since Lee assumed command over a year before.

Federal authorities first sent Archer to Fort McHenry in Baltimore, then Fort Delaware, and finally Johnson's Island prison in Ohio, where he remained until exchanged in the summer of 1864. Archer assumed command of a brigade in the Army of Tennessee on August 9 but ten days later was reassigned to Lee's army. His imprisonment, however, had broken his health. Archer died in Richmond on October 24, 1864, and was buried in Hollywood Cemetery in the city.

James Archer had been a capable regimental and brigade commander. He had fought bravely and skillfully during the Seven Days Campaign, at Cedar Mountain, Second Manassas, Sharpsburg, and Chancellorsville. His troops defended their position against overwhelming numbers at Fredericksburg, and elicited the praises of Archer's superiors. His worst battle, Gettysburg, proved to be his final one.

Jeffry D. Wert

Taken at the same sitting, this pose is only a slight variant. (Museum of the Confederacy, Richmond)

⋆ *Lewis Addison Armistead* ⋆

No wartime photograph of Armistead has yet come to light. This prewar image shows him in uniform, probably as a captain in the 6th United States Infantry, circa 1860. (Cook Collection, Valentine Museum, Richmond)

Born in New Bern, North Carolina, on February 18, 1817, Armistead entered West Point in 1834 after preparatory schooling. Two years later, he was dismissed from the academy after breaking a plate over the head of fellow cadet Jubal A. Early. But a military career appealed to Armistead, and he secured a direct appointment in the Regular Army in 1839. Breveted twice for gallantry during the Mexican War he remained in the service until the beginning of the Civil War, resigning as captain of the 6th Infantry on May 25, 1861.

Armistead received a commission of colonel of the 57th Virginia on September 25, 1861. The regiment briefly served in western Virginia and North Carolina before being stationed in eastern Virginia. On April 1, 1862, Armistead was promoted to brigadier general effective immediately and assigned a brigade of Virginia troops in the division of Benjamin Huger at Norfolk. When the advance of the Union Army of the Potomac up the Virginia peninsula forced the evacuation of Norfolk, Huger's Division joined Joseph E. Johnston's army in the defense of Richmond.

Armistead directed his brigade in combat for the first time at the Battle of Seven Pines on May 31—June 1, 1862. His performance earned the praise of D. H. Hill, who described Armistead as "that gallant officer." During the Seven Days Campaign at the end of June, Huger's lackluster performance kept his division out of much of the combat. At Malvern Hill, on July 1, however, the advance of Armistead's brigade acted as the signal for the assault of the Confederate Army. The Rebel lines melted before the massed Union artillery and infantry fire with Armistead losing nearly 400 men.

After the campaign, Richard H. Anderson replaced Huger as division commander. At the Battle of Second Manassas, Anderson's command acted primarily in a reserve position, suffering modest casualties. When the Confederates crossed into Maryland, Robert E. Lee assigned Armistead the duty of provost marshal in an effort to stem the flow of thousands of stragglers from the ranks. At Sharpsburg on September 17, Armistead's Brigade was attached to the division of Lafayette McLaws and joined that command in its riveting counterattack into the West Woods. During the action Armistead suffered a wound and relinquished command of the brigade to one of his colonels.

Lee reorganized his army during the fall. George E. Pickett was given a new division that included Armistead's Brigade. Pickett's command acted as a reserve during the Battle of Fredericksburg and in the spring of 1863 served on detached duty in southeastern Virginia, missing the Battle of Chancellorsville. Its rendezvous with glory came on the afternoon of July 3, 1863, at Gettysburg.

Armistead's brigade—the 9th, 14th, 38th, 53d and 57th Virginia—occupied the left of Pickett's line, overlapping and behind the brigade of Richard Garnett. During the preliminary artillery bombardment, Armistead walked among his troops, assuring them: "Lie still, boys, there is no safe place here." When the order came to advance, he shouted his familiar command to the brigade: "Men, remember your wives, your mothers, your sisters and your sweethearts!"

As Pickett's lines stepped forward, Armistead, instead of positioning himself in the brigade's rear, walked to a point about twenty paces in front of the ranks, placed his hat on the point of his sword, holding it in above his head as a guide. Through a terrible cauldron of fire the Virginians advanced. As they closed on the stone wall before the copse of trees, the commands intermingled into a mass of struggling, dying men. Garnett fell dead, and Armistead, endeavoring to uncork the mass, shouted: "Boys, give them the cold steel! Who will follow me."

Between 150 and 300 troops followed Armistead over the stone wall toward a Union battery and the crest of the ridge. Armistead reached the cannon when a volley from Union infantry ripped into the left flank of the Confederates. Armistead reeled and fell near an artillery piece with wounds in an arm and a leg. The Federals overwhelmed the attackers who with hundreds of comrades retreated back across the fields.

Union soldiers carried Armistead to a field hospital where surgeons tended to the wounds. Neither wound was mortal but on July 5 Armistead died from exhaustion. His enemies buried him on the George Spangler farm. Weeks later, a Philadelphia physician had Armistead's body disinterred and embalmed. The doctor hoped to receive financial reimbursement from the general's friends but, when that did not transpire, the remains were eventually shipped to Baltimore and interred in St. Paul's Cemetery.

Lewis Armistead, according to one of his men, was a "gallant, kind and urbane old veteran." A friendly man with a casual manner, Armistead was nevertheless a strict disciplinarian. To him, "obedience to duty" was "the first qualification of a soldier." He held his officers accountable for their actions and those of their men. But he had earned the respect and devotion of those in his command. Lee in his Gettysburg report wrote that Armistead possessed "devotion that never faltered and courage that shrank from no danger," and died in the "highest duty of patriots." At the time he fell, Armistead seemed destined for higher rank and command.

Jeffry D. Wert

Armstrong appears post-January 1863 in this portrait, with his brigadier's collar insignia sewn onto his colonel's blouse. (William Turner Collection)

⋆ Frank Crawford Armstrong ⋆

Armstrong was born on November 22, 1835 at the Choctaw Agency, Indian Territory (now Oklahoma) where his army officer father was stationed. Armstrong later graduated from Holy Cross Academy and College in Massachusetts, and in 1854, he accompanied his stepfather, General Persifor F. Smith, on an expedition into New Mexico. He distinguished himself in a fight with Indians near Eagle Spring and, as a result, received a commission as a 2d lieutenant in the 2d U.S. Dragoons on June 7, 1855. Armstrong participated in Colonel Albert Sidney Johnston's expedition to Utah, 1858–1859, and was promoted to captain in June 1861. He led a company of the 2d Dragoons in the Battle of First Manassas, July 21, 1861, but resigned from the U.S. Army shortly afterwards. The War Department accepted his resignation on August 13 although he had already gone over to the Confederacy. Armstrong served as a volunteer aide on the staff of Brigadier General Ben McCulloch at the Battle of Wilson's Creek, Missouri, on August 10. He then acted in the same capacity on the staff of Colonel James McQ. McIntosh during operations in the Indian Territory from November 19, 1861, to January 4, 1862. He saw action in a fight at Chustenahlah in the Cherokee Nation on December 26. Shortly, he received a commission as a lieutenant and adjutant general on McIntosh's staff.

After McIntosh was killed in the Battle of Pea Ridge, Arkansas, on March 7, 1862, Armstrong first acted on the staff of Colonel Elkanah B. Greer and later on that of Major General Earl Van Dorn. The latter recommended Armstrong for promotion to lieutenant colonel in the Provisional Army of the Confederate States for his services. He accompanied the Army of the West when it moved from Arkansas to Corinth, Mississippi, to reinforce the army of General Pierre G. T. Beauregard. On May 8, Armstrong was named colonel of the 3d Louisiana Infantry Regiment. One of his men remembered that Armstrong "required and expected a strict observance of every military regulation and order" while his men were on duty but "was always affable, kind, and courteous" in his dealings with the men when off duty.

Major General Sterling Price appointed Armstrong an acting brigadier general on July 7 and gave him command of all of the cavalry in the Army of the West. His resignation as colonel of the 3d Louisiana was not accepted until November. He led an expedition from Tupelo to Courtland, Alabama, capturing an enemy force at the latter place on July 25. The next month, Armstrong's force conducted a raid into western Tennessee and successfully engaged the Federals in skirmishes at Boliver on August 30 and at Britton's Lane on September 1. Price wrote, "The highest praise should be awarded to General Armstrong for the prudence, discretion, and good sense with which he conducted this expedition." Armstrong's cavalry covered the retreat of the armies following the battles of Iuka, September 19, and Corinth, October 3–4, and was credited by some with saving both armies from destruction.

Subsequently, Armstrong was given command of a brigade in Brigadier General William H. Jackson's Division of Van Dorn's cavalry corps, Army of Tennessee. With this brigade, Armstrong fought in the engagements at Thompson's Station (or Spring Hill), Tennessee, on March 4–5, 1863; Brentwood on March 25; Franklin on April 10; and again at Franklin on June 4. Union troops captured Armstrong during the last named fight, but he managed to escape.

Winning actual promotion to brigadier general on April 23 to date from January 20, Armstrong in June obtained command of a brigade in Brigadier General Nathan Bedford Forrest's Division, and he participated in the Tullahoma Campaign in central Tennessee that month. Just before the Battle of Chickamauga, Georgia, September 19–20 Armstrong was given a division of two brigades in Forrest's corps.

Armstrong's men fought dismounted during the second day of battle and at one point conducted an attack against the Union right flank. Forrest wrote: "The charge made by Armstrong's Division (while fighting on foot)...would be creditable to the best drilled infantry." Armstrong led a division in Brigadier General William T. Martin's cavalry corps during Lieutenant General James Longstreet's Knoxville Campaign, November 17–December 5, 1863, and later remained in eastern Tennessee and engaged the enemy several times during December 1863 and January 1864. On February 6, 1864, Armstrong was reported as being on leave "with authority to ask for a brigade under General S. D. Lee." Armstrong hoped to serve again under Forrest, who commanded Lee's cavalry, but the War Department relieved him from duty with the Army of Tennessee on March 5 and ordered him to report at Demopolis, Alabama. There, Lieutenant General Leonidas Polk, who had succeeded Lee, assigned Armstrong to command of a brigade under Brigadier General William H. Jackson. The latter's division accompanied Polk's infantry when it left Mississippi to reinforce the Army of Tennessee in northern Georgia in May 1864. Armstrong served credibly during the retreat from Dalton to Atlanta, and briefly during the campaign, he commanded Jackson's Division. That division came under Forrest's direction when General John Bell Hood took the Army of Tennessee toward Nashville in November. Armstrong's men fought in skirmishing at Murfreesboro on December 7 and helped cover the retreat of the army after the disastrous Battle of Nashville on December 15–16. In late November, Beauregard wrote from Macon, Georgia, that he wanted a major general who was "active, energetic, bold, and a good disciplinarian" to take over Major General Joseph Wheeler's cavalry then opposing Major General William T. Sherman's "March to the Sea." Hood replied that he had no one of that rank to spare but stated, "Brigadier General Armstrong is the best person I could recommend from this army, provided he could be promoted to the proper rank." Nothing ever came of this proposal, but it demonstrates Armstrong's high standing in the estimation of his superiors. In mid-February 1865, Armstrong's brigade was transferred from Jackson's Division to that of Brigadier General James R. Chalmers. Armstrong and his men participated in the unsuccessful defense of Selma, Alabama, on April 2, 1865, then in late April

Armstrong assumed command of Chalmer's Division. His command was surrendered as a part of the Department of Alabama, Mississippi, and East Louisiana on May 4. Following the war, Armstrong was in the Overland Mail Service. From 1885 to 1889, he was United States Indian Inspector, and he served as Assistant Commissioner of Indian Affairs from 1893 to 1895. Armstrong died on September 8, 1909, in Bar Harbor, Maine; his body was buried in Rock Creek Cemetery, Georgetown, District of Columbia.

Arthur W. Bergeron, Jr.

Armstrong is still a lieutenant, standing at the right with this group of staff officers, including future general Lunsford Lomax, seated at left, and probably taken in early 1862. (William Turner Collection)

Armstrong's first commission was as a lieutenant and adjutant general on the staffs of Generals James McIntosh and Ben McCulloch. This portrait was probably taken in 1861. (William Turner Collection)

Ironically, the only known wartime photo of Ashby in uniform was taken in death, probably on June 7, 1862, in Winchester, Virginia. He appears to have flowers in his hands. (Chicago Historical Society)

⋆ *Turner Ashby* ⋆

Turner Ashby, grandson of Captain Jack Ashby, a veteran of the American Revolutionary War, and son of Colonel Turner Ashby, an officer in the American Army during the War of 1812, was born at his father's home, "Rosebank," in Fauquier County, Virginia, on October 23, 1828. Ashby's mother, Dorothy Green Ashby, tutored her son until he enrolled in Major Ambler's private educational program.

When Ashby completed such formal education as he was able to obtain from private sources, he engaged in commerce and in agriculture on a farm he purchased within sight of his father's home. Ashby's residence, located near Markham and Farrowsville, was known as Wolfe's Craig, and it remained his home for the remainder of his life. An energetic outdoorsman, an excellent horseman, and a natural leader, he never married.

Ashby provides a prime example of the circumstance faced by many Virginians during the 1850s: a patriot of Virginia, he nonetheless revered his country and honored the roles played by his family members in establishing and preserving the nation. Because he was raised in a slave state, Ashby accepted that institution as a way of life without being an unquestioning advocate, although he did bristle at the abuse abolitionists heaped upon the South. Apparently Ashby did not take an active role in advocating secession as a way to preserve slavery. In fact, in the election of 1860 he supported the Union ticket of John Bell and Edward Everett, as did a slight majority of his fellow Virginians. Of this futile effort to preserve the Union, he said, "If war ensues, we will have the consolation that we have done all in our power to avert it."

By 1860 Ashby already had played a minor role in one of the incidents that provoked the war he wanted to avoid. John Brown seized the Federal armory at Harpers Ferry, Virginia, on October 16, 1859. Federal troops handled the situation well, but fearing that the raid would spark violence elsewhere, or cause others to try to rescue the captured Brown, Governor Henry A.

Wise ordered Virginia troops to be prepared. Ashby, as a captain of volunteers, gathered a company of men and rode to Harpers Ferry. There they mingled with others of their kind who came to do a job that no longer needed doing. He did meet Major T. J. Jackson, a professor at Virginia Military Institute, who was there with the troops. Ashby witnessed Brown's hanging on December 2, 1859, before returning to Wolfe's Craig. In January 1860, his company presented him with a dress sword and a silver service as testimony of their admiration, a kind of prophecy of Ashby's relations with his men during the early years of the Civil War.

When Virginia reluctantly bowed to the Southern majority and seceded in April 1861, Ashby once again gathered his mounted company and reported for duty at Harpers Ferry. He moved to Winchester in June, where his command became part of the 7th Virginia Cavalry. For eight months he engaged in picket and scouting duty, sometimes impersonating a rambling horse-doctor to gather information. John D. Imboden wrote in 1885 that "the career of Ashby was a romance from that time on until he fell." During this time Ashby operated in the area of Romney, Bath, Martinsburg, and Harpers Ferry, and he became involved with J. E. B. Stuart's cavalry and helped to cover Joseph E. Johnston's movement from Winchester to Manassas in July 1861.

Ashby earned promotion to lieutenant colonel on July 23, 1861. Operating now more or less independently, he organized Chew's Horse Battery in November 1861, and soon thereafter assumed command of a regiment. From that time forward, Ashby was associated with the command of General T. J. Jackson, and was the one commander from whom Jackson would suffer much independence. They enjoyed an easy confidence in each other. Jackson did lament at Winchester, "Oh, that my cavalry were in place!" but he never questioned Ashby's courage or devotion. Ashby covered Jackson's retreat from

Charlestown to Swift Run Gap in March 1862, fighting ably at Kernstown. While Jackson moved against General Milroy, Ashby watched Banks at Harrisonburg until he rejoined Jackson to march on Front Royal. He then attacked Federal troops at Buckton Station, joined Jackson again at Front Royal, and they moved toward Middletown to strike Banks once more. His command took part in the action at Winchester on May 25, 1862. On May 27 he was commissioned a brigadier general, but survived only until June 6, when he was struck down while fighting a rear-guard action near Harrisonburg. First his horse was shot, but he continued to lead his men on foot. Waving his sabre and shouting, "Charge, men; for God's sake, charge," he took a bullet in the chest.

Ashby's death affected Jackson personally. Upon hearing the news he withdrew from his staff for a time. Later, he said, "As a partisan officer I never knew his superior. His daring was proverbial; his endurance almost incredible; his tone of character heroic, and his sagacity almost intuitive in divining the purposes and movements of the enemy." One of Ashby's men attempted a eulogy: "We shall miss you mightily, General, we shall miss you in camp, we shall miss you when we go on scout. But we shall miss you most of all when we go out…"; the soldier could not continue.

Despite such praise, and his unquestioned courage, Ashby had deficiencies as a general. Douglas S. Freeman states that he was not an able administrator, and all generals must be administrators as well as leaders in battle. Jackson's biographers, including Frank E. Vandiver, speak of the lack of discipline among Ashby's men, who followed him because of his daring and his devotion to the Confederate cause. For one thing, says Vandiver, "he looked the part of a hero." A soldier described him thus: "He will quit a meal…for a chance at a Yankee…perhaps killed more of them with his own hand than any one man in the State. He is the *bravest* man that I ever saw. I'll describe him. Imagine a man with thick coal black hair, heavy black beard, dark skin, large black eyes, sleepey looking except when the Yankees are in sight…Then they do flash fire…His person is small and slight. Say five feet 8", weight about 130, shape elegant—the best and most graceful rider in the Confederacy."

Archie McDonald

Long believed to be an image of Ashby made just before the war, this shows him as captain of Ashby's Mountain Rangers, a militia group that he raised. (Museum of the Confederacy, Richmond)

✷ *Alpheus Baker* ✷

Alpheus Baker was born in Clover Hill, South Carolina, on May 28, 1828. His father was an educator and scholar from Massachusetts, his mother an Irish immigrant. Educated by his father, Baker became a teacher himself by the age of sixteen and eventually taught schools in Abbeville, South Carolina, Lumpkin, Georgia, and Glennville, Alabama. Moving to Eufaula, Alabama, in 1848, Baker gave up his teaching career and began to read law. He was admitted to the bar in 1849 and opened a practice in Eufaula. Prior to the Civil War, Baker was outspoken in his politics. Returning from a trip to Kansas in 1856, he endorsed making Kansas a slave state in order to restore a balance of power between the North and the South. Barbour County chose Baker to represent it at the 1861 Alabama constitutional convention, but he resigned his seat to join the Eufaula Rifles as a private. Elected captain of his company, Baker was first ordered to Pensacola, Florida, and then in November 1861 to Fort Pillow, Tennessee. There he was elected colonel of the regiment that became known as the 1st Alabama, Tennessee, Mississippi Regiment, because of its multi-state composition. In Mach 1862, Baker was placed in command of a steamboat used to withdraw several Confederate cannon from New Madrid, Missouri, to Island No. 10. When Island No. 10 was surrendered on April 10, Baker became a prisoner of war. After being exchanged in September, Baker's reg-iment was reorganized and four Tennessee companies were replaced with four from Alabama and the regiment was renamed the 54th Alabama, after briefly being called the 50th Alabama.

During the Vicksburg Campaign, Baker served in William W. Loring's Division and saw action at Fort Pemberton on the Yazoo River. On May 13, 1863, he was severely wounded in the foot at the Battle of Champion's Hill where Loring characterized him as "the brave Alpheus Baker."

While the actual date and seniority of Baker's promotion is uncertain, on March 7, 1864, Richmond informed him of his promotion to brigadier general and ordered him to Dalton, Georgia to take command of John C. Moore's Alabama Brigade, ultimately composed of the 37th, 40th, 42d and 54th Alabama Regiments and assigned to Maj. Gen. Alexander Stewart's Division. Some sources claim March 5 as his commission date. Baker's Brigade engaged in skirmishing on May 9 at Rocky Face Ridge and formed the army's rear guard on the retreat from Dalton to Resaca. On May 14 Baker held the extreme right of Joseph E. Johnston's Army of Tennessee, having his right regiment touching the Oostenaula River. An advance late

Baker served through the entire war, but seems not to have left behind a photograph of himself in uniform. This image probably dates from the 1870s. (Museum of the Confederary, Richmond)

in the afternoon easily pushed the Union forces back a mile and a half, but the movement was halted and Baker returned to his original position. On May 15 his brigade participated in Stewart's attack during the Battle of Resaca. Brought up from a supporting position, Baker led his men in an assault after the lead Confederate brigades were repulsed. Baker's Brigade hit Ohio and New York troops posted behind entrenchments and was badly shot up. The futile assault lasted only minutes, but in that time Baker had his horse killed and lost 176 men.

Baker was then only lightly engaged until the Battle of New Hope Church on May 25. There A. P. Stewart praised his men for helping repulse the Union assaults while losing only eighty-seven men. Two days later the brigade came under heavy artillery fire and lost approximately fifty more men. Such action quickly wore out Baker's Brigade. From May 7 to June 2, his unit suffered 311 casualties.

By the Battle of Atlanta on July 22, 1864, Baker's brigade was part of Henry Clayton's Division. Little is known of Baker's role in the July 22 attack except that his brigade was in Clayton's front line. When John Bell Hood lashed out at William T. Sherman's army again at Ezra Church on July 28, Clayton intended for Baker to the the division's reserve brigade, but Baker was sent into battle by the corps' assistant adjutant general without Clayton's knowledge. When Baker drove the federal skirmishers back onto their main line, Clayton advanced the rest of the division. Baker again charged "with spirit," Clayton wrote, but was repulsed with the rest of the Confederate forces. Although Baker's brigade "had fought with gallantry," the Rebels failed to achieve a victory and Baker lost half of his men.

Baker had been praised by his division commander several times during the Atlanta Campaign, but he was criticized by corps commander, Stephen D. Lee. On August 3, Union forces attacked Baker's picket line outside Atlanta and seized the position. Baker apparently ordered a subordinate officer to retake the rifle pits, but the attempt failed. On August 8 Lee wrote Clayton demanding to know why Baker did not lead the counterattack personally, since it involved over half the brigade. Baker, Lee complained, "does not seem to have acted with any degree of energy upon the occasion," and the officer in charge showed "indecision and vacillation." Lee fumed that Baker's Brigade "had lost its picket lines oftener than any

other brigade in this corps and had never retaken them." Much of the blame for the failure to retake the pits, he said, was due "to a want of energy and promptness on the part of the brigade commander." Lee then tempered the rebuke by noting that Baker had shown improvement since the incident in question. On August 5, Lee noted, Baker's pickets were again attacked but instead of fleeing, they put up a stubborn fight and lost half their complement before withdrawing.

Lee's criticism of Baker seems overly harsh in light of the brigade's good record. But perhaps because of Lee's feelings, Baker's Brigade was transferred to Mobile, Alabama, that August. Baker continued to serve in the Department of the Gulf until early 1865 when his brigade was transferred to the Carolinas to help stop Sherman. As part of Clayton's Division, Baker's men took part in the Battle of Bentonville on March 19, 1865. In that fight his 350 men captured 204 Union prisoners. In May Baker's command was surrendered to Sherman along with the rest of Johnston's army.

After the war, Baker returned to the practice of Law and became well known for his use of eloquence and use of humor in court. In 1878 he moved to Louisville, Kentucky, and established a law office there. He died on October 2, 1891, and is buried in Louisville.

Terry Jones

Thomas Connelly, *Autumn of Glory* Baton Rouge, 1971

Baker, recuperating from one of his several wartime wounds, appears in brigadier's uniform sometime after July 1863, and probably prior to his 1864 posting to North Carolina. (Cook Collection, Valentine Museum, Richmond)

⋆ *Laurence Simmons Baker* ⋆

Born in Gates City, North Carolina, on May 15, 1830, to a distinguished family, Baker received a good education at the Norfolk Academy before he entered West Point in 1847. Graduating 42d in the class of 1851, he served in the cavalry on the frontier, rising to the rank of captain of the 3d United States Cavalry by 1861.

Although he opposed secession, Baker resigned his commission on May 18, 1861, approximately two weeks before his native state seceded. He had already been appointed lieutenant colonel of the 1st North Carolina Cavalry, to rank from March 16. The regiment transferred to Virginia to the command of J. E. B. Stuart, and the following spring the members of the regiment elected Baker their colonel, his rank to date from March 1, 1862.

The 1st North Carolina did not participate in Stuart's ride around the Union Army in mid-June and saw only limited action during the Seven Days Campaign. After the latter series of battles, Baker's command was assigned to the brigade of Wade Hampton, and his performances during the campaigns of Second Manassas and Sharpsburg earned the praises of his superior officers.

During the winter of 1863, a subordinate officer accused Baker of drunkenness. Stuart investigated and secured a written pledge from Baker that the colonel would not drink whiskey for the duration of the war. Stuart asserted later that Baker's conduct improved, but he seemed not as "dashing" as before.

Baker's first significant role in action came at Brandy Station on June 9, 1863. In that swirling engagement, the regiment made a dismounted charge upon Union infantry and undertook two mounted charges upon Union cavalry. The North Carolinians routed the 10th New York Cavalry, capturing its flag and over 130 troopers. In his report, Hampton cited Baker's "skill and judgment" and "conspicuous gallantry."

Twelve days later, on June 21, at Upperville, Virginia, Hampton's brigade engaged the Union brigade of Judson Kilpatrick. The opponents crashed into each other in and around the village in a chaotic struggle marked by hand-to-hand combat. Baker's North Carolinians were in the midst of the fury and fought well.

At Gettysburg, on July 3, Hampton's brigade once again bore a crucial role. During the cavalry fight east of the main battlefield, the 1st North Carolina and the Jeff Davis Legion broke through the Federal ranks and pursued. Encountering Union reserves, the two units fought hand-to-hand. Hampton was wounded in the combat, and Baker, as senior colonel, took command of the brigade and extricated it although suffering a slight wound.

During the retreat back to Virginia, Stuart's cavalrymen screened the army's rear. Baker's troopers were engaged in skirmishes at a number of places. On July 31, the brigade repulsed a Federal sortie across the Rappahannock River. Robert E. Lee, writing of the action, stated: "Hampton's Brigade behaved with its usual gallantry, and was very skillfully handled by Colonel Baker." Lee previously recommended the North Carolinian for promotion to brigadier general, which Baker subsequently received on July 30, to rank from July 23.

Baker, however, was severely wounded in the arm during the fighting on the 31st. The arm bones had

---

A slight variant made at the same sitting is this bust portrait of Baker. (U.S. Army Military History Institute, Carlisle, PA.)

been shattered, rendering the limb useless and ending his career as a cavalry officer. Baker required months to recuperate.

When Baker returned to duty in May 1864, Wade Hampton, now commanding the cavalry corps because of Stuart's death, requested that Baker be given a division and promotion to major general. His disability, however, precluded his acceptance, and Confederate authorities assigned Baker to command of a military district in North Carolina.

Baker's forces in the district were stationed at Goldsboro, Kingston, Wilmington, Plymouth, and Weldon. His primary responsibility was to protect the Weldon Railroad. Late in the year, authorities dispatched his troops to Savannah as the Union armies of William T. Sherman closed on the city. After the fall of the city, Baker returned to North Carolina and assumed command of a brigade of reserve troops in the division of Robert Hoke. His brigade fought in the Battle of Bentonville on March 19–21. The Confederates launched three assaults on the first day, but Sherman's Federals held, and Joseph E. Johnston's army withdrew during the night of the 21st. Baker was not with the Confederate Army when Johnston formally surrendered on April 26. He accepted a parole in Raleigh in May.

Baker had a varied postwar career. He was a farmer, an insurance agent and, after 1877, a station agent for the Seaboard Air Line Railroad in Suffolk, Virginia. He died in Suffolk on April 10, 1907, and was buried in the Cedar Hill Cemetery in that community.

Laurence S. Baker had a solid career as a cavalry officer in the Civil War. In a corps filled with Virginians, the North Carolinian had distinguished himself on a number of battlefields and would have most likely attained divisional command had he not been crippled by a wound. Baker was typical of the many fine field officers that made Jeb Stuart's command such an excellent fighting force.

Jeffry D. Wert

Possibly another variant from the same sitting. (Cook Collection, Valentine Museum, Richmond)

✴ *William Edwin Baldwin* ✴

Baldwin appears in his uniform as colonel of 14th Mississippi Infantry, in this image made prior to February 1862. (Museum of the Confederacy)

William Edwin Baldwin was born July 18, 1827, in Statesburg, South Carolina, but at an early age moved to Columbus, Mississippi. As an adult Baldwin sold books and stationery. He joined a militia known as the "Columbus Riflemen" in 1849, and served as an officer for twelve years. When the Civil War began he became captain of Company K, 14th Mississippi Infantry, took his men to Pensacola, and was soon elected as the regiment's colonel. His command was ordered to east Tennessee, and in August he was instructed to move to the Johnson County line where he was to scout, obtain information about Unionists in the area, and seize the leaders. In September his regiment was ordered to the Cumberland Gap, and by October he was in command of the 2d Infantry Brigade composed of his regiment and the 26th Tennessee. On February 11, 1862, he left Cumberland City for Fort Donelson with his two regiments. His own regiment, the 14th Mississippi, had been sent to Fort Donelson in advance. When he arrived he became an acting brigadier general and assumed command of the 26th Mississippi, the 26th Tennessee, and, temporarily, the 20th Mississippi. Baldwin's brigade constituted the front of the attacking force on February 15, and along with Colonel Wharton, took the first shock of the battle. Of the 1,358 men he led into battle, 42 were killed and 216 wounded. General Buckner wrote that Baldwin was "conspicuous on every occasion" for his "gallantry and military judgment," and he should "merit the special approbation of the Government." He was captured at Fort Donelson, imprisoned at Fort Delaware, then sent to Fort Warren.

After being exchanged in August 1862, Baldwin was promoted to brigadier general on October 3, to rank from September 19, 1862. He took part in the battle at Coffeeville in early December where his commander claimed he "displayed the greatest good judgment and gallantry." In February 1863 he was ordered to report to General M. L. Smith for duty with his division in the defense of Vicksburg and Port Hudson. Baldwin's brigade included the 17th and 31st Louisiana, the 4th and 46th Mississippi, the 1st Mississippi Light Artillery, and the Mississippi Partisan Rangers. In late May he reported 1,448 men present, and 1,450 guns. On May 1 he participated in the battle of Port Gibson where he had 12 killed, 48 wounded, and 27 missing. From there he moved to the Vicksburg defenses, arriving on May 4. The next evening he moved his command about five miles southeast of the city and remained there until the 8th when he moved ten miles from Vicksburg on the Warrenton and Hall's Ferry road. His regiments served as picket and some of the men spent part of the time reconnoitering. On the 15th he was ordered by Major General Forney to take command of all troops guarding Big Black Bridge and its approaches, front and rear. On May 17 he was instructed to concentrate all of his command at Bovina, if possible, and take a position on the left of the bridge, to cover the crossing of the Confederates from the left bank. He was ordered to move all troops in the direction of Vicksburg, and his command was instructed to bring up the rear. On the 18th Major General Smith directed him to occupy the outer line of defenses covering the left of the main works. However, at 3 a.m., he was ordered to evacuate the outer line, and occupy the inner and principal line of entrenchments.

On the 22d Baldwin received a severe wound about 12 o'clock and left the field, although General Smith reported that Baldwin returned to duty before the battle closed. Smith observed that Baldwin "receives my special acknowledgements for gallant service." As a result of the wound, Baldwin was out of action until June 13, when he returned to active duty and commanded his brigade for the remainder of the siege.

On July 3, when Pemberton brought his officers together to consider Grant's term of surrender, he reported: "These terms, it may be proper to add, were approved by every division and brigade commander with one exception (Brigadier General [W. E.] Baldwin), who, without offering any objection to them, insisted on holding out, but assigned no reason for it." That night Baldwin penned a short note to General Smith that read: "I object to the surrender of the troops, and am in favor of holding the position, or attempting to do so, as long as possible." After the surrender, Baldwin recalled: "My command marched over to the trenches and stacked their arms with the greatest reluctance, conscious of their ability to hold the position assigned them for an indefinite period of time." Baldwin's brigade included 1,734 men: the 4th and 46th Mississippi, the 17th and 31st Louisiana, and a Tennessee battery command by Captain Thomas F. Tobin. On July 13 Baldwin was among those declared exchanged, and part of his troops rejoined him and were rearmed. By November he commanded a new brigade in Forney's Division, Department of Mississippi and East Louisiana. When Braxton Bragg requested reinforcements in Tennessee, Baldwin's brigade, along with that of William A. Quarles, was temporarily detached and sent. Baldwin's brigade became part of Hardee's Corps, Walker's Division, and consisted of the 4th, 35th, 40th, and 46th Mississippi. After the battle at Missionary Ridge there was some confusion over which department Baldwin belonged to and Polk pointed out that because of the threat to Mobile, the men should be ordered to the Department of the Gulf. General J. E. Johnston agreed, and on January 15, 1864, instructed Baldwin to move to Mobile. Upon his arrival there he commanded 1,659 effectives. Scarcely a month later, on February 19, Baldwin died in an unfortunate accident near Dog River Factory, Alabama, when his stirrup broke and he suffered a fatal fall from his horse. He was first buried at Mobile, but his body was later moved to Friendship Cemetery in Columbus.

Anne Bailey

✴ *William Barksdale* ✴

No wartime uniformed photograph is currently known of Barksdale, the only portrait available being this prewar view taken in the 1850s. (Miller, *Photographic History*)

Born in Smyrna, Tennessee, on August 21, 1821, Barksdale attended the University of Nashville, then moved to Columbus, Mississippi, where he practiced law and edited the Columbus *Democrat*. During the Mexican War, he served both as an enlisted man and as an officer in the 2d Mississippi, then in 1852, won election to the United States House of Representatives. For eight years the Mississippian espoused the doctrine of state rights in Congress and, when his state seceded in early 1861, he returned home and embraced the Southern cause.

From March 18, 1861, Barksdale acted briefly as quartermaster general of Mississippi troops before receiving the colonelcy of the 13th Mississippi on May 14. The regiment arrived in Virginia in time for the Battle of First Manassas, serving in the brigade of Jubal A. Early. The only serious fighting the Mississippians encountered in the engagement occurred late in the day when roughly fifty of them stumbled into a nest of wasps. The insects shattered the Rebels' ranks, and Barksdale, trying to restore order, rode into the swarm.

In the fall of 1861 the 13th Mississippi was combined with three other Mississippi regiments into a brigade under Richard Griffith. By the spring of 1862, Griffith's command was sent to the Peninsula where it served under John B. Magruder. The Mississippians did not see significant action until the Seven Days Campaign. On June 29, at Savage's Station, Griffith fell mortally wounded, and Barksdale assumed command of the brigade. Two days later, at Malvern Hill, the Mississippians charged across an open field, in Barksdale's words, "under a terrible fire of shell, grape, canister, and Minie balls." Robert E. Lee cited Barksdale in his report, writing that the colonel displayed the "highest qualities of the soldier."

Barksdale received promotion to brigadier general on August 12, to rank from the same date, and official command of the brigade which consisted of the 13th, 17th, 18th and 21st Mississippi. As a part of Lafayette McLaws' division, Barksdale's brigade missed the Battle of Second Manassas.

During the Maryland Campaign, Barksdale distinguished himself. On September 13, his brigade and Joseph Kershaw's drove Federal troops from the crest of Maryland Heights, sealing the fate of the garrison in Harpers Ferry. Four days later at Sharpsburg, McLaws once again had Barksdale and Kershaw spearhead his counterattack. McLaws claimed that Barksdale possessed "radiant wild joy" when leading a charge. On this day Barksdale must have been ecstatic as his veterans assisted in the rout of John Sedgwick's Union division, sweeping the West Woods clean of Federals.

Barksdale's finest day as a brigadier came three months later at Fredericksburg on December 11. The Mississippians occupied the town with orders to resist Federal efforts to cross the Rappahannock River. The Northerners opened with a heavy bombardment of artillery as engineers tried to lay a pontoon bridge. Despite the storm of artillery fire, the Mississippians drove back the bridge builders. An admiring staff officer wrote later of the Southerners: "The brave fellows were there, however, to stay."

Barksdale was a large, portly man who embraced the Confederate cause as fervently as he had argued for Southern rights in Congress. During some of the worst action on the day, he ordered a courier to "tell General Lee that if he wants a bridge of dead Yankees I can furnish him with one!" But the Union fire continued; the engineers finished the bridge and infantry crossed the river. Barksdale finally withdrew after dark but not until McLaws had sent a second order to do so. McLaws asserted afterwards that the Mississippians held for sixteen hours, writing: "A more gallant and worthy service is rarely accomplished by so small a force." In the ensuing battle, fought on the 13th, Barksdale's troops held a reserve position.

During the Chancellorsville Campaign, May 1–5, 1863, Barksdale's troops once again found themselves defending the heights behind Fredericksburg. While the bulk of Lee's army fought the Federals around Chancellorsville, a contingent of Confederates, including the Mississippians, protected Lee's rear against another force of Northerners. It was a game of bluff for the outnumbered Southerners, but they held the ground throughout May 2, until the morning of the third. Barksdale's conduct added to his laurels.

With the victory at Chancellorsville, Lee's army marched northward into Pennsylvania. On the afternoon of July 2, 1863, Barksdale's Mississippians formed for battle in Pitzer's Woods west of the Emmitsburg Road. It was a kind of day Barksdale relished—his Mississippians were under orders to attack the enemy. To his right, units of James Longstreet's First Corps moved to the offensive. As the echelon assault unfolded and drew nearer to Barksdale, the impetuous brigadier twice asked McLaws and Longstreet if he could advance. They told him to wait. Moments before the order finally came, Barksdale told his regimental officers: "The line before you must be broken—to do so let every officer and man animate his comrades by his personal presence in the front line." Then, with a yell, the 1,400 Mississippians emerged from the woods, storming toward the road. Nothing seemed to stop the Rebels as they wrested the Peach Orchard from its defenders and drove along the Wheatfield Road. The combat raged, and Barksdale toppled from his horse. He had been hit in the chest and in the left leg, with the bullets puncturing a lung and fracturing a leg bone.

After the Confederate repulse, Union soldiers found the wounded brigadier and carried him to an aid station along the Taneytown Road. He suffered intensely and died on the morning of July 3, 1863. The Federals put him in a temporary grave nearby, but ultimately his remains were returned to Mississippi and buried in Greenwood Cemetery in Jackson. William Barksdale had fallen as perhaps he would have wished—at the head of his charging Mississippians.

Jeffry D. Wert

The Richmond firm of Vannerson & Jones made this portrait of Barringer, probably not long after his June 1864 promotion to brigadier, for he still wears his colonel's blouse. (Museum of the Confederacy, Richmond)

⭑ *Rufus Barringer* ⭑

He was born in "Popular Grove," Cabarrus County, North Carolina, on December 2, 1821. His grandfather, Paulus Behringer, who had emigrated to Philadelphia from Wurtemburg in 1743, promptly Anglicized the family name. Rufus' father was Paul Barringer, a brigadier general of militia during the War of 1812 and a vigorous politician; his mother was Elizabeth Brandon.

After attending Sugar Creek Academy and graduating from the University of North Carolina in 1842, Barringer studied law with Richmond Hill. In 1844 he began practicing his profession in Concord, North Carolina, where he quickly distinguished himself among his peers. Politically a Whig and Presbyterian by faith, Barringer also avidly supported the temperance movement. In 1848, at the age of twenty-seven, he was elected to the state assembly, and he was reelected in 1850. The following year he was elected state senator and, in conjunction with William S. Ashe, he lobbied for a railroad charter and other internal improvements to enhance commercial development. He retired from political life in 1852, probably because of the demise of the Whig party. An avowed Unionist, Barringer served as a presidential elector for John Bell in 1860. Although opposed to secession, he accepted the final decision of his state, and continuing in his father's footsteps he volunteered for military service. During the conflict he chose to remain with the army despite repeated offers of a seat in the Confederate Congress.

Barringer raised a company of cavalry and entered the Confederate Army as its captain on May 16, 1861. Assigned to the 1st North Carolina Cavalry as Company F, Barringer led his men throughout the Peninsular, Second Manassas, Sharpsburg, Fredericksburg, and Chancellorsville Campaigns. Despite this service, he remained a captain until after the battle of Brandy Station in June of 1863 where he received a severe face wound and earned the praise of his brigadier, Wade Hampton. When writing of Barringer's performance during the fighting near

Gettysburg, Hampton reported, "Barringer...acted as a field officer...and bore himself with marked coolness and good conduct..."

Barringer now rose rapidly through the ranks, being promoted to major on August 26, 1863, and to lieutenant colonel three months later through his participation in the Bristoe Campaign. During that campaign he is credited for leading a charge at Buckland Mills and aptly fighting at Auburn Mills, which led to his nomination for brigadier general on June 1, 1864, to rank immediately. On June 4 he received command of a brigade of cavalry in Major General William H. F. Lee's division on the fourth. Barringer led his brigade, which consisted of the 1st, 2d, 3d, and 5th North Carolina regiments, until April 3, 1865, when it was literally destroyed while covering the Army of Northern Virginia's retreat from Richmond.

During the last year of the war Barringer occasionally held divisional command, including during the Battle of Reams' Station in August of 1864. Hampton, now a major general and commanding Robert E. Lee's cavalry corps, noted in his report of that engagement: "General Barringer commanded [W. H. F.] Lee's division to my satisfaction..." Robert E. Lee, in a letter to North Carolina Governor Zebulon Vance, wrote "the brigade of General Barringer bore a conspicuous part in the operations of the cavalry which were not less distinguished for boldness and efficiency than those of the infantry. If men who remain in North Carolina share the spirit of those they have sent to the field, as I doubt not they do, her defense may be securely entrusted to their hands."

On March 31, 1865, he won the last substantial Confederate victory in Virginia at Chamberlain Run. Barringer led his brigade across that stream at a point one hundred yards wide, saddle-girth deep, and in the face of heavy enemy fire, and successfully drove a Federal cavalry division from the field.

On April 3, 1865, Barringer was captured by troopers of Colonel John J. Coppinger's 15th New York Cavalry. Initially escorted to City Point along with

Lieutenant General Richard S. Ewell, Barringer met President Abraham Lincoln there before continuing to the old Capitol Prison. After a brief confinement in Washington, he was transferred to Fort Delaware. Barringer took the oath of allegiance in June, was released July 24, and reached his home in August. His distinguished military career was over. It is claimed by one source that he "had fought in seventy-six actions, been three times wounded, and had two horses shot under him." One of his subordinates described him as being a "prudent, methodical, and cautious" soldier.

Barringer relocated to Charlotte and returned to the practice of law. He accepted the defeat of the Confederate in much the same vein he had the secession of his native state four years earlier, and actively worked to restore the Union. He encouraged acceptance of the policies of the national government—including Negro suffrage—and became an active member of the Republican Party. He participated in the Constitutional Convention of 1875 and was the Republican candidate for lieutenant governor in 1880. Despite the demands of a distinguished career as an attorney and politician, Barringer found the time to pursue affairs of the heart. In 1854 he married his first wife, Eugenia Morrison, a sister of the wives of Lieutenant Generals Thomas J. "Stonewall" Jackson and Daniel Harvey Hill. Following Eugenia's death in 1858, Barringer married Rosalie Chunn of Ashville and, later, Margaret Long of Orange County. His wives gave birth to three sons, the most prominent of whom was Dr. Paul B. Barringer.

He gave up his law practice in 1884 and retired to his estate. He maintained an intense interest in educational matters, particularly those items of interest to the small farmer, and occasionally wrote historical papers. Most of his articles related to his activities during the Civil War or North Carolina history. From what proved to be his death-bed, he wrote a history of his old regiment. He died in Charlotte on February 3, 1895, and is buried there.

Lawrence L. Hewitt

Hill, D. H., Jr. *North Carolina*. Atlanta: 1899. Vol. IV of Clement A. Evans, ed., *Confederate Military History*.

A late 1864 or early 1865 image of Barringer shows him with a brigadier's button arrangement on his blouse. (U.S. Army Military History Institute, Carlisle, Pa.)

A variant image, probably made on the same occasion. (Warner, *Generals in Gray*)

✫ John Decatur Barry ✫

Taken probably when Barry was a major in the 18th North Carolina, sometime between Antietam and Chancellorsville, this is to date the only wartime image of him known. (Virginia Historical Society)

This native of Wilmington, North Carolina, was born June 21, 1839. After graduating with honors from the University of North Carolina in 1859, he worked as a banker in Wilmington.

The prewar militia company of youths in which Barry served as a private, the Wilmington Rifle Guards, turned out on April 15, 1861, promptly after the fall of Fort Sumter, but over a month before North Carolina seceded. On June 15, the Rifle Guards entered state service for a year, and the following month they became Company I of the 8th North Carolina Volunteer Infantry. On August 20, the regiment was transferred to national service. Its designation was changed from the 8th North Carolina to the 18th North Carolina on November 14, 1861.

Barry continued as a private in Company I during its early service at Fort Fisher, Coosawhatchie, and Kinston. While at the latter town, the regiment reorganized on April 14, 1862, for three years service. In the resulting elections, only the major, quartermaster, three surgeons, and one company commander were retained in those offices. The Rifle Guards elevated Barry from private to captain of Company I.

Thus far, the 18th had seen little action. It had reached South Carolina after Port Royal fell and had returned to its own state too late to save New Berne. In May 1862, however, it transferred to Virginia; thenceforth to the end of the war it was heavily engaged. Barry evidently fought in the 18th's first combat at Hanover Court House—where some companies of the 18th lost half their men killed or wounded—and a month later at Gaines' Mill. At Frayser's Farm, he was severely wounded.

Whether he returned in time to fight at Cedar Mountain and Second Manassas is not clear. He was definitely present in the Maryland Campaign, where his regimental commander singled him out for "special mention…for his coolness and gallantry and devotion to duty." On November 11 came promotion to major of the 18th. His first battle in field grade was presumably Fredericksburg the following month.

Barry's most memorable, and most tragic, day in the Civil War occurred on May 2, 1863, at Chancellorsville. Late that afternoon, the great Confederate flank attack rolled up the Union right. To exploit that victory, the Light Division, to which the 18th belonged, moved up from reserve for night-time pursuit. The graycoats deployed astride the Orange Plank Road, with the 18th immediately north of that highway. In the darkness and confusion, the Tarheels heard horsemen approaching them from the direction of Yankee lines. Fearing a cavalry charge, Barry ordered the regiment to fire. When the riders cried out that they were friends, Barry suspected a trick, denounced them as liars, and kept firing. Only too late did he learn that the horsemen really were friends; it was his fire that mortally wounded "Stonewall" Jackson.

When fighting resumed on May 3, Barry was heavily engaged. He "rendered me great assistance," reported Brigadier General James H. Lane, the brigade commander. Of the thirteen field officers in that brigade, Barry was the only one to emerge unscathed. His colonel was killed and eight days later his wounded lieutenant colonel resigned to take his legislative seat in Raleigh. On May 27, Barry was promoted colonel of the 18th, to rank from May 3. In just thirteen months, he had risen from private to colonel.

In less time than that, he would receive brigade command. He led the 18th at Gettysburg, where it participated in "Pickett's Charge", and subsequently at Jack's Shop, Culpeper, and Mine Run. When fighting resumed in 1864, he saw much action at the Wilderness, Spotsylvania, North Anna, and Pole Green Church. His operations in the Wilderness prompted Lane to report that "Barry is deserving great praise for the manner in which he handled his regiment in protecting our right flank on the 5th. He has shown himself fully competent to fill a more responsible place than that which he now holds."

Opportunity to fill that higher office came late on June 2, when Lane was critically wounded at Turkey Hill. Command of the brigade devolved on Barry as senior colonel. His force now included not only his own 18th but also the 7th, 28th, 33d, and 37th North Carolina Infantry Regiments. He saw little action at Second Cold Harbor and Second Riddel's Shop but was heavily engaged in the great Confederate victory at First Weldon Railroad.

On July 25, R. E. Lee endorsed Barry's promotion to brigadier general. A temporary assignment was made on August 8, ranking from August 3; he was formally assigned to command Lane's Brigade on August 11—and at the time the fifth youngest general in the Confederate army (by war's end, the youthful Carolinian was the eighth youngest of the 425 Southern generals). In the meantime, however, Barry was severely wounded by a sharpshooter while reconnoitering the Northern position at Deep Bottom early on July 27. The wound cost him two fingers and disabled him for the rest of the year. With Barry out of action and with another colonel back with the brigade, Lee, on August 13, recommended that the promotion be cancelled. Around September 18 the War Department vacated the appointment.

Though he had led the brigade in battle as a colonel, the convalescing Barry never actually served as a general under his brief appointment. He did return to duty with the 18th in 1865 and again commanded the brigade as ranking colonel while Lane temporarily headed the Light Division as the end of February. In March, Barry was transferred to "departmental duty" in North Carolina. He was paroled at Raleigh on May 12.

Postwar, he edited the *Wilmington Dispatch*. He was buried in that city following his death on March 24, 1867.

A brave, hard-fighting, yet cool officer, Barry earned the respect of his superiors and men. He gave promise of fulfilling their confidence that he would make a good brigadier. Before those expectations could be tested, a marksman's bullet cut short his career just as his own volleys the previous year had tragically cut short the career of Stonewall Jackson and perhaps of the Confederacy itself.

Richard J. Sommers

Barton posed sometime after March 1862 for this half-length portrait. (William C. Davis collection)

⋆ *Seth Maxwell Barton* ⋆

The son of Thomas Bowerbank Barton, an attorney in Fredericksburg, Virginia, he was born in that city on September 8, 1829. All of Thomas Barton's four sons eventually served in the Confederate Army. Seth Barton entered the United States Military Academy just shy of his sixteenth birthday and was graduated in the lower half of the class of 1849. Barton's class standing is surprising in light of the fact that classmates and instructors regarded him as more mature than the average cadet despite the youthful age at which he was admitted. One classmate suggested that Barton's academic performance suffered because of his preference for reading unrelated literature: "he was fond of reading and gave more attention to the pursuit of general knowledge than to the specific requirements of the course."

Following graduation, Barton was commissioned into the infantry since he did not have a choice of the other services. His first assignment was at Fort Columbus, New York, and he spent his time in New York Harbor on Governor's Island. Within a year he was promoted to brevet second lieutenant, 3d Infantry, and reassigned to a post in New Mexico. Barton remained in the Southwest until the beginning of the Civil War. After first being posted in New Mexico, but also serving at various installations in Texas, he served as adjutant to his regimental commander 1855–1857, and fought in engagement against the Comanche Indians. In 1853 he won promotion to 1st lieutenant, and advanced to a captaincy four years later.

Barton participated in a march to Fort Leavenworth, Kansas, in 1861, then resigned his commission, effective June 11. Three days earlier, he was appointed lieutenant colonel of the 3d Arkansas regiment, under Colonel Albert Rust. The 3d Arkansas was part of the command of General Henry R. Jackson, and was engaged in the West Virginia Campaign and in the Shenandoah Valley late in 1861. In this capacity, Barton helped to fortify Camp Bartow, located on the Greenbriar River, and participated in action at Cheat Mountain and in the defense of Camp Bartow in October, at the head of his regiment. Barton also acted for a time during the winter of 1861–1862 as General T. J. Jackson's chief engineer.

Barton was nominated for a brigadier generalcy in January 1862, but his nomination was withdrawn from the Confederate Senate, then resubmitted on March 18, to date from March 11, and the Senate immediately confirmed him. Placed at the head of a brigade, he was assigned to the command of General Edmund Kirby Smith in the Department of East Tennessee. He commanded the 4th Brigade, consisting of units from Alabama, Georgia, and Virginia during the Cumberland Gap Campaign.

Later in 1862, Barton's command was assigned to assist in the defense of Vicksburg, Mississippi. His command occupied the Confederate center during General William T. Sherman's attempted approach along the Chickasaw Bayou in December 1862, and they succeeded in holding their ground despite three days of rifle and artillery firing and five attempted assaults on December 29. Barton continued to serve in the defense of Vicksburg, seeing action at Chickasaw Bluffs and Champion's Hill, until the city was surrendered to General Ulysses S. Grant on July 4, 1863.

When formally exchanged, Barton received a command in the Eastern Theater. He commanded Armistead's Brigade in General George Pickett's Division, a position vacated by Armistead's death at Gettysburg. Barton joined the command in Kinston, North Carolina, and led it in action at New Berne early in 1864.

On May 10, 1864, Barton's command was engaged at Drewry's Bluff against General Benjamin F. Butler. His men fought bravely, and eventually captured the enemy's position. Nonetheless, Pickett criticized Barton's leadership, if not his bravery, and he was relieved of command by General Robert Ransom. His

A later war view, probably taken in Richmond in 1864. (Cook Collection, Valentine Museum, Richmond)

regimental officers twice petitioned that he be reinstated, and Barton himself requested a hearing which was not granted. Even Ransom admitted that Barton's personal bravery was not in question.

Barton retained his commission but had no command until assigned a brigade composed of infantry and artillery during the defense of Richmond, Virginia, in the fall of 1864. His brigade became part of General G. W. C. Lee's Division in January 1865, and he continued to serve in this capacity until captured at Sailor's Creek on April 6. Barton was imprisoned at Fort Warren with more important Confederate figures until his release on July 24, 1865. While there he joined other prominent prisoners in condemning the assassination of President Abraham Lincoln.

Following his release from Fort Warren, Barton returned to Virginia. He lived in Fredericksburg, but died in Washington, D.C. on April 11, 1900. He is buried in Arlington Cemetery.

Archie McDonald

A very slight variant taken at the same sitting. (William Turner Collection)

Quite probably a late 1864 or 1865 portrait, this image shows Bate's beard graying, and somewhat longer than in earlier photographs. (William Turner Collection)

✶ *William Brimage Bate* ✶

Bate was born in Bledsoe's Lick (now Castalian Springs), Sumner County, Tennessee, on October 7, 1826. His early education was in a log schoolhouse which later became known as the Rural Academy. When his father died in late 1842, sixteen-year-old William left school to become second clerk on the steamboat *Saladin*, which steamed the Cumberland and Mississippi Rivers between Nashville and New Orleans.

Upon the advent of the Mexican War, the impassioned Bate, whose ancestors included Generals Thomas Sumter and John Coffee, enlisted in New Orleans as a private in a Louisiana company. Purportedly, he was the first Tennessean to reach Mexican soil. Before that the conflict ended, Bate had achieved the rank of 1st lieutenant in Company I of the 3d Tennessee Infantry.

When his military service concluded in 1849, Bate settled in Gallatin, Tennessee, and established and edited the *Tenth Legion*, an ardent Democratic newspaper. Before the end of that year he was elected to the state legislature. When that term expired in 1851, he opted for a career in law and pursued his studies at the Law School in Lebanon, Tennessee, now part of Cumberland University. He received his degree in 1852 and opened a practice in Nashville. In 1854 he was elected attorney general of the Nashville District, which embraced three counties. He held this post until 1860 and, despite his limited knowledge and experience, he apparently performed his duties in a satisfactory manner. In 1856 he married Julia Peete of Huntsville, Alabama. An outspoken believer in state rights and secession, he had achieved sufficient prominence to serve as a presidential elector on the Breckinridge-Lane ticket in 1860.

Bate entered Confederate service as a private in a company composed of men from Gallatin and soon became their captain. Elected colonel of the 2d Tennessee infantry, Bate commanded his regiment at Columbus, Kentucky, and at Shiloh, where four of his

An earlier sitting produced portraits showing Bate not long after his February 1864 promotion to major general. (William Turner Collection)

The same sitting, probably in Atlanta, produced this half-length view. (U.S. Army Military History Institute, Carlisle, Pa.)

relatives were killed or wounded. Bate also sustained a severe wound in that conflict. While leading his regiment in a charge through a murderous cross-fire, a minie ball broke his leg; the wound disabled him for several months.

Both Brigadier General Patrick R. Cleburne and Major General Joseph Hardee praised Bate for his heroism. Appointed a brigadier on October 3, 1862, to rank from that date, Bate commanded the garrison at Huntsville, Alabama, and temporarily, the District of Tennessee. When he returned to active duty in February of 1863, he assumed command of a brigade in Major General Alexander P. Stewart's Division of Lieutenant General Leonidas Polk's Corps which he led with distinction during the Tullahoma Campaign and at Chickamauga, where his artillery reportedly fired the last shot of the battle. Of Bate at Chickamauga, Stewart reported, "During this charge, which was truly heroic, General Bate and several of his staff had their horses killed—the second lost by General Bate that morning."

Bate again distinguished himself at Chattanooga, where, with the personal assistance of General Braxton Bragg, he successfully organized a rear guard. Bragg officially commended Bate for his "coolness, gallantry, and successful conduct throughout the engagements and in the rear guard in the retreat," and he was promoted to major general on March 6, 1864, to rank from February 23. In the spring of 1864, Bate would lead his division in the Army of Tennessee from Dalton, Georgia, through the Atlanta Campaign, and in the fateful invasion of Tennessee. After supporting Major General Nathan Bedford Forrest's operation against Murfreesboro, Bate returned with his division to the outskirts of Nashville where some of his regiments were virtually annihilated and all three of his brigade commanders were captured. Bate commanded the remnant in the closing actions in the Carolinas and surrendered at Greensboro, North Carolina, in April of 1865.

Bate was a fighting general, second only to Forrest among Tennesseeans. During the war Bate sustained wounds on three different occasions and had six horses killed under him in battle. While in the field he received official notification of his nomination for governor of Tennessee in June of 1863. His answer became historic in a half-dozen versions: "While an armed foe treads our soil and I can fire a shot or draw a blade, I will take no civic honor. I had rather, amid her misfortunes, be the defender than the Governor of Tennessee." His performance on the field made him the hero of Resaca and earned him the praise of his superiors for gallantry at Franklin.

When he returned to his home near Nashville, the regime of Governor William J. Brownlow disfranchised him. He resumed his law practice and, although still disfranchised, served as a delegate to the National Democratic Convention in 1868 and as a member of both the state and the national Democratic executive committees until the late 1870s. He also worked to maintain the peace in Tennessee, where Brownlow's hatred of former Confederates threatened to bring civil war within the state. On August 1, 1868, Bate, along with ten other Confederate generals (including Forrest), signed a memorial to the legislature protesting Brownlow's policies. Despite their action, the former Confederates did not have their political rights restored until after Brownlow left the state in 1869.

In 1876 Bate was a presidential elector on the Tilden-Hendricks ticket and in 1882 he was elected governor of his state and reelected in 1884. In 1886 the legislature, after sixty-eight ballots, elected him to the U.S. Senate. His main accomplishments while governor included the restructuring of the state debt in 1883, which repudiated a sizeable portion of the debts incurred during the Brownlow administration that were tainted with fraud, and his securing the establishment of a state-wide railroad commission.

In the Senate, Bate became extremely influential as a leader of the strong delegation of former Confederates within that body. In 1893, he authored the act which repealed all laws providing for the supervision of local elections by Federal officials—thus effectively ending Reconstruction. Bate's position in Washington and his former association with the Confederacy prompted the Secretary of War to invite him to speak for the Confederates at the dedication of the Chickamauga-Chattanooga National Park. Bate remained in the Senate until his death in Washington, D.C., on March 9, 1905. He is buried in Mount Olivet Cemetery, Nashville.

This view may also come from that same sitting. (Alabama Department of Archives and History, Montgomery)

Laurence L. Hewitt

Marshall, Park. *William B. Bate*. Nashville, 1908.

Porter, James D. *Tennessee*. Atlanta: 1899. Vol. VIII of Clement A. Evans, ed., *Confederate Military History*.

✶ *Cullen Andrews Battle* ✶

Cullen Andrews Battle was born at Powelton, Hancock County, Georgia, on June 1, 1829. In 1836 the boy's father, a physician, moved the family to Eufaula, Alabama. Young Cullen entered the University of Alabama from Eufaula and graduated there in 1850. For the next two years Battle read law in the office of John Gill Shorter, making an important early acquaintance that would serve him well during the war when Shorter occupied the governor's chair in Alabama. In 1852 Battle won admittance to the state bar and began a career that mixed legal and political matters in proportions familiar to students of the antebellum South. A canvass by Battle of southern Alabama in 1856 on behalf of James Buchanan's Presidential bid prompted one listener to write of "the witchery of his eloquence."

Cullen Battle's prewar politics ran along sternly secessionist lines, as evinced by his intimate friendship with William Lowndes Yancey. Yancey nominated his friend as Presidential elector and delegate to the Charleston Convention in 1860. In the campaign that followed Battle shared platforms with Yancey on a speaking tour that covered not only Alabama and the South but also such Northern destinations as Boston, New York, Chicago, St. Louis, Philadelphia, and Cincinnati.

Battle's slender prewar military experience came as a result of the John Brown raid on Harpers Ferry in 1859. Battle organized and commanded a volunteer company at Tuskegee in the excitement attending Brown's trial and execution. Within six days after the raid he was able to offer its services to Virginia's Governor Wise. Although Wise of course declined, the company maintained its organization and became a part of the 3d Alabama Infantry soon after the Civil War broke out. Battle's first Confederate duty was as lieutenant colonel of an Alabama state regiment posted at Pensacola. When Alabama's troops went into Confederate service the state commissions became void, but Battle won election as major of the 3d Alabama and accompanied the regiment when it went to Virginia as the first Alabama unit on that front.

The promotion of Colonel Jones M. Withers of the 3d Alabama in July 1861 advanced the much-admired Tennent Lomax to command of the regiment and Battle to the lieutenant colonelcy. In the regiment's, and Battle's, baptism of fire at Seven Pines the regiment lost heavily. A Federal volley killed Colonel Lomax as he pulled the regiment back after an unsuccessful attack, leaving Lieutenant Colonel Battle—himself slightly wounded—to lead

Battle posed for this portrait sometime between August 1863 and October 1864. (U.S. Army Military History Institute, Carlisle, Pa.)

the 3d Alabama. As the ranking field officer, the lieutenant colonel stood in line for routine promotion to the rank of colonel and permanent command of the regiment. Battle assumed colonel's rank informally, but for some reason the official promotion was long delayed. He continued to lead the 3d through the summer, suffering wounds at both South Mountain and Sharpsburg, but with such growing concern over his rank that he attempted to resign in December. Battle's formal promotion to colonel came on Christmas Eve of 1862, and was confirmed on March 26, 1863, to take rank from May 31, 1862 (on the mistaken notion that Lomax had died then, rather than on June 1).

Meanwhile, Governor John Gill Shorter had written to Jefferson Davis on October 27, 1862, touting his protege and former legal student for further promotion to brigadier general, asserting that Battle's "daring, courage and gallantry...are notorious in the army." General William Mahone, in whose brigade the 3d Alabama had fought at Seven Pines, added his recommendation on November 12, attesting to the "high evidence of his gallantry and of ability as an officer." Forty-one members of the Alabama legislature addressed Jefferson Davis on November 25 for the same purpose, insisting that they knew that Battle was, among other strengths, "well versed in military science." Battle, ever the politician, accumulated these various recommendations personally and forwarded them to his friend in President Davis' cabinet, Thomas Hill Watts.

After its brief stint as part of Mahone's Brigade, the 3d Alabama had transferred in June 1862 to the all-Alabama brigade commanded ably by General Robert E. Rodes, with which both the regiment and Battle would be associated for the rest of the war. Despite political support that continued to arrive by mail, Battle's promotion would be largely dependent on how his performance impressed his military commanders. The colonel's misfortunes during the Chancellorsville Campaign kept him from any role in the brigade's stellar performance there. On April 29, 1863, as the campaign opened, Battle was "seriously injured by his horse rearing and falling in a ditch." Two days later Battle rode gingerly back to his command, only to suffer at once another equestrian accident that wrenched his back badly.

With Rodes promoted to division command, Edward A. O'Neal of the 26th Alabama commanded the Alabama brigade at Gettysburg with such a complete lack of success that his promotion to brigadier general was revoked. General Rodes' summary of the officers in his old brigade capable of rectifying the mess left by O'Neal damned Battle with faint praise. The colonel "has always done his duty," Rodes wrote to Lee on August 1, 1863, but had he "not recommended him heretofore decidedly because I preferred" both John B. Gordon and John T. Morgan (of the 6th and 5th Alabama respectively) over Battle. With Gordon and Morgan assigned elsewhere, that left Battle as Rodes' alternate choice. Battle's promotion to brigadier general—dated August 25, 1863, to rank from August 20—eventually was confirmed by the Senate on February 17, 1864.

General Battle commanded Rodes' old brigade for the rest of the war in a manner that displayed competence and reliability. A manuscript letter from Battle to Rodes defending his brigade's performance at the beginning of the Spotsylvania Campaign suggests that the division commander had been displeased with it there. Sickness and wounds kept General Battle away from his command on furlough for several extended spells: in the fall of 1863 for bronchitis; in the summer of 1864 for dysentery; and from October 1864 to the end of the war due to a wound suffered at Cedar Creek. On October 24 Battle left a Richmond hospital for a sixty-day furlough. He was still at Tuskegee on wounded leave at the end of February. Battle's war reached an official end on May 16, 1865, when he was paroled at Montgomery as a brigadier general. Another set of political endorsements in late 1864 had encouraged the President and the War Department to promote Battle to the rank of major general. That never happened, despite the unsubstantiated claims of several secondary sources.

Political disabilities during Reconstruction denied General Battle a seat he won in the United States House of Representatives and also a likely nomination for the United States Senate. He moved in 1880 to Newbern, North Carolina, where he edited a newspaper and served as may or the city. Later in life the general moved to Greensboro, North Carolina, where he died on April 8, 1905. Battle is buried in Petersburg, Virginia.

Robert K. Krick

⋆ Richard Lee Turberville Beale ⋆

Beale served throughout the war with the Army of Northern Virginia, yet apparently left behind no image of himself in uniform. This postwar portrait dates probably from the 1870s or later. (Museum of the Confederacy, Richmond)

Beale was born at "Hickory Hill," Westmoreland County, Virginia, on May 22, 1819. His family had been prominent in the area for nearly two hundred years. Richard attended Northumberland and Rappahannock Academies and Dickinson College before graduating from the University of Virginia Law School in 1838. Admitted to the bar the following year, he began practicing at Hague in Westmoreland County. An Episcopalian and a Democrat, he was married and had at least one son who fought in the Confederate Army. Elected in 1846, he served one term in the U.S. Congress from 1847 to 1849. Although he declined to run for a second term, he remained active in politics. He was a delegate to the state reform convention of 1851, and a state senator from 1858 to 1860.

In May of 1861 Beale entered Confederate service as a 1st lieutenant of a cavalry company known as "Lee's Legion," or "Lee's Light Horse." His first action came the following month when he led a small force aboard two flatboats from Mathias Point to seize a vessel that had grounded in the Potomac River. His participation on the twenty-seventh of that month in repulsing an attack upon Mathias Point earned him special mention by Colonel Daniel Ruggles, the ranking officer on the scene. In July the company was ordered to Manassas, but arrived the day following the battle. Before the end of the month Beale was promoted to captain and he and his cavalrymen returned to patrolling the banks of the Potomac. The company was expanded into a battalion, and he became major of the larger unit in October and placed in command of the Northern Neck. His district commander Major General Theophilus H. Holmes, described Beale at this time as "a man of cool discrimination, great intelligence, and in every way perfectly reliable."

When the legion was merged with other companies to form the 9th Virginia Cavalry in April of 1862, Beale was appointed lieutenant colonel. When William H. F. Lee became a brigadier general in October, Beale became colonel of the regiment and was given command of Camp Lee, which was located near Hague on the lower Potomac; the following month his regiment reported only ninety effective men present for duty. In December he made a daring raid into Rappahannock County and captured the Federal garrison at Leeds' Ferry without losing a man. General Robert E. Lee wrote Major General J. E. B. Stuart regarding the raid: "The boldness of Colonel Beale's plan was equaled by the success of its execution, and reflects great credit upon himself and the officers and men engaged."

Although Beale served creditably throughout the war, for some unknown reason he was dissatisfied. He submitted his resignation on three separate occasions: November 22 1862, February 8, 1863, and August 25, 1863—none were accepted. His latest letter included a plea that he be authorized to organize a company of partisan rangers or allowed to serve as a private.

In 1863 Stuart praised Beale's thwarting of Major General George Stoneman's raid on April 18, Beale being one of three individuals who, because of "their heroic lead, deserve the highest praise for their distinguished bravery under circumstances of great personal peril." Later that month Beale again successfully engaged Stoneman. Beale fought at Brandy Station, Gettysburg, and Culpeper Court House (where he commanded his brigade), and participated in Stuart's raid into Maryland. During a skirmish in September of 1863, Beale sustained a severe wound that necessitated a three-month convalescence—his only absence during the entire war.

In March of 1864, Beale made a forced march from the Northern Neck to intercept Colonel Ulric Dahlgren's raiders near Richmond. A detachment of his regiment killed Dahlgren and captured Union correspondence that called for the burning of Richmond and the assassination of President Jefferson Davis and his cabinet members. Beale distinguished himself during the fighting in northern Virginia during the spring and early summer of 1864, especially at the engagement at Stony Creek on April 2 and at Reams' Station on June 28.

At Reams' Station, Beale's regiment was the first to engage the advancing Federals. The Virginians immediately charged and drove the enemy a considerable distance. Confederate reinforcements soon routed the enemy, at which time Major General Wade Hampton reported:

"I sent Colonel Beale, of the 9th Virginians, with two or three squadrons in pursuit. He followed them four miles, capturing a large number and scattering the rest. The force of the enemy was entirely broken and the fragments were seeking safety in flight in all directions. They scattered through the woods, and night coming on the pursuit had to cease."

During the engagement, Beale's men captured two colors and Beale, apparently unaware that he was violating military regulations, gave the banners as personal gifts to Hampton. Hampton requested he be allowed to keep them, and General Lee seconded the request; their final disposition is unknown. Undoubtedly, Beale would have been commended for his performance in the engagement, but his brigade commander, Brigadier General John R. Chambliss, apparently failed to submit a report of the action to Hampton prior to the former's death on August 16.

Following the death of Chambliss, Beale was appointed a brigadier general on January 13, to rank from January 6. In March 1865 Beale captured Dinwiddie Court House. He was only of only two cavalry generals to surrender with General Lee at Appomattox Court House.

He returned to Hague, resumed his law practice and farmed. Disfranchised until the end of Reconstruction, he won election to the U.S. Congress in 1878 and served from 1879 to 1881. An active member in veterans organizations and activities, he also wrote a history of his regiment, *History of the Ninth Va. Cavalry in the War between the States*, which was published posthumously. He died on April 21, 1893, in Hague, and was buried at Hickory Hill.

Lawrence L. Hewitt

Hotchkiss, Maj. Jed. *Virginia*. Atlanta: 1899. Vol. III of Clement A. Evans, ed., *Confederate Military History*.

An 1864-65 image of Beall made by J. Gurney & Son of New York, while the general was a prisoner of war on parole. (Kentucky Historical Society, Frankfort)

✯ *William Nelson Rector Beall* ✯

William Nelson Rector Beall was born in Bardstown, Kentucky, on March 20, 1865. Before he reached the age of ten, his family relocated to Arkansas, and it was an appointment from Arkansas that enabled him to enter West Point on September 1, 1844. Graduating thirteenth in his class of thirty-eight, he received an appointment as brevet 2d lieutenant in the 4th Infantry on July 1, 1848. On April 30, 1849, he was commissioned as 2d lieutenant in the 5th Infantry and ordered to the northwestern frontier. On March 3, 1855, he was promoted to 1st lieutenant in the 1st Cavalry and ordered to Indian Territory; twenty-four days later he was promoted to captain. He participated in several skirmishes against the Plains Indians, in the civil war in Kansas in 1856–1857, and in the 1860 expedition against the Kiowas and Comanches before resigning his captaincy on August 20, 1861.

Beall promptly entered the Regular Confederate Army with the rank of captain of cavalry—his commission dating from March 16, 1861. While stationed in Arkansas, he so impressed Major General Earl Van Dorn, who took command of the Trans-Mississippi District of Department No. 2 on January 29, 1862, that the new commander made Beall his assistant adjutant general and later major in the commissary, and twice recommended him for promotion to colonel. However, the Confederate Congress decided otherwise and confirmed Beall as a brigadier general on April 7, 1862, to rank from April 11. Within two weeks he assumed command of all mounted troops in the vicinity of Corinth, Mississippi.

Despite his having had little combat or independent command experience, on August 29 he was placed in command of the District of East Louisiana which pri-

Another Gurney image from the same sitting. (Museum of the Confederacy, Richmond)

Possibly made earlier than the previous portraits, this, too, almost certainly was taken while Beall was in New York. (National Archives)

marily consisted of the thousand-man garrison at Port Hudson. Beall immediately asserted himself by designing a new line of fortifications to prevent the batteries that overlooked the Mississippi River from being taken from the rear. His plan called for a continuous parapet and ditch, as opposed to the previously adopted design that consisted of detached lunettes at four-hundred-yard intervals. The new 4 1/2 mile line was barely half the length of the original. Nevertheless, Beall lacked the infantry and artillery to man even this more consolidated line.

During the fall, he struggled to strengthen the defenses of Port Hudson, but Union warships, raids moving northward from New Orleans along the New Orleans, Jackson, & Great Northern Railroad, and, after December 17, a strong garrison at Baton Rouge hampered his efforts. On October 14, Beall's district was extended to incorporate that portion of Mississippi between the Big Black and Mississippi Rivers and the above mentioned railroad and the two counties on the Gulf Coast. Two-thirds of his 3,600 men occupied Port Hudson, while the remaining third manned smaller garrisons at Ponchatoula, Baton Rouge, Covington, and Camp Moore.

Almost immediately after the district's expansion, Brigadier General John B. Villepigue arrived and relieved Beall of all his responsibilities beyond Port Hudson. Shortly after his arrival, Villepigue became ill and died on November 9. Beall immediately resumed command of the district, a position he retained until the arrival of Major General Franklin Gardner on December 27, when he reverted to command of the Port Hudson garrison.

The arrival of reinforcements at Port Hudson during the first week of 1863 prompted Gardner to reorganize the garrison, and he reduced Beall's command to one of the three brigades and assigned him to the left wing of the fortifications. When the enemy advanced from Baton Rouge in March, Beall's situation remained unchanged, although the garrison had been increased to four brigades. After the Federals began to withdraw on the morning of the fifteenth, Beall's brigade and one other pursued them until the following evening, although no serious fighting occurred. When he returned to the garrison, he found that his brigade had been further reduced by the transfer of some of its units to a newly organized, fifth brigade.

In response to Major General Ulysses S. Grant's crossing of the Mississippi, Gardner relinquished

A different pose, quite probably from the same sitting. (Museum of the Confederacy, Richmond)

command of both the district and the garrison to Beall on May 6 and departed for Mississippi with approximately half of the effective troops in the district. Beall now had approximately 5,000 men to defend Port Hudson, less than one-fourth of the garrison's strength in mid-March and too few to successfully defend 4 1/2 miles of earthworks.

Five days later, Gardner returned to Port Hudson with approximately 2,000 troops and resumed command of both the district and the garrison. He divided the earthworks into three sections and gave Beall the largest portion of the garrison and assigned him to the center of the fortifications. Beall's timely reinforcement of the Confederate left flank on May 27 enabled the garrison to successfully repulse the enemy's principal assault that day, and his defense on June 14 of his own sector, better known as the Priest Gap, proved equally successful. The surrender of Vicksburg prompted Gardner to follow suit, and although the non-commissioned officers and enlisted men were paroled, Beall found himself a prisoner of war on July 9.

Soon incarcerated on Johnson's Island, Beall remained a captive until he was paroled in 1864, in accordance with a special agreement negotiated by officials of the opposing governments. They had selected Beall to serve as the Confederate agent in the North in charge of purchasing supplies for Confederate prisoners of war—a formidable assignment. Union authorities opened a cotton brokerage office for Beall in New York City and allowed him to contract for the exportation of cotton from the Confederacy. His ships could pass through the Federal blockade unmolested and he used the proceeds from the sale of the cotton to purchase clothing, blankets, and food for incarcerated Confederate soldiers. On February 8, 1865, 830 bales auctioned in New York City netted $331,789.66. Beall continued to operate the brokerage office until August 2, 1865, by which time most Confederate soldiers had been paroled.

After the war Beall moved to St Louis where he labored as a general commission merchant. He died in McMinnville, Tennessee, July 26, 1883, and is buried in Mt. Olivet Cemetery in Nashville. Confederate Major General James F. Fagan was his brother-in-law by the former's first marriage.

Lawrence L. Hewitt

Another view of Beall taken in New York, showing a uniform immaculate thanks to
no battlefield exposure. (William Turner Collection)

Beauregard in his prime, probably photographed about 1864. (Museum of the Confederacy, Richmond)

✳ *Pierre Gustave Toutant Beauregard* ✳

The fourth ranking officer of the Confederacy was born on May 28, 1818, at "Contreras," his father's plantation just below New Orleans in St. Bernard Parish, Louisiana. Christened Pierre Gustave Toutant Beauregard, he entered a world in which his family occupied a position of great local influence. He attended a school in New York City run by two brothers who had served as officers under Napoleon, where he learned English and developed a passionate admiration for France's greatest soldier. Drawn to the military life by his study of Napoleon, he entered West Point as a sixteen-year-old plebe in 1834 and graduated second in his class on July 1, 1838, with a commission as 2d lieutenant in the 1st Artillery (on July 8, 1838, he became 2d lieutenant of engineers). He had dropped the hyphen between Toutant and Beauregard at the beginning of his career at West Point, and by the mid-1840s ceased to use his given first name—for the remainder of his life he was Gustave Toutant Beauregard. Some have speculated that he sought by the changes to become more American; Beauregard himself explained in 1845 that it "was merely for the sake of brevity, my name being rather a long one I endeavor to shorten it as much as possible."

Promoted to 1st lieutenant on June 16, 1839, Beauregard participated in the Mexican War as a member of Winfield Scott's brilliant group of engineers and earned brevets at Contreras and Churubusco (captain) and Chapultepec (major). He received his Regular Captaincy on March 3, 1853, and spent most of the 1850s performing engineering duty in New Orleans. Although a secessionist, he assumed the superintendency of West Point on January 23, 1861, but held that post just two days before being instructed to give it up by chief of the Engineer Department Joseph G. Totten. Louisiana seceded on January 26, and Beauregard left the Academy on the 28th. He resigned from the U.S. Army on February 20, 1861, and was appointed a brigadier general in the

Provisional Army of the Confederate States to rank from March 1, 1861, assigned to command the Southern forces at Charleston, South Carolina.

As he entered the Confederate service, Beauregard was 5'7" tall, weighed about 150 pounds, had dark eyes and hair (the hair would quickly turn quite gray, either from the burden of duties or the absence of dyes available in the pre-blockade days), and spoke with a faint French accent. Edward Porter Alexander, a member of Beauregard's staff early in the war, thought he "had more courtesy of manner than any of the other generals with whom I had ever served" and described him as "quick & alert, of fine carriage & aspect, & of unusual strength & activity."

Diversity and controversy marked Beauregard's career in the Confederate Army. He accepted the surrender of Fort Sumter in April 1861, becoming the first military idol of the Confederacy, and commanded the largest Southern force in Virginia preceding the battle of First Manassas. From the beginning he championed a strategy of concentration against the Federal armies rather than a place-oriented policy designed to protect cities and territory. But he compromised this realistic approach by consistently suggesting grand strategic combinations that paid scant attention to the realities of Confederate transportation, logistics, and manpower. Poor staff work and a welter of conflicting orders characterized his generalship at First Manassas, where he exhibited personal bravery but was lucky to win a victory.

A fresh torrent of public praise came in the wake of the battle, followed by promotion to full general on August 13, 1861 (to rank from the date of First Manassas, leaving Beauregard junior only to Samuel Cooper, A. S. Johnston, R. E. Lee, and J. E. Johnston). The first signs of serious bickering with the Davis administration appeared at about the same time. For the rest of the war Beauregard complained of ineptitude and malice on the part of the government

Possibly the earliest wartime photo of Beauregard, this shows him in uniform as a colonel of engineers in the Provisional Army of Louisiana, and was probably taken in February 1861. (Old Courthouse Museum, Vicksburg, Miss.)

Another pose taken at the same session, and in the same uniform. (U.S. Army Military History Institute, Carlisle, Pa.)

Beauregard's first sitting as a Confederate brigadier was made in Charleston, probably in March or April 1861. (Museum of the Confederacy, Richmond)

(Commissary General Lucius B. Northrop and Secretary of War Judah P. Benjamin were prime early targets), and Jefferson Davis returned this ill will with full measure.

Transferred to the west in the winter of 1862, Beauregard became Albert Sidney Johnston's second in command. He disapproved of Johnston's strategic deployment, called for concentration, and orchestrated the shifting of troops by rail that brought an army of 40,000 together at Corinth by the end of March 1862. He planned the Battle of Shiloh and falteringly directed the fighting on April 6–7 after Johnston's mortal wounding. The subsequent retreat to Corinth and abandonment of that city spurred critics, most notably Jefferson Davis, to question his actions, and when he took sick leave from the Army of Mississippi in June 1862, the President replaced him with Braxton Bragg. Appointed on August 19, 1862, to head the Department of South Carolina and Georgia, he chafed at the loss of field command: "If the country is willing I should be put on the shelf thro' interested motives, I will submit until our future reverses will compel the Govt to put me on duty. I scorn its motives, and present action."

An embittered Beauregard reached Charleston on September 15, 1862, and soon made improvements in its defenses. In April 1862 his batteries easily repulsed a Federal naval attack against the city; in the summer and fall of that year, he directed a masterful defense against Union General Quincy A. Gillmore. The winter of 1863–64 proved an unhappy one, during which he urged a concentration in the west, railed against Davis, and considered resigning. The Confederacy had not produced a great captain like Napoleon, he suggested in one letter, because "we have a power near the *throne* too egotistical and jealous to allow such a genius to develop itself."

April 23, 1864, brought another transfer, this time to the Department of North Carolina and the Cape Fear. This command, which Beauregard renamed the Department of North Carolina and Southern Virginia, included all of Virginia south of the James River. Beauregard's principal task was to keep Federals away from Lee's rear and protect the back door to Richmond, and he succeeded admirably. On May 16 he turned back Benjamin F. Butler's Army of the James at Bermuda Hundred; a month later, between June 15–18, his badly outnumbered forces held off the advance of Grant's army at Petersburg

Several standing poses were shot. (William Turner Collection)

With the war barely begun, Beauregard made himself in this single session probably the most photographed general in the new Confederacy. (William Turner Collection)

A variant from the same session. (Old Courthouse Museum, Vicksburg, Miss.)

Beauregard's temperament was well suited for striking poses for the camera. (U.S. Army Military History Institute, Carlisle, Pa.)

until Lee could shift the Army of Northern Virginia southward.

This success represented the high point of Beauregard's Confederate career, but he hoped for a more active assignment. During the early summer of 1864, he wanted to lead either the Confederate Army in the Shenandoah Valley or the Army of Tennessee—appointments that went to Jubal A. Early and John Bell Hood respectively. On October 17, 1864, Davis named him to a primarily administrative post as head of the new Military Division of the west, a sprawling geographical area that covered parts of five states and included responsibility for contesting William T. Sherman's march across Georgia. Facing an impossible situation Beauregard watched Hood's disastrous Tennessee campaign of late fall 1864 and proved unable to slow Sherman's inexorable advance. Blamed in part for these failures, Beauregard was assigned command of the state of South Carolina on February 16, 1865, and soon found himself subordinate to Joseph E. Johnston, who took charge of all forces opposing Sherman on February 22. After Lee surrendered at Appomattox, Johnston and Beauregard advised Davis that further resistance would be futile. Johnston capitulated on April 18; a month later, Beauregard was back in New Orleans, a civilian for the first time in his adult life.

The postwar years were generally kind to Beauregard. After a somewhat unsettled decade, during which he considered leaving the United States to take military positions in Brazil, Mexico, and Egypt, he regained full United States citizenship on July 24, 1876, and decided to spend the rest of his life in his native country. He made a considerable amount of money as a railroad executive in the 1860s and early 1870s, but real financial success began in February 1877 when he accepted a position with the Louisiana Lottery. For the last seventeen years of his life, Beauregard lived comfortably, served for a time as commissioner of public works in New Orleans and as adjutant general of Louisiana, and wrote *Military Operations of General Beauregard* (a two-volume memoir credited to Alfred Roman, a former officer on Beauregard's staff) and several shorter pieces relating to the war. He died on February 20, 1893, in New Orleans, and was buried in the vault of the Army of Tennessee in Metairie Cemetery.

Gary W. Gallagher

On March 31, 1861, Beauregard sat for this portrait in Charleston. The absence of hair coloring shows just how gray he had become. (Kentucky Historical Society, Frankfort.)

Probably by 1863 Beauregard had adopted major general's button arrangement on his uniform, though now he was a full general. This portrait shows how he artificially darkened his nearly white hair. (Miller, *Photographic History*)

By about 1864 Beauregard showed ageing from the pressures of the war. In probably his last wartime sitting he looked more contemplative, less jaunty. (U.S. Army Military History Institute, Carlisle, Pa.)

He still showed his pride and self-confidence, however. (Library of Congress)

⋆ *Barnard Elliott Bee* ⋆

No photo had emerged from Bee's one-month career as a general. This image probably shows him in his old U.S. Army uniform as a captain of the 10th Infantry. (William Turner Collection)

Barnard Elliott Bee was born on February 8, 1824, in Charleston, South Carolina, the son of Barnard E. Bee and younger brother of Hamilton Prioleau Bee. The elder Barnard Bee migrated in 1835 to Texas, where he played a leading role in the creation of the Republic and later served as its secretary of state. Bee's family joined him in Texas in 1839, and young Barnard spent about two years there before gaining an at-large appointment to West Point in 1841. Known as a friendly, quiet, and gentle individual, Bee impressed others with his qualities as a man but not as a student. Bee's closest friend at the Academy was William Farrar "Baldy" Smith, who noted in his memoir that Bee's classmates called him "Bubble." Smith also observed that Bee's friendship was "of that quality that carried such perfect confidence that a support to any extent was ready at anytime in any difficulty." Apparently unconcerned about his academic standing, Bee graduated 33d in the class of 1845, was commissioned brevet 2d lieutenant in the 3d infantry, and soon joined Zachary Taylor's American military force on the Texas frontier.

Bee saw considerable action during the war with Mexico. He fought at Palo Alto and Resaca de la Palma in 1846, earning promotion to 2d lieutenant on September 21 of that year, and later joined Winfield Scott's army for the campaign from Vera Cruz to Mexico City in 1847. He received a wound and a 1st lieutenant's brevet at the battle of Cerro Gordo on April 18, recovering in time to win a captain's brevet for his role at Chapultepec on September 13. In 1854, the state of South Carolina presented Bee with a sword in recognition of his "patriotic and meritorious conduct" in Mexico.

Between the end of the war with Mexico and the secession winter of 1860–61, Bee was promoted to 1st lieutenant of the 3d Infantry on March 5, 1851, and to captain of the 10th Infantry on March 3, 1855. He served as adjutant of the 3d Infantry (1848–1855), accompanied Albert Sidney Johnston's column to Utah in 1857, and held posts at various times in Minnesota, the Dakotas, and in the cavalry school at Carlisle. Far from a rabid secessionist, Bee blamed politicians for bringing on a crisis that soldiers would have to settle. He suggested to "Baldy" Smith that they avoid the coming strife by moving to the far Texas frontier, where they could settle on some of his brother's vast land holdings and raise cattle. But sectional tensions eventually engulfed Bee; he resigned from the U. S. Army on March 3, 1861, and was commissioned lieutenant colonel of the 1st South Carolina Regulars (an artillery regiment) on June 1, 1861.

On June 17, 1861, to rank from that date, Bee was promoted to brigadier general and assigned to Joseph E. Johnston's Army of the Shenandoah, then stationed near Winchester in the lower Shenandoah Valley. His 3d Brigade consisted of the 4th Alabama, 2d and 11th Mississippi, and 6th North Carolina infantry regiments and John Imboden's battery of artillery. Bee's command remained in the Lower Valley until July 18, when it moved with the rest of Johnston's Army toward Manassas Junction to reinforce P. G. T. Beauregard's Army of the Potomac; Bee and Johnston reached Manassas Junction together on July 20. During the battle of First Manassas on July 21, Bee's brigade entered the fighting about 11:00 A.M., engaging the Federals first on Matthews Hill and subsequently on Henry Hill. After hard fighting and heavy casualties, Bee's units fell back, giving way to a fresh brigade under Thomas J. Jackson. "General, they are driving us," Bee admitted to Jackson. "Sir," answered Jackson, "we will give them the bayonet." About three hours later a discouraged Bee, who had been separated from his command for at least an hour and seemed confused, found a part of the 4th Alabama and, pointing toward the fighting, shouted: "Yonder stands Jackson like a stone wall; let's go to his assistance." Although not uttered at the moment of crisis when Jackson's brigade first came up (as usually supposed),

Bee's statement nonetheless fastened on Jackson his legendary sobriquet and forever yoked Bee with his more famous comrade. Shortly after leading a part of the 4th Alabama back into the fight, Bee fell mortally wounded near the crest of Henry Hill. He survived a painful night before dying on the morning of July 22, 1861. His remains lay in state with a guard of honor in Richmond before his transfer to Pendleton, South Carolina, for burial.

Bee became the subject of heroic tributes in South Carolina and elsewhere in the South. The Charleston *Mercury* described his gallant attempts to keep his men in line. Beauregard's report stated that the Confederacy had "sustained an irreparable loss" and spoke of Bee's "great personal bravery and coolness, he possessed the qualities of an accomplished soldier and an able, reliable commander." "Baldy" Smith's memoirs echoed Beauregard's estimate, averring that had Bee lived he would have ranked among the great Southern captains. Other contemporary evidence, however, raises questions about Bee's conduct at First Manassas. Accounts by members of the 4th Alabama hint that he was disoriented after his brigade retreated. Thomas J. Goree of James Longstreet's staff lent credence to such a view in a letter of November 1861: "I would not detract from the noble dead, but from all I can learn, both Genls. Bee and Bartow went themselves, and carried their men into places on 21st July, which they could and would have avoided, had they been entirely free from the influence of liquor." In truth, Bee's career with the Confederate Army was far too brief to permit sound conclusions about his potential. He must remain an unknown quantity in any reckoning of Southern military leadership.

Gary W. Gallagher

⋆ Hamilton Prioleau Bee ⋆

This photo of Bee has been heavily retouched sometime in the past, and the uniform is probably an addition. No genuine uniformed pose has surfaced to date. (Special Collection, Tulane University Library, New Orleans)

This son of Barnard E. Bee and his wife, Anne, was born in Charleston, South Carolina, on July 22, 1822. Thomas Bee, his grandfather, served as a Federal judge. His younger brother, Barnard Elliott Bee, served in the Confederate Army in the eastern theater and is noted for naming General T. J. Jackson "Stonewall."

Bee's father, who served on the staff of South Carolina Governor James Hamilton, became unhappy with his state's stand over nullification and moved to Texas in 1832. In Texas he served in the army and filled the posts of secretary of state and treasury during the interim administration of President David G. Burnet. His family, including Hamilton Bee, moved to Texas in 1839, where Hamilton Bee was appointed secretary of the commission that determined the border between Louisiana and Texas.

Bee's father opposed the annexation of Texas by the United States and returned to South Carolina, but Bee stayed on in Texas to accept a position as secretary of the Texas Senate. When war developed between Mexico and the United States in 1846 over Texas and other issues, Bee resigned to enter the army as a private in a cavalry company commanded by Ben McCulloch. He was commissioned a lieutenant before the end of the war, and also served in the Texas Rangers and in a regiment of Texas Volunteers under General Zachary Taylor in northern Mexico.

After the Mexican-American War Bee lived in Laredo, and for the remainder of his life he lived principally in the southern Texas area. He represented the area in the Texas legislature from 1849 until 1859, and was speaker of the House of Representatives for the Sixth Legislature from 1855 until 1857. Bee married Mildred Tarver of Alabama in 1854, and they had six children.

At the beginning of the Civil War, Bee was commissioned a brigadier general of state troops, and on March 6, 1862, received similar rank in the Confederate Army, to rank from March 4. In both positions he was assigned the duty of protecting the southern Texas coast and facilitating the exporting of Confederate produce and importing goods needed for the war effort. Bee's headquarters were at Brownsville. He applied for the post, saying in part that "I am not much of a military man but was under fire at Monterrey and did not run." He emphasized his familiarity with the area and its people, including the Spanish language. Bee filled this post until 1864 with more skill than he exhibited in field commands after that time. With little military action in his theatre of operations, he mostly worked with shipping interests on both sides of the border to export cotton and import munitions, and in this capacity performed ably but failed to develop battle skills because of the lack of opportunity. In 1864 that opportunity was presented by the Red River Campaign of General Nathaniel Prentiss Banks.

When General Banks began his campaign in the late spring of 1864, troops from throughout Texas were massed on the state's eastern border to repel the invasion. Bee took three cavalry regiments under Colonels Xavier Blanchard de Bray, August C. Buchel, and Alexander W. Terrell from Columbus, Texas, to join General Richard Taylor's army, and commanded these regiments during the battles at Mansfield (Sabine Cross Roads) and Pleasant Hill in Louisiana in June 1864. Bee commanded the right flank of General J. G. Walker's sector of the battlefield throughout the fighting on June 8, 1864 in an area called the Peach Orchard and was in an advanced position in the maneuvering and subsequent fighting at Pleasant Hill and Monett's Ferry.

Bee led a charge in the battle at Mansfield in which he had two horses shot from under him and was wounded slightly in the face but not incapacitated. Nevertheless, there was criticism of Bee's leadership, both by contemporaries and later by scholars. Taylor criticized Bee's defense of his position at Monett's

Ferry, and Walker praised his courage, honor, and integrity, but claimed that "I would regard it as a public calamity to know of his being assigned to an important command." Edmund Kirby Smith apparently discounted the criticism, however, praising Bee's actions and calling him a "brave and gallant soldier."

After the action in northwest Louisiana, Bee succeeded to the command of General Thomas Green's cavalry after that officer's death and was assigned to patrol the Red River area. In the winter of 1864–1865 Bee served under General Samuel B. Maxey in the Indian Territory, being paroled on June 26, 1865, at Columbus, Texas, at war's end.

Following the Civil War, Bee moved his family to Mexico where they lived until 1876 when they relocated in San Antonio, Texas. Bee died on October 2, 1897, and is buried in San Antonio. At his request, a Confederate flag presented to him at the beginning of the war was draped around his casket.

Archie McDonald

★ *Tyree Harris Bell* ★

The only known uniformed portrait of Bell is this small pose which shows him sometime post-1861, and probably as lieutenant colonel or colonel of the 12th Tennessee. (*Confederate Veteran*, X, p. 464)

Tyree Harris Bell was born on September 5, 1815, in Covington, Kentucky. His family moved to Gallatin, Tennessee, and he grew up on his father's plantation. As an adult he became a planter in Sumner County. When the war began he raised the New Bern Blues or Company G (later designated A) of the 12th Tennessee and soon became the regiment's lieutenant colonel.

Bell led his regiment in the Battle at Belmont. On the morning of November 7, he was ordered to cross the Mississippi River, and upon reaching the Missouri shore moved his men into line of battle. His command took a position on the extreme right with its left resting on Colonel James Tappan's regiment. After being attacked, Bell led his men in a charge and drove the Federals back thirty to forty yards before realizing he was exposed and returned to his former position. Bell held the line for almost four hours, or until his men ran out of ammunition and had to return to the river. Rearmed, Bell reformed his regiment, then attacked again before the Federals withdrew and the battle ended.

At the Battle of Shiloh, Bell again led the 12th Tennessee. During the fighting on the morning of April 6 he had two horses shot from under him, and received a slight wound from a fall of his horse. On the 7th he was ordered to form a line of battle, but he turned the command over to Major R. P. Caldwell because he was unable to perform any duties as a result of the injuries that he had received the day before. When the battle ended, however, Colonel R. M. Russell reported that Bell had been "distinguished" by his "courage and energy." In July he became colonel of the 12th and 22d Tennessee Consolidated and fought at Corinth, Mississippi, and Richmond, Kentucky. After the Battle of Perryville the command was consolidated with the 47th Tennessee. At the army's reorganization following Stone's River, Bell was determined to be an excess officer, and General Pillow sent him into western Tennessee to recruit cavalry. He raised 400 men, obtained arms from Braxton Bragg in middle Tennessee, and went back to western Tennessee. In September 1863 he was reported at Paris, Tennessee, raiding between there and the Tennessee River. December reports showed him at Trenton, Kentucky, and moving toward Paducah. Bell eventually had between 1,100 and 1,200 or enough for three regiments. In December he was reported in Dyer County waiting for Forrest.

When Forrest arrived at Jackson, Tennessee, the troops in western Tennessee were organized with Bell commanding a brigade, known as Bell's Brigade. On January 25, 1864, he was officially assigned to Forrest, and initially led an independent brigade in Forrest's Cavalry Corps, but in February was assigned the 4th Brigade in Buford's Division. In February he was with Forrest at Grenada in a fight with A. J. Smith, and in March Forrest requested that Bell be made a brigadier general. Just a few days later, General Polk repeated the request that Bell be promoted. Bell was involved in Forrest's attack on Fort Pillow in April where Brigadier General B. G. Chalmers reported that he deserved "special mention" for the "gallantry" with which he led his brigade. "Colonel Bell, with his gallant brigade of Tennesseans, from Buford's division, temporarily attached to my command, stormed the works at Fort Pillow, in the face of the incessant fire from two gun-boats and five pieces of artillery from the fort." Bell was with Forrest at Tishomingo Creek, Harrisburg, Brice's Crossroads, and in the Tupelo Campaign. Forrest later reported that Bell "added new laurels to the chaplet" which his "valor and patriotism has already won." He fought against A. J. Smith in August 1864, and was with the Army of Tennessee at Spring Hill and Franklin. Forrest recalled that on November 29 "Colonel Bell reported that he had only four rounds of ammunition to the man when I ordered him to charge the enemy. This order was executed with a promptness and energy and gallantry

which I have never seen excelled." He was commissioned a brigadier general on March 2, 1865, ranking from February 28, 1865, and took part in the defense against Wilson's raid through Alabama and Georgia in 1865. In May he reported 122 officers and 1,140 men present, and his brigade was composed of the 9th Tennessee, 10th and 11th Tennessee, 19th and 20th Tennessee, 2d and 21st Tennessee. When the war ended he returned to his home in Tennessee, but about ten years later moved to Fresno County, California, where he took up farming and was prominent in civic affairs. He died September 1, 1902, while in New Orleans on a trip which had included a visit to his former home in Tennessee, and a meeting of Confederate veterans. Bell is buried in Bethel Cemetery near Sanger, California.

Anne Bailey

★ Henry Lewis Benning ★

Henry Lewis Benning was born on April 2, 1814, in Columbia County, Georgia. The third of eleven children, he attended the best preparatory schools in the state before entering Franklin College (later the University of Georgia) where, at the age of twenty, he finished first in his class. Following graduation he moved to Columbus where he resided for the remainder of his life. He studied law in the office of George W. Towns, who later served in Congress and as governor of Georgia. Benning gained admittance to the bar at the age of twenty-one, and two years later was appointed to fill the vacancy of solicitor general for the Chattahoochee Circuit, which included Columbus. He also served a term in the general assembly. On September 12, 1839, he married Mary Howard Jones, the only daughter of his law partner, Colonel Seaborn Jones. The Bennings' only son was mortally wounded during the Civil War.

Benning believed that ultimately the only social and economic security for the deep South would be a Southern Republic. Having many of the characteristics and beliefs of John C. Calhoun, Benning in 1850 supported the movement to hold a conference in Nashville. He was one of only a few secessionists in Georgia to be elected a delegate to that conference. Supposedly in an attempt at compromise, Benning introduced a resolution at Nashville that stated that the least the South could accept as a settlement of the question of slavery in the Mexican Session was the extension of the Missouri Compromise line. Actually he believed that the South would agree with this position and the North would reject it, which would lead to secession. Instead, even his own state accepted the compromise proposed by Henry Clay and Stephen Douglas.

In 1851 Benning was defeated in his bid for Congress, but in 1853 the general assembly elected him an associate justice of the Supreme Court, where in the case of *Padleford v. Savannah*, he held that a state supreme court was not bound by the U.S. Supreme Court regarding constitutional questions, rather that the two courts were "coordinate and co-equal." His eighty-page decision might represent the most assertive argument of the doctrine of "strict constriction" ever written. His failure to be reelected in 1859 apparently had nothing to do with his secessionist beliefs, although by 1860 he appears to have become more moderate when he remained within the regular Democratic Party. That year he served as a delegate at the Charleston convention in 1860 and as a vice-president of the Baltimore convention that nominated Douglas for President.

In 1861 Benning was active in the Georgia secession convention and served that body as its commissioner

No uniformed photo of Benning seems to have survived. This civilian view probably dates from immediately before or after the war. (Miller, *Photographic History*)

to the Virginia Convention, which he addressed. Although considered for a position in the Confederate cabinet, Benning chose to raise a regiment in Columbus and he entered Confederate service on August 29 as colonel of the 17th Georgia Infantry.

Benning's actions on the battlefield earned him the sobriquet "Old Rock." He led his regiment in the battles of Malvern Hill, Second Manassas, and Sharpsburg. At the latter, Benning commanded the brigade of Brigadier General Robert Toombs and Toombs had posted him opposite the upper bridge over Antietam Creek. Benning's defense of what has since been known as Burnside's Bridge was legendary. Finally outflanked on both sides in the afternoon, Benning had to withdraw from the heights overlooking the bridge but managed to keep what remained of his command intact. In the closing action of the battle Benning rode at the head of the brigade when it drove the Federals from the town. Although Benning credited Toombs for the brigade's performance that day, it was he who warranted the recognition.

Benning commanded the brigade at Fredericksburg in December and, following Toombs' resignation, he was deservedly commissioned a brigadier general on April 23, 1863, to rank from January 17, and given permanent command of the brigade. Engaged at Gettysburg, his brigade secured Devil's Den for the Confederates on July 2 but, at least according to one of his subordinates, when the order arrived to assault Little Round Top "Benning refused to have his troops butchered and sent word back that he wouldn't obey the order."

Detached with Lieutenant General James Longstreet to Georgia, he arrived in time to participate in the Battle of Chickamauga. After having three horses shot from under him, he commandeered a fourth from an artillery limber and led his brigade in a charge using a piece of rope for a whip and without taking time to remove the harness. His efforts saved General Evander M. Law's brigade from a flank attack and captured eight cannon. Benning participated in the engagement at Wauhatchie, Tennessee, on the outskirts of Chattanooga, October 28–29, and in the assault against Fort Sanders at Knoxville on November 29 before returning to Virginia in the spring of 1864.

Severely wounded in the arm during the second day's fighting in the Wilderness, May 6, 1864, Benning returned to command his brigade during the Siege of Petersburg, where, on one occasion, it successfully withstood an overwhelming enemy assault for hours. Apparently he never thought that the South would lose the war and was heartbroken when Lee surrendered at Appomattox.

Benning participated in every major action of the Army of Northern Virginia with the single exception of Chancellorsville, which he missed because his unit was detached with Lieutenant General James Longstreet in southeastern Virginia, and his later performance in Georgia and Tennessee more than compensated for this single absence. No other brigadier present at the surrender could boast of so distinguished a career. Although the claim has been made that he was appointed a major general, and he did command a division on several occasions, Benning was never officially commissioned at that grade.

Paroled on April 9, 1865, Benning was penniless at the end of the war. He returned to Columbus to find that his property had been confiscated or destroyed and that his dependents now included his fallen brother-in-law's widow and children and his sister's orphans. To support his extended family, Benning resumed his law practice with the same tenacity he had displayed on numerous battlefields. On July 8, 1875, he was struck with apoplexy on his way to court in Columbus and he died two days later. He is buried in Columbus. Fort Benning, Georgia is named in his honor.

Lawrence L. Hewitt

Faust, Patricia L., ed. *Historical Times Illustrated Encyclopedia of the Civil War*. New York, 1986.

Rozier, John, ed. *The Granite Farm Letters: the Civil War Correspondence of Edgeworth and Sallie Bird*. Athens, Ga.

Tucker, Glenn. *Chickamauga: Bloody Battle in the West*. Indianapolis, 1961.

✯ *Samuel Benton* ✯

This portrait shows Benton as a colonel of the 37th/34th Mississippi Infantry, and was taken between early 1862 and his death in July 1864. (Virginia Historical Society)

Samuel Benton, nephew of the famous United States Senator Thomas Hart Benton, was born on October 18, 1820. His place of birth is uncertain, but Confederate historian Ezra J. Warner deducted from family letters that it was probably in Williamson County, Tennessee. After a brief tenure as a schoolteacher, Benton moved to Holly Springs, Mississippi, where he became a prominent lawyer and politician. One wartime document notes that he was personally known to Jefferson Davis, but the extent of their relationship is unknown. Benton eventually was elected state representative for Marshall County and became a member of Mississippi's secession convention in 1861, where he voted for secession.

Although Benton had no prior military experience, he was appointed captain of the 9th Mississippi Infantry, a twelve-month regiment. In early 1862 he was appointed colonel of the 37th Mississippi and was said to have led the regiment at the Battle of Shiloh that April, although his actions in the battle are unrecorded. This regiment was reorganized sometime in early 1862 and renamed the 34th Mississippi. Official records, however, still referred to it as the 37th Mississippi for some time. On May 9, 1862, Benton's regiment participated in a spirited skirmish at Farmington, Mississippi, and although the regiment's casualties were limited to only one man wounded, his brigade commander, General J. Patton Anderson, gave a "special commendation" for the regiment. Anderson also noted that the 37th Mississippi "made a most gallant charge" against the enemy.

For the next sixteen months the 34th Mississippi garrisoned north Mississippi and middle Tennessee. Then, as part of General Edward C. Walthall's Mississippi brigade, the regiment participated in the Battle of Chickamauga in September 1863. At that time, however, Benton was absent from his command and the regiment was led by a major. The colonel's absence was not explained. It is known that in the spring of 1864 Benton was temporarily commanding the 24th and 27th Mississippi regiments in Walthall's brigade, but it is unclear whether he led them at Chickamauga. He resumed command of the 34th Mississippi on May 11, 1864, at the beginning of the Atlanta Campaign.

Little is known of Benton's activities during the campaign. On May 15 at Resaca, his regiment was attacked heavily in the center of the Confederate line by Union artillery, infantry, and sharpshooters. But losses were surprisingly light, amounting to only fifteen dead and wounded out of 298 engaged. It was reported that his regiment did suffer heavy casualties at Kolb's Farm on June 22, but Benton's role in the battle is not known. When Walthall was promoted to major general in early July, Benton was elevated to command Walthall's Mississippi brigade.

On July 22 during the Battle of Atlanta, Benton was supervising the brigade when an artillery shell exploded nearby and shrapnel tore through his body. One piece mangled a foot and another lodged in Benton's chest over his heart. Benton's foot was amputated and he was sent to a hospital in Griffin, Georgia, where he died on July 28, 1864. Belatedly, his commission to brigadier general arrived shortly afterwards, dated from July 26, to rank from the same date. Having lived only two days after his promotion, Benton must have been the shortest surviving general in Confederate history. He was temporarily buried at Griffin, but his body was exhumed and reburied at Holly Springs, Mississippi. Although Benton's grave bears an elegant tombstone, there is no mention on it of his having served in the Confederate Army.

Terry Jones

Thomas Connelly, *Autumn of Glory* Baton Rouge, 1971

⋆ *Albert Gallatin Blanchard* ⋆

This portrait probably shows Blanchard in mid-1861 when he was colonel of the 1st Louisiana Infantry, though it could possibly date from his Mexican War service. (Virginia Historical Society)

Blanchard was born in Charlestown, Massachusetts, on September 10, 1810. He attended the United States Military Academy at West Point and graduated twenty-sixth in a class of forty-six in 1829. His classmates included Robert E. Lee and Joseph E. Johnston. Breveted a 2d lieutenant in the 3d United States Infantry, Blanchard served primarily on frontier duty but was involved in making improvements on Sabine River and Sabine Lake in Louisiana. He resigned as a 1st lieutenant on October 1, 1840, then moved to New Orleans, Louisiana, and became a merchant. From 1843 to 1845, he served as director of the state's public schools. He led an independent company of Louisiana volunteers in the Mexican War and performed well in the Battle of Monterrey. On May 27, 1847, Blanchard received a commission as major of the 12th United States Infantry and was honorably discharged on July 25, 1848. He returned to New Orleans, where he worked as a civil engineer, schoolteacher, and railroad executive.

When the Civil War started, Blanchard was elected colonel of the 1st Louisiana Infantry Regiment on April 28, 1861. His regiment went to Richmond, Virginia, in early May and received orders to report for duty at Norfolk. There Blanchard soon assumed command of the western division of the Department of Norfolk under Benjamin Huger. On September 21, Blanchard received an appointment as brigadier general, to rank from the same day, and he took charge of a brigade at Portsmouth composed mostly of Georgia regiments. George W. Randolph replaced Blanchard as brigade commander on February 21, 1862, and the latter complained to the War Department about being displaced, expressing the hope that the War Department did not disapprove of his conduct.

By April 18, Blanchard had resumed command of a brigade and received orders to move to South Mills, North Carolina. His troops reached Richmond about the time of the Battle of Seven Pines. While some sources state that he led his brigade in that engagement, no conclusive proof of that service has surfaced. After Robert E. Lee succeeded to command of the Army of Northern Virginia, he directed Blanchard's release from active duty. Blanchard received orders on June 21 to go to Louisiana and assume command of camps of instruction in that state west of the Mississippi River with his headquarters in Monroe. He reached that town and assumed his duties on July 20.

Richard Taylor, after taking command of the District of Western Louisiana in August, assigned Blanchard to immediate command of that portion of the district north of the Red River. Union troops made several landings along the west bank of the Mississippi River north of Vicksburg, Mississippi, in December 1862 and conducted destructive raids into the Louisiana countryside. President Jefferson Davis and the War Department directed Taylor to investigate the lack of any response by Blanchard to these raids.

The War Department relieved Blanchard of command on February 11, 1863, and ordered him to report to Alexandria, Louisiana. Taylor reported that Blanchard had either not carried out Taylor's instructions for protecting the area or had executed those instructions very badly. He felt that Blanchard was utterly incompetent for command. When Blanchard applied to the War Department for relief from conscript duty, thinking he might receive field command, he received instructions in late April 1863 to proceed to the capital for further orders, but he got no new assignment. After several months of unsuccessful attempts to obtain a new brigade, Blanchard moved his family to Warrenton, North Carolina. He sent letters to the War Department begging for employment to escape his "disgraceful idleness," but Secretary of War James A. Seddon reported that he had "really no brigade to assign [Blanchard] to with propriety." On May 27, 1864, the War Department assigned Blanchard to a court of inquiry that would investigate charges against Seth M. Barton; however, the court never convened.

In January 1865, Blanchard was reported as commanding several regiments of South Carolina reserves in Ambrose R. Wright's division of the Department of South Carolina, Georgia, and Florida. The next month, Blanchard was leading a brigade of reserves in Lafayette McLaws' division at Cheraw, South Carolina. His brigade apparently accompanied Johnston's army on its retreat into North Carolina. On March 31, he wrote Adjutant General Samuel Cooper that he had received orders dated February 11 dropping him from Confederate service, but no other references to this action have been found. Blanchard's reserves were consolidated with South Carolina regiments in John D. Kennedy's brigade of the Army of Tennessee.

Apparently, no record of Blanchard's parole at the end of the war exists. He returned to New Orleans and again worked as a civil engineer and surveyor. From 1870 to 1878, he served as deputy surveyor of the city and as assistant city surveyor from 1878 to 1891. Blanchard died in New Orleans on June 21, 1891, and was buried in St. Louis Cemetery No. 1. Blanchard's advancing age when the war began undoubtedly prevented him from serving his country as well as he would have liked. Richard Taylor's judgment was perhaps too harsh. One assessment that seems to ring true is that Blanchard "seems to have bungled every command" he held and "showed...little insight into the limitations of his talent."

Arthur W. Bergeron, Jr.

⋆ *William Robertson Boggs* ⋆

In this very dim group photo, taken in 1864 or 1865, Boggs sits in full uniform third from the left. Just left of him is General Edmund Kirby Smith, and to the left of Smith is General Henry W. Allen, in civilian garb as governor of Louisiana. (William C. Davis Collection)

Boggs, the son of Archibald and Mary Ann Robertson Boggs, was born in Augusta, Georgia, on March 18, 1829. His father was a merchant in Augusta. Boggs attended the Augusta Academy before being admitted to the United States Military Academy in 1849, graduating fourth in the class of 1853. He served briefly in the Corps of Engineers before accepting a position with the Topographical Bureau of the Pacific Railroad Survey. In 1854 Boggs was made a 2d lieutenant in the Ordnance Bureau and was stationed in New York. On December 19, 1855, Boggs married Mary Sophia Symington, and they had five children, three sons and two daughters.

In 1856 Boggs was promoted to 1st lieutenant, and in 1859 he became inspector of ordnance stationed at Port Isabel, Texas, until ordered to Charleston, South Carolina, where he was serving when that state seceded from the Union in December 1860. Boggs resigned his commission in the United States Army in February 1861 and immediately entered the Confederate Army as a captain. He served under the command of General P. G. T. Beauregard in Charleston. Because he was a staff officer, his first duties involved the designing of weapons and fortifications, but at the request of Governor Joseph Brown of Georgia, he was transferred to Savannah despite Beauregard's efforts to retain his services.

In April Boggs was assigned to assist General Braxton Bragg in the Pensacola, Florida area, where he became a colonel on July 14, 1862. Bragg commended Boggs for "close reconnaissances on which the expedition was based, and the secret and complete organization which insured its success," in his report on the action at Santa Rosa Island. In October 1862 Bragg further commended Boggs in a letter of recommendation containing a list of officers whom he recommended for promotion to brigadier general. Bragg was noted for a brusque personality, and Boggs exhibited a similar quarrelsome nature. Before long the two became estranged over the promotion issue, and Boggs resigned his commission on December 21, 1861 to accept a position as chief engineer for the state of Georgia. However, Boggs continued to respond to requests for his services in both Georgia and Florida from General John C. Pemberton.

Boggs was named a brigadier general on November 4, 1862, with seniority from that date, and directed to join General Edmund Kirby Smith in the Department of the Trans-Mississippi. He served as Smith's chief of staff until after the Red River Campaign in the summer of 1864. Boggs again resigned his commission following a dispute with Smith. He then served as commander of the Louisiana District, and attempted an aborted military expedition into Mexico. Boggs was not present at any surrender ceremony and apparently never considered that he had in fact surrendered.

Following the Civil War, Boggs moved to Savannah and worked for a time as an architect. After a year he moved to St. Louis, Missouri, to become chief engineer of the Lexington & St. Louis Railroad, a post he held for two years. He also worked as a civil and mining engineer in St. Louis from 1870 until 1875, when he accepted a position at Virginia Polytechnic Institute at Blacksburg, Virginia, to teach mechanics and drawing. Boggs wrote his military reminiscences, *Military Reminiscences of General William R. Boggs*, which was published posthumously at Durham, North Carolina in 1913.

Boggs died in Winston-Salem, North Carolina, on September 11, 1911, and is buried in Salem Cemetery.

Archie McDonald

⁂ *Milledge Luke Bonham* ⁂

Bonham here appears as major general in command of South Carolina state forces sometime in the early months of 1861. The palmetto insignia on his hat is clearly evident, as is the state insignia on his belt plate. (U.S. Army Military History Institute, Carlisle, Pa.)

Bonham was born in the Edgefield District, now Saluda County, near Red Bank, South Carolina. The majority of sources list his birth date as December 25, 1813, but some claim May 6, 1815. Bonham, the son of James and Sophia Smith Bonham, was the eighth child born to his parents. He was descended from a Mayflower Pilgrim, and his grandfather, Major Absalom Bonham, served in the army during the American Revolution. A brother, James Butler Bonham, died in 1836 in defense of the Alamo during the Texas Revolution.

Bonham was educated in "old field" schools in Edgefield, at Edgefield and Abbeville academies, and in 1834 was graduated from South Carolina College—now the University of South Carolina. He practiced law and served as adjutant general of the South Carolina militia. During the Seminole War, Bonham served in the company of Captain James Jones until promoted to brigade major, a position similar to adjutant general of brigade. Following his active service in this conflict, Bonham held the post of major general of militia for several years, and served in the South Carolina legislature as a representative of the Edgefield District from 1840 until 1844. On November 13, 1845 he married Ann Patience Griffin and they had fourteen children.

When the war with Mexico began in 1846, Bonham was appointed lieutenant colonel of the 12th United States Infantry. Winfield Scott Hancock served as Bonham's adjutant, and together they served in the brigade of future President and General Franklin Pierce, who cited him for conspicuous service. Bonham served as governor of one of the conquered Mexican provinces for a year before returning to South Carolina to practice law. In 1848 he was elected solicitor of the southern district of South Carolina, a post he filled until 1857 when he won election to the United States House of Representatives to fill the unexpired term of his cousin, Preston S. Brooks, who had resigned from Congress following his famous caning of Charles Sumner. Bonham remained in Congress until South Carolina seceded from the Union in December 1860. An advocate of secession, he also played a role in seeing that Mississippi followed South Carolina's lead in leaving the Union.

Bonham returned to South Carolina and accepted appointment as commander-in-chief of state forces in the Charleston area. He worked well with General P. G. T. Beauregard, who commanded Confederate forces in the area. On April 23, 1861 he received a commission as a brigadier general in the Confederate service, ranking from that date, and was transferred to Virginia. Bonham led his brigade in battles at Fairfax, Centerville, Vienna, and First Manassas (Bull Run), where he commanded the center of Beauregard's forces.

Bonham lost his commission on July 14, 1861, when his brigade was disbanded, but President Davis reappointed him on October 21, with seniority from July 14. Nevertheless, on January 29, 1862, Bonham resigned his commission as a result of a dispute with Davis over the loss of seniority, which he felt should have dated back to April 23. Immediately elected to the Confederate House of Representatives, Bonham devoted himself chiefly to military affairs. He served on the House Ways and Means Committee, opposed the suspension of habeas corpus, and was an advocate of states' rights.

Bonham won the governorship of South Carolina in 1862 and served until December 1864. As governor, he supported the central government with troops. He was also noted for prosecuting deserters and using slave labor to construct defenses.

Bonham reentered the army as a brigadier general on February 20, 1865, to date from February 9, serving in cavalry under General Joseph E. Johnston in his last command of the Army of Tennessee. Bonham was involved in the last campaigns in North Carolina until Johnston surrendered.

Following the war Bonham farmed and practiced law until he was elected to the South Carolina legislature (1865–1867), and was a delegate to the Democratic National Convention in 1868. He also became involved in the insurance business in South Carolina and Georgia, and had little to do with politics from 1868 until he became involved in Governor Wade Hampton's activities to restore white supremacy in South Carolina. In 1878 Bonham was appointed railroad commissioner of South Carolina, and held the post of chairman of the commission when he died on August 27, 1890 at Sulphur Springs, North Carolina. He is buried in Elmwood Cemetery in Columbia, South Carolina.

Clement Evans quotes a soldier's description of Bonham. The soldier remembered his commander as "one of the finest looking officers in the entire army. His tall graceful figure, commanding appearance, noble bearing, and soldierly mien, all excited the admiration and confidence of his troops. He wore a broad-brimmed hat with a waving plume, and sat his horse with the knightly grace of Charles the Bold or Henry of Navarre. His soldiers were proud of him, and loved to do him homage. While he was a good disciplinarian, so far as the volunteer service required, he did not treat his officers with any air of superiority."

Archie McDonald

☆ *John Stevens Bowen* ☆

Bowen was born on October 30, 1830, at Bowens Creek, Georgia. His father, a prosperous merchant in nearby Savannah, saw that young John received a good education and at 18 he graduated from a Milledgeville preparatory school. Appointed to the U.S. Military Academy, Bowen arrived at West Point in May 1848. A good student with an aptitude for the military, John as a second-classman was named a cadet lieutenant and stood in the top third of his class. But, in March 1851, Bowen ran afoul of the honor system. He failed to report one of his classmates for an unauthorized absence. Court-martialed, Bowen was found guilty of unsoldier-like conduct and his dismissal from the corps of cadets recommended. President Millard Fillmore, on reviewing the records, reduced the expulsion to a year's suspension.

Bowen returned to the academy after the twelve-month absence, but he had lost much of his enthusiasm for the military. During his last year he received eighty-two demerits and on June 1, 1853 was graduated, ranking 13th in his class of fifty-two. Other future Civil War generals in the class that Bowen would either serve with or fight against were: James B. McPherson, William R. Boggs, William R. Terrill, Alexander Chambers, and William McE. Dye.

Commissioned a brevet 2d lieutenant in the Mounted Rifles, Bowen was billeted to the cavalry school at Carlisle Barracks, Pennsylvania. His next assignment took him to Fort McIntosh, Texas, by way of Jefferson Barracks, Missouri. While in Missouri, he met, courted, and married a 19-year-old St. Louis belle,

Mary Kennerly. The newly-weds did not remain long in Texas, for Bowen resigned his commission on May 1, 1856.

After returning to Savannah to become an architect, Bowen soon relocated to St. Louis, where he entered partnership with C. C. Miller. By 1859 the Bowens and their two children were living in Carondelet, and he had joined the Missouri militia. In November 1860, following the election of Abraham Lincoln, pro-secessionist Governor Claiborne Fox Jackson called out the Missouri militia and sent them into the state's western counties to guard against raids by Kansas "Jayhawkers" and to coerce those Missourians opposed to Jackson's policies. Bowen, first a major and then a lieutenant colonel and Brigadier General Daniel Frost's adjutant, participated in this "Southwest Expedition." He remained in western Missouri guarding the Kansas frontier until April 1861, when he returned to a St. Louis that had been aroused by the bombardment and capture of Fort Sumter, President Lincoln's call for 75,000 volunteers, and Governor Jackson's bitter denunciation of the call.

Colonel Bowen, along with other members of the militia, reported to Camp Jackson on May 3. The camp was surrounded by a formidable force of pro-Union volunteers, many of them Germans, led by Captain Nathaniel Lyon. On the 10th, General Frost sent Bowen

---

The only uniformed pose of Bowen is this, probably pre-war, image, showing him in U.S. Army uniform, and taken between 1853 and 1856. (U.S. Army Military History Institute, Carlisle, Pa.)

to meet with Captain Lyon. The latter refused to negotiate and General Frost, assured by Bowen that the prosecessionists were outnumbered ten to one, surrendered. Bowen was paroled on his promise not to serve "in any military capacity against the United States" unless exchanged. He did not honor his parole, holding that it was invalid. (After his capture and parole at Vicksburg, a Union officer, recalling the incident, protested, accusing Bowen of violating his parole).

Bowen headed for Memphis, where he opened a recruiting depot and camp of instruction for secessionist Missourians. He enlisted more than 1,000 men, organized into ten companies, which were designated the 1st Missouri Infantry. He was commissioned colonel of this unit on June 11. Bowen and his regiment pulled duty at New Madrid, Missouri, and in southern Kentucky during the next five months. Bowen in the late autumn led a division for a few weeks and was also post commander at Bowling Green. While at Bowling Green in mid-February 1862, Bowen was named to lead a brigade. A strict disciplinarian who insisted that his people be indoctrinated in the school of the soldier, Bowen was viewed by a number of his officers and men as a martinet. As one of his officers recalled, he "made us soldiers but sometimes made soldiering irksome."

On March 14, 1862, four weeks after the Confederate evacuation of Bowling Green, Kentucky, and while the Army of the Mississippi was being regrouped and reorganized in and around Corinth, Mississippi, Bowen was promoted to brigadier general to rank from that date. As a brigade commander, he saw his first combat at Shiloh where, in savage fighting near the Peach Orchard on April 6, he had two horses shot from under him and was wounded and incapacitated for duty. Released from a Memphis hospital, he rejoined his troops at Corinth, Mississippi, in early May. He and his brigade, in late June, accompanied Major General Earl Van Dorn to Vicksburg, then under attack by Union naval forces. Bowen and Van Dorn's relations soon soured and exploded in the weeks following the Battle of Corinth, October 3–4, and the Confederate retreat to Holly Springs. As a result of two charges and five specifications brought against him by Bowen for his erratic and lackluster conduct of the Corinth Campaign, Van Dorn faced a court of inquiry, held at Abbeville, Mississippi, in mid-November. Van Dorn vigorously defended himself, and the court held that the evidence submitted "fully disproves every allegation contained in said charges."

In the weeks following the court of inquiry, the retrograde of Lieutenant General John C. Pemberton's troops behind the Yalobusha, and the redeployment of U. S. Grant's army to the Louisiana parishes across the Mississippi and upstream from Vicksburg, Bowen's brigade was posted first at Big Black Bridge and then rushed to Grand Gulf. Bowen turned the latter position into a stronghold that would be tested as Union columns felt their way south from Milliken's Bend, Louisiana, and as Union gunboats and transports successfully ran the Vicksburg gauntlet. Bowen, his command increased to a division, between mid-April and July 3 demonstrated remarkable talents as an outstanding combat leader with an uncanny feel for defensive-offensive tactics, a keen appreciation of terrain, and an ability to divine the enemy's intentions. After standing tall at Grand Gulf, on April 29, Bowen, though outnumbered three to one at Port Gibson, held Grant at bay for sixteen hours before numbers told. His May 16 charge at Champion Hill was magnificent and for a time seemingly turned the tide. At Big Black Bridge on May 17, Bowen's reinforced division was routed, but General Pemberton noted that he "did not believe [Bowen] to be responsible."

At the Vicksburg siege, May 9–July 4, Bowen and his troops constituted Pemberton's strategic reserve and were thrown in wherever the fighting was the most savage and there was the threat of a Union breakthrough. His gallantry and leadership earned a promotion to major general, to rank from May 25.

Bowen, though weakened by dysentery, remained with his troops and played a key role in arranging the July 3 armistice and in the discussion that led to the surrender by General Pemberton of his army and Vicksburg on July 4. His health worsened in the week while the Confederates were being paroled. On July 11, Bowen's troops marched out of Vicksburg en route to the Demopolis, Alabama camp of instruction to await exchange. Bowen, too weak to ride, traveled in an ambulance. His wife Mary joined him near Edwards Station, but it was too late. Bowen died on July 13, 1863, in the garden of the Valley Farm, seven miles southeast of Edwards, Mississippi. He was buried in a nearby cemetery, but in 1887 his remains were disinterred, shipped to Vicksburg, and reburied in the Confederate section of the City Cemetery.

Edwin C. Bearss

A magnificent unpublished portrait of Bragg, probably made late in the war when he had grayed considerably. (Mansfield State Commemorative Area, Louisiana Office of State Parks)

✶ *Braxton Bragg* ✶

Braxton Bragg was born on March 22, 1817, at Warrenton, North Carolina. After receiving his early education there, he entered West Point in 1833. He finished fifth among fifty graduates in the class of 1837 and entered the army as a 2d lieutenant in the 3d Artillery on July 1, 1837. He served as the 3d's regimental adjutant from November 19, 1837 to March 8, 1838. Promoted to 1st lieutenant on July 7, 1838, Bragg experienced combat against the Seminoles in Florida during the 1830s before he joined Major General Zachary Taylor's forces in Texas in 1845.

During the Mexican War, Bragg earned the brevet of captain for his gallant and distinguished conduct in defense of Fort Brown, Texas, on May 9, 1846, a rank he actually achieved on June 18. His performance in several engagements near Monterrey, Mexico earned him the brevet of major on September 23. As captain of Battery C, 3d Artillery, he truly distinguished himself at Buena Vista on February 23, 1847, where he managed his artillery in such a way as to fill the gaping holes in the American infantry lines and finally repulse the numerically superior Mexican force. The victory largely won by Bragg helped make Taylor and, to a lesser extent, Mississippi Colonel Jefferson Davis national heroes. In return, the young captain received a brevet lieutenant colonelcy from Taylor and inaugurated a longtime bond with Davis.

Described as being "naturally disputatious" by Ulysses S. Grant, Bragg had difficulties in almost every relationship with either a superior or subordinate officer. Unable to have his way regarding the use of horse artillery in the army or duty stations, Bragg resigned on January 3, 1856. He had married a wealthy woman from Louisiana, Eliza Brooks Ellis, in 1849, and now he moved to Thibodaux, Louisiana, to become a substantial sugar planter. He also served his adopted state as a commissioner on the Board of Public Works, a position that involved his designing of the state's drainage and levee system. Bragg soon realized the need for trained engineers in Louisiana and worked to establish the State Military School in 1860, now Louisiana State University.

In December 1860 Louisiana Governor Thomas O. Moore appointed Bragg to the state military board to organize a 5,000-man army, and on January 11, 1861, Bragg captured the Baton Rouge Arsenal at the head of 500 volunteers. Following the secession of Louisiana and its creation of an army, Bragg became its commander with the rank of major general on February 6. On March 7, he was commissioned a brigadier general in the Confederate Army to rank from that date, and assigned to command a portion of the Gulf Coast which included Mobile and Pensacola. On September 12, 1862 he was appointed a major general, to rank

A late war portrait of Bragg, and the only one that shows him in a uniform with buttons arranged for major general or higher rank. (William Turner Collection)

113

Another outstanding view of Bragg was taken in Montgomery, Alabama, by the photographer A.C. McIntyre, probably in 1862 or 1863. (Confederate Museum, New Orleans, La)

immediately, and on February 15, he suggested to the secretary of war that his forces along the Gulf be ordered north. Bragg's advice was accepted, and he moved to Corinth, Mississippi, where he helped General Albert Sidney Johnston organize what eventually became the Army of Tennessee. Bragg served as chief of staff and commanded the II Corps. At Shiloh, much of the Confederate success on April 6 resulted from Bragg's supervision of the right flank.

Promoted to full general on April 12, Bragg relieved General P. G. T. Beauregard of command of the army at Tupelo on June 27. Following the breakup of the Union forces at Corinth, Bragg determined to strike Corinth and continue to Nashville. Threats to east Tennessee and especially Chattanooga forced Bragg to modify his original plan; instead, most of Bragg's army moved by rail via Mobile to Chattanooga.

On August 27, Bragg headed northward from Chattanooga. Bypassing Nashville, he entered Kentucky in the wake of Confederate Major General Edmund Kirby Smith. Although he captured Munfordville on September 17, Bragg felt his force insufficient to assault the enemy at Bowling Green. While Bragg busied himself meeting with Kirby Smith and installing a Confederate governor in Frankfort, Major General Leonidas Polk moved Bragg's army eastward into central Kentucky. The campaign culminated on October 8 at Perryville, where a bizarre chain of circumstances enabled the heavily outnumbered Confederates to win a tactical victory. By darkness Bragg had learned his opponent's true strength and wisely withdrew during the night. The retreat continued into Tennessee where, despite substantial criticism of him by his corps commanders and others, he retained command of the army.

On December 31, Bragg countered the Union advance from Nashville by attacking it near Murfreesboro. The considerable success achieved by the Confederates that day was followed by a day of inactivity, and then heavy fighting on January 2. The next day Bragg withdrew to Tullahoma. Between June and September 1863, Federal forces fought a campaign of maneuver that culminated in Bragg's withdrawal into northwestern Georgia. After receiving substantial reinforcements from Virginia, however, Bragg assumed the offensive.

He fought at Chickamauga September 19–20, the only major victory he ever won, but failed to quickly follow it up. Instead, he laid siege to Chattanooga, which gave the Federals time to reinforce the beleaguered town while reducing Confederate chances for capturing it because of the strained relations between Bragg and numerous subordinates. These tense relations resulted in the transfer of senior officers and substantial numbers of troops to other regions. When the Confederate line cracked on Missionary Ridge on November 25 and his troops retreated into Georgia literally on the run, Bragg asked to be relieved. His career as the commander of the principal field army in the western theater ended on December 2, 1863.

During 1864 Bragg served in Richmond, nominally as general-in-chief but actually only as a military advisor to President Davis. He held several minor commands during the final six months of the war, primarily in North Carolina. His last battle as senior officer on the field occurred at Kingston on March 8, 1865. He joined Davis in his flight from Richmond and was captured in Georgia on May 9 and paroled.

After the war Bragg worked as a civil engineer, first in Mobile and later in Texas. He also served at Commissioner of Public Works for the state of Alabama for four years, during which time he supervised harbor improvements at Mobile. Later he briefly served as chief engineer of the Gulf, Colorado, and Santa Fe Railroad. His death came unexpectedly in Galveston on September 27, 1876, while employed by the state of Texas to monitor the progress of railroads being constructed that involved state land grants. His body was returned to Mobile for interment in Magnolia Cemetery.

In Bragg, the Confederacy found its strictest disciplinarian and, at least in the western theater, its best organizer. Long the most detested of Confederate generals, Bragg is enjoying somewhat more favorable treatment by Civil War historians and some of the tarnish is receding from Bragg's star. However he is regarded, Bragg's association with the American military will continue as long as Fort Bragg, the enormous military base in North Carolina named in his honor, continues to operate.

Bragg's best known portraits come from an early war sitting that cannot be dated, but was probably 1863 or before. (Chicago Historical Society)

Lawrence L. Hewitt

Hewitt, Lawrence L. "Braxton Bragg and the Confederate Invasion of Kentucky in 1862," Roman J. Heleniak and Lawrence L. Hewitt, eds., *The 1989 Deep Delta Civil War Symposium: Leadership During the Civil War,* Shippensburg, Pa, 1991.

A variant pose from the same sitting. (Chicago Historical Society)

One of Bragg's last wartime portraits shows his hair retouched by an artist to take out some of the gray. (Confederate Museum, New Orleans, La.)

✶ *Lawrence O'Bryan Branch* ✶

Branch was born at Enfield, Halifax County, North Carolina, on November 28, 1820, into a wealthy and prominent family. When both parents died before his seventh birthday, he became the ward of his uncle, John Branch, who was much distinguished in North Carolina and national politics. L. O'B. Branch's preparatory education included terms at various schools and under a succession of tutors. After a stint at the University of North Carolina, Branch enrolled in the College of New Jersey (Princeton University), from which he earned a degree in 1838.

The young graduate emigrated to Tennessee, where he studied law in Nashville and edited a political newspaper for a short time. In 1840 Branch moved to Florida, won admittance to that state's bar while still a minor, and practiced law in Tallahassee. His first military experience—and the only that he would gain before the Civil War—came during the latter stages of the Second Seminole War, when he served for about six weeks during 1841 as a general's aide-de-camp. Seven years later Branch returned to North Carolina, settling in 1852 in Raleigh. He engaged extensively in business there, especially railroads, in addition to his legal practice and management of the family's considerable estate. In 1860 he owned ten slaves. Branch ran the Raleigh & Gaston Railroad between 1852 and 1855, and held the position of president.

From 1852 until his death Branch was deeply involved in Democratic party politics. In that year he was chosen Presidential elector on the Pierce ticket. Two years later Branch won election to the United States House of Representatives, although he was nominated for the post, he wrote, "against my most active and sincere protests." He remained in the House until March 1861, espousing positions notably moderate on matters of interest to the South. When Branch did not stand for renomination in 1860, President Buchanan offered him in December of that year the post of Secretary of the Treasury, but he declined the position, as he had the earlier offer by Buchanan of the postmaster generalship.

After North Carolina seceded, Branch assumed the duties of quartermaster general of the state on May 20, 1861. A contemporary North Carolina historian later complained mildly that the Branch tenure in that department left a disappointing lack of records behind, but he loyally asserted that the quartermaster function was apparently well discharged during Branch's reign. On September 20, 1861, the state legislature passed a bill reorganizing the quartermaster department and on the same day Branch was commissioned colonel of the 33d North Carolina Infantry. After less than two months in that role, Colonel Branch received promotion to brigadier general. His brigadier general's commission on November 16, 1861, took rank from the same date and was confirmed on December 13.

No uniformed photo of Branch has appeared that is genuine. This portrait was probably made while he sat in Congress in the latter 1850s. (Miller, *Photographic History*)

The brigade that Branch led would become famous under his name and that of his successor as the Branch-Lane Brigade of the Army of Northern Virginia. It included five North Carolina infantry regiments: 7th, 18th, 28th, 33d, and 37th. The first serious battle action for the brigade and its leader came in March 1862 around New Berne. Federal General Ambrose E. Burnside drove the brigade and other troops under Branch out of the town, inflicting a serious loss on the Confederacy and pulling another important nautical access point within Federal grasp. Because Burnside comfortably outnumbered the Southerners, Branch generally escaped criticism for the result, and was even applauded in some quarters for his successful retreat.

Branch and his brigade moved to Virginia in the immediate aftermath of the New Berne disaster. During much of the period of Stonewall Jackson's legendary Shenandoah Valley Campaign that spring, the North Carolinians hovered in Piedmont, Virginia on the verge of a call to that theater that never came. Branch suffered considerable frustration during this period of apparently fruitless marching and countermarching. With an arrogance typical of much of his wartime writing, and with the anti-professional slant so common in political generals, he blamed the confusion on stupid military men. In a letter to his wife in mid-May, Branch assigned the responsibility for what he saw as chaos to "rivalry and jealousy between Gens. Jackson and Ewell." "It is very unfortunate," he declared, "that our Govt is under the necessity of suddenly transforming so may Lieuts. and Captains of the old army into...Generals."

The self-confident Branch must have welcomed the opportunity that came just a few days later to escape the incompetent clutches of Jackson and Ewell. His brigade was ordered on a rapid rail move from Gordonsville to Hanover Court House. Near there on May 27, 1862, Branch commanded a small Confederate force in his second independent action. Once again his troops suffered a thorough beating, although as at New Berne the odds against Branch attracted much of the blame for his failure.

Just before Lee's first operation in command of the Army of Northern Virginia in the Seven Days Campaign, Branch and his brigade were assigned to A. P. Hill's new "Light Division." Through most of the summer of 1862, Branch outranked the other five brigade commanders in that large division by virtue of his date of commission. In private correspondence, Branch referred derogatorily to several of his fellow brigadiers, and even to Hill, as "West Point Lieuts." During the Seven Days, Hill's troops performed splendidly under difficult circumstances and Branch's Brigade bore its full share of the hardship and shared in the credit. The brigade made the advance that opened Lee's offensive on June 25 when it lunged across the Chickahominy at Half Sink to signal the army's movement.

Hill's Division, including Branch's command, moved toward Gordonsville during July to support Jackson's command in its response to a new Federal threat under General John Pope. At Cedar Mountain on August 9, Branch led his men against a Northern thrust at a critical moment and contributed solidly to the Confederate victory there. After the battle, however, he wrote immodestly and somewhat inaccurately to his wife about his role and deprecated other Confederate units in the process. Perhaps this was prompted by what he saw as mistreatment, since he assured his wife that she would not see his accomplishments "acknowledged in the Virginia papers," or in North Carolina either. "Little will be said about it," he grumbled suspiciously, "lest it may redound to my credit."

Branch's Brigade fought on the far Confederate left at Second Manassas, and arrived on the battlefield of Sharpsburg on September 17 as part of Hill's exhausted division that saved the day. Just after the crisis passed, a Federal bullet hit General Branch in the right cheek and killed him instantly. He is buried in Old City Cemetery, Raleigh.

Robert K. Krick

✭ *William Lindsay Brandon* ✭

The uniform, though indistinct in this portrait of Brandon, appears to be genuine and not an artist's addition. This would date the photo to sometime after June 1864, taken probably in Mississippi. (Virginia Historical Society)

Brandon was born a few miles northeast of Natchez, Mississippi, near the village of Washington in Adams County. Most accounts place his birth in either 1800 or 1802; however, Brandon stated in a letter of October 1863 that he was then fifty-nine years old, which suggests that his birthdate was 1803 or 1804 (family records that could resolve the question fell victim to a fire in 1831). Brandon attended Washington College and the College of New Jersey at Princeton before settling down in 1824 on "Arcole," a plantation near Pinckneyville, Mississippi. His antebellum activities included a stint in the Mississippi Legislature in the mid-1820s and service as a major general of the state militia. During the war with Mexico, he sought the colonelcy of the 1st Mississippi Infantry (Mississippi Rifles), losing out to Jefferson Davis. Brandon's prewar interests also extended to the study of medicine, a field in which he acquired a reputation as an expert.

On June 11, 1861, some five months after Mississippi had seceded from the Union, Brandon accepted a commission as major in the Provisional Army of the Confederate States. Promoted to lieutenant colonel on July 17, 1861, he commanded the 1st Mississippi Battalion. In the fall of 1861, two companies were added to the battalion to form the 21st Regiment Mississippi Infantry under the leadership of fellow-Mississippian Colonel Benjamin G. Humphreys. Brandon's first exposure to serious combat came during the Seven Days, where he and the 21st Mississippi fought in Colonel William Barksdale's 3d Brigade of Major General John Bankhead Magruder's division. In temporary command of the regiment on July 1, Brandon led it forward about 6:30 that evening in an assault against the Federals on Malvern Hill. "We advanced in line of battle until within 200 yards of the enemy's battery," reported Captain William C. F.

Brooks of the 21st, "and finding no support either right or left were ordered to retire, which we did in good order, losing Lieut. Col. W. L. Brandon (the only field officer), being wounded by a grape shot." Magruder lauded Brandon's performance in the battle, while Barksdale's report noted that the lieutenant colonel was "severely wounded while gallantly and nobly" leading the regiment into action.

Brandon's medical experience probably told him, even before he was carried from the field at Malvern Hill, how serious a wound he had suffered. Surgeons removed his right leg, after which he began a long convalescence. Such a trauma tested the physical resources of even strong young men; for Brandon, edging toward old age by mid-19th century standards, recovery was painful and incomplete. Promoted to colonel on August 12, 1863, he took command of the 21st Mississippi when Humphreys moved up to replace Barksdale, who had been killed at Gettysburg. Brandon and his regiment rode the trains to north Georgia in late summer 1863, travelling with Lafayette McLaws' division of Longstreet's First Corps in the strategic shuffling that resulted in the battle of Chickamauga and the siege of Chattanooga.

The rigors of active campaigning soon overwhelmed Brandon, who tendered his resignation on October 10, 1863. Writing from his regimental headquarters near Chattanooga, he informed Adjutant and Inspector General Samuel Cooper that a combination of age and lingering problems with his amputated leg left him unfit for service with his regiment. "Having lost my right leg at Malvern Hill, I had a substitute made, with which I expected to be able to serve in the field," he explained. "I was encouraged in this hope from the reported experience of others, but I am disappointed in this. The attachment is weak & insecure, & very defective, so much so, that on horseback the stump slips up & down in the socket, & disarranges the padding so as to prevent my walking with comfort when I dismount."

Brandon's inability to campaign in the field neither diminished his devotion to the Southern cause nor ended his Confederate service. On June 18, 1864, he received promotion to brigadier general, to rank from that date, and orders to assume command of the reserve troops in his native state. President Davis believed that Mississippi should mobilize a larger proportion of its male population and wanted Governor Charles Clark and Brandon to oversee the process. Establishing a headquarters in Enterprise, Mississippi,

on July 23, 1864, Brandon quickly threw himself into his new work and within three months had enrolled about 3,000 reserves. During the balance of 1864 and well into 1865, Brandon waged a bureaucratic contest with Governor Clark for control of Mississippi's manpower. Clark called out the state militia on several occasions between July and September disrupting Brandon's efforts to place those men in the Confederate reserves. The governor complained about Brandon to President Davis and persuaded General Richard Taylor, who commanded the department embracing Mississippi, that it mattered little whether the troops went into state or national service because all were led by Confederate officers. General Cooper and Secretary of War James A. Seddon, however, supported Brandon's position that he had precedence over the state. Two decisions by Chief Justice A. H. Handy of the Mississippi High Court went against Clark, and by February 1865 all but two companies of the militia had passed under Brandon's control.

The stress of contending with Clark might have contributed to renewed physical ailments that forced Brandon to take leave of absence in the spring of 1865. Confined to his house for at least a month in February and March, he returned to his post at Enterprise in April to find serious problems of morale. Many of the reserve troops had "deserted their regiments and joined other commands," Brandon wrote Taylor on April 5—an offense for which Brandon asked permission to prefer charges. About one month later, on May 4, Brandon's part in the war ended when Taylor surrendered all Confederate forces in the Department of Alabama, Mississippi, and East Louisiana.

Brandon returned to his plantation after the war, a battle-scarred reminder of the failed Southern experiment in rebellion. More than six feet tall, well educated, and affable, he enjoyed a wide circle of friends and admirers and took an active part in state politics, serving as lieutenant governor. Former Confederate general St. John R. Liddell, who had known Brandon before the war in Mississippi, described him as a "Southern paladin" who, after the war, "still lives to bear, as bravely as he had fought, the misfortunes of the 'fallen cause.'" Brandon died on October 8, 1890, at "Arcole" and was interred in the family burial ground.

Gary W. Gallagher

⋆ *William Felix Brantley* ⋆

Despite his long service, Brantley seems not to have had his photograph taken in uniform, and this postwar view taken prior to his death in 1870 is all that survives. (Miller, *Photographic History*)

Brantley was born in Greene County, Alabama, on March 12, 1830. His parents soon relocated to Mississippi with their family and he grew to manhood in the latter state. After reading law, he was admitted to the bar and opened his law office in Greensboro in 1852. A pro-secessionist, he represented Choctaw County in the convention that met in Jackson and voted Mississippi out of the Union on January 9, 1861. Brantley was elected captain of the Wigfall Rifles of Choctaw County, and he and his unit were mustered into state service at Greensboro on April 20, 1861. One month later, Brantley and the Wigfall Rifles were at Corinth, Mississippi, where they were redesignated as Company D, 15th Mississippi Infantry, and mustered into Confederate service for twelve months. He was promoted to major and, during his year with the regiment first camped and trained in western Tennessee and then camped, marched, and fought in eastern Tennessee and southeastern Kentucky. Brantley saw his first combat at Camp Wildcat, Kentucky, on October 21 and participated in the Battle of Mill Springs on January 19, 1862. He accompanied the regiment on the long march to Corinth and was present at "Bloody Shiloh."

In early May, the 15th Mississippi reorganized and reenlisted for two years. Coincidentally, the 29th Mississippi was organized at Grenada and Brantley was promoted to lieutenant colonel and assigned to the latter unit. Brantley, along with the regiment, was in the Siege of Corinth, April 29–May 30, and in Braxton Bragg's Kentucky Campaign, August 20–October 23, where he participated in the savage fighting that led to the capture of Munfordville on September 17. At Stones River, having been promoted to colonel, Brantley commanded the regiment and, in the desperate December 31 fighting in the cedar glades north of the Wilkinson pike, he was "knocked down by concussion" from an exploding shell. Following the retreat from Stones River to Shelbyville in early January 1863, the 24th and 29th Mississippi were temporarily consolidated under Colonel Brantley. He led the 29th at Chickamauga, September 18–20, and at Chattanooga, November 23–25. At Lookout Mountain, on the 24th, his immediate superior called attention to Brantley's "skill, activity, zeal, and courage" in the fighting near the Cravens House.

May 7, 1864 found Brantley commanding the consolidated 29th and 30th Mississippi Infantry Regiments in Walthall's Brigade, Hindman's Division, Hood's Corps. Alerted to the advance of William T. Sherman's army and at the opening of the four-month Atlanta Campaign, Brantley sent his Mississippians into the rifle-pits at Alt's Gap. At Resaca, May 14–15, Brantley and his people held the left of Hood's Corps in support of Confederate artillery emplaced on a bald knob. Here they were assailed three times by Union troops, but they stood tall and grimly held their breastworks of logs and earth in the face of the enfilading fire of 24 enemy cannon. Brantley led his consolidated regiment into the lines at Cassville, May 19, the bitter eleven days at New Hope Church, May 25–June 5, the fight with Union cavalry at Big Shanty, June 9, and Kolb's Farm on June 22.

South of the Chattahoochee, on July 17, John Bell Hood replaced Gen. Joseph E. Johnston as army commander. The Army of Tennessee during the next ten days on three occasions came out from behind their earthworks to unsuccessfully carry the fight to Sherman. On July 22, Brigadier General Samuel Benton, the brigade commander, was mortally wounded and Brantley succeeded him, having been commissioned brigadier general on July 26, to rank from that date. At Ezra Church, two days later, Brantley led his Mississippians forward along the Lickskillet Road and drove Union soldiers from their field works but, as Brantley wrote, "being greatly weakened by the killed and wounded, and the innumerable cases of utter exhaustion among the best men…as well as the absence of a goodly number who had no legitimate excuse, I was unable to hold the works."

At Jonesboro, the last battle before Atlanta was evacuated, Brantley's Brigade, on August 31, suffered heavy losses in an attack on Federals posted behind earthworks.

Brantley and his brigade—assigned to Johnston's Division, Lee's Corps—were active and tragic participants in Hood's Middle Tennessee Campaign, November 21–December 27, 1864. At the Battle of Franklin on November 30, Johnston's was the only one of Lee's three divisions that engaged in the Confederate attacks that exceeded the Pickett-Pettigrew Gettysburg onslaught in gallantry, desperation, and futility. Writing of the assaults, Gen. S. D. Lee noted that the brigade of Sharp and Brantley (Mississippians) and of Deas (Alabamans)…distinguished themselves. Their dead were mostly in the trenches and on the works of the enemy, where they fell in desperate hand-to-hand combat. Brantley was exposed to a severe enfilade fire.

At Nashville, on December 16, Brantley and his Mississippians were on the Confederate right guarding the easterly approach to Overton Hill, where they repulsed a desperate lunge by Steedman's black brigades.

Following the retreat from Tennessee and their return to Tupelo, Mississippi, Brantley and his officers and men were furloughed until February 12, 1865. Brantley reassembled and reorganized his brigade—152 strong—at Meridian, Mississippi, on February 14, and four days later they boarded cars for the first leg of the trip that, by the last day of March, brought them to Smithfield, North Carolina, by way of Montgomery, Alabama, and Augusta, Georgia. Brantley and his consolidated brigade, now including regiments from Alabama and North Carolina, as well as Mississippi, were surrendered by Joseph E. Johnston at Durham Station, North Carolina, on April 26. Brantley signed his parole at nearby Greensboro on May 1.

He returned to Mississippi and his law practice but did not live long. Ironically, like a number of other Confederate generals who had lived through four years of savage combat, he died violently. On November 2, 1870, while riding in his buggy, he was shot and killed near Winona. Brantley's murder—his killer was never identified or brought to trial—was associated with a bitter feud. The general is buried "behind the church at Old Greensboro," three miles north of Tomnolen, Webster County, Mississippi.

Edwin C. Bearss

⋆ *John Bratton* ⋆

While Bratton's uniform is indistinct in this portrait, it appears to be that of a field grade officer, and probably shows him as a lieutenant colonel or colonel prior to May 1864. (Virginia Historical Society)

John Bratton was born on March 7, 1831, in Winnsboro, Fairfield County, South Carolina. After attending Mount Zion Academy (later Mount Zion College), he entered South Carolina College. Graduating in 1850, he studied medicine and received a diploma from the South Carolina Medical College in Charleston in 1853. Shortly thereafter he established a medical practice and became a planter in Fairfield County and remained active in both professions until he joined the Confederate Army in 1861. He married Elizabeth P. Du Bose in 1859 and they had three children.

Bratton entered South Carolina military service as a private in an independent company but was immediately elected its captain. At that rank he participated in the bombardment of Fort Sumter. When his company failed to enlist in Confederate service, Bratton organized a new company for the 6th South Carolina Infantry Regiment. As second lieutenant in Company C, he accompanied the regiment to Virginia, where it arrived shortly after the First Battle of Manassas.

The only action he saw in 1861 was at Dranesville, but near the end of that year Bratton attracted the attention of his superiors by proposing that his entire regiment reenlist for the war. Although his proposition failed, he reenlisted the first company for the war in General Joseph E. Johnston's army. When five other companies of the 6th reenlisted, the men elected Bratton their commander; when four more were added to complete the regiment, he was promoted to colonel. Although worried about his lack of military experience, he wrote his wife, "My first drill will be on the battlefield."

His regiment was assigned to the brigade of Brigadier General Richard H. Anderson, whom Colonel Micah Jenkins soon succeeded. With the latter exercising command over several regiments including the 6th South Carolina, Bratton fought at Williamsburg and Seven Pines. Bratton distinguished himself at the latter before being wounded and captured; his regiment had 269 men killed or wounded out of the 521 who entered the battle.

After spending several months in Fort Monroe, Bratton was exchanged and rejoined the army in time to participate in the Battle of Fredericksburg. In the spring of 1863, Bratton missed the Battle of Chancellorsville because of service with Lieutenant General James Longstreet in southern Virginia. During the Siege of Suffolk, Bratton commanded his brigade in the absence of new Brigadier General Micah Jenkins. In June, his regiment garrisoned Richmond and therefore missed the Battle of Gettysburg. It accompanied Longstreet to Georgia that fall, but failed to arrive in time to participate in the Battle of Chickamauga.

During the early stages of Chattanooga, Bratton commanded the brigade while Jenkins led the division of the wounded Major General John Bell Hood. Bratton led the brigade in a night assault at the Battle of Wauhatchie on October 28. Their gallant charge "drove the enemy through their camp, and entirely beyond their wagon camp," but the South Carolinians, lacking support, had to withdraw before two additional Union divisions arrived. The fruitless charge cost the brigade 356 casualties. Ill, homesick, and tired of the responsibilities of command during the winter of 1863–64, Bratton wrote in January, "It has been one protracted, head-cracking job for me."

Despite having grown tired of the war, when the same Confederate volley that wounded Longstreet killed Jenkins in The Wilderness on May 6, 1864, Bratton assumed command of the brigade with enthusiasm. His brigade covered the Confederate withdrawal from the "bloody angle" at Spotsylvania on May 12. After participating in an assault near Kingsland Creek, between the James and Appomattox Rivers on June 17, the brigade moved into the Petersburg trenches near the future site of the Battle of the Crater. In this position, the brigade endured its severest test of the war—enemy sharpshooter fire around the clock for five days. When finally relieved on June 24, they were transferred to New Market Heights, north of the James River. Bratton had led the brigade so well since May 6 that he had earned the sobriquet "Old Reliable" from his men and a brigadier general's commission from the government on June 9, 1864, to date from May 6. Before the end of the year a superior described him as "the best commander of the best brigade in the Army of Northern Virginia."

Following its relocation to New Market Heights, the brigade did not participate in any serious fighting until August 15, when it held its sector of the line during the fighting around Chaffin's Farm. Following this engagement, the brigade returned to the Petersburg trenches until September 29, when it received orders to move north of the James to the New Market road to participate in the efforts to recapture Battery Harrison the following day. Bratton lost 377 out of the 1,294 officers and men who participated in the unsuccessful charge.

The brigade fought along the Darbytown Road on October 7 and, on December 23, moved by rail to Gordonsville, Virginia, to confront the enemy moving toward Richmond from the Shenandoah Valley. It never encountered the Federals in central Virginia, however, and soon returned to Petersburg. At Appomattox Court House, Bratton had the distinction of commanding the largest and most coherently organized brigade in what remained of General Robert E. Lee's army. Larger than some of Lee's Divisions, Bratton's Brigade numbered 1,500 men and was the only unit to make an organized march to Danville, Virginia, where the men secured railroad transportation to hasten their return home.

Bratton abandoned the practice of medicine following the war, turning instead to farming. He quickly became active in political matters, serving as a member of the state constitutional convention in 1865, a state senator in 1865–66, a delegate to taxpayers' conventions, and as chairman of the South Carolina delegation to the 1876 Democratic National Convention. Chairman of the state Democratic committee in 1880, Bratton was elected state comptroller in 1881 and won a seat in Congress in 1884.

A member of the conservative party headed by Wade Hampton, Bratton labored to end Republican rule in the state. Although a farmer, he never supported the Farmer's, or Populist, Movement. In 1890 he became his party's gubernatorial candidate because he stood the best chance of uniting the Democrats against the Farmer's candidate, "Pitchfork Ben" Tillman. Although he conducted an admirable campaign, Bratton went down to defeat, a fate he shared with virtually all of the conservatives at the hands of the Tillmanites. Following the governor's race, Bratton retired from politics. He died at Winnsboro on January 12, 1898, and is buried there.

Lawrence L. Hewitt

Faust, Patricia L., ed. *Historical Times Illustrated Encyclopedia of the Civil War* (New York, 1986.)

⋆ *John Cabell Breckinridge* ⋆

While at least two other uniformed wartime portraits are known to have been taken, this view by Minnis and Cowell, taken in Richmond in January 1864, is the only one of Breckinridge known to survive. (Cook Collection, Valentine Museum, Richmond)

Born January 16, 1821, in Lexington, Kentucky, young Breckinridge came into an old and honored Bluegrass family that included an attorney general in Jefferson's cabinet. Following early education in local schools, he attended Centre College in Danville, the College of New Jersey (now Princeton), and finally Transylvania University where he received a law degree.

Breckinridge practiced law briefly in Kentucky before removing to Burlington, Iowa, but then returned to his native state where he married Mary Cyrene Birch, began a family, built his law practice, and took an interest in Democratic party affairs despite a strong Whig tradition in his family. When war came with Mexico in 1846, he did not initially show an interest in participating, but a eulogy delivered over the Kentucky dead returned from the Battle of Buena Vista made him an instant celebrity, and almost overnight he was commissioned a major in the 3d Kentucky Volunteers. Subsequently he marched to Mexico City, but saw no action.

Returning to Kentucky in 1848, Breckinridge won a seat in the commonwealth's legislature in 1849, and two years later successfully won election to Congress from Henry Clay's old district, despite its heavy Whig sentiment. Reelected two years later, he retired in 1855 to attend to his practice and growing family but in 1856 the Democrats turned to the handsome and popular young Kentuckian at their national convention, making him James Buchanan's running mate. "Buck and Breck" were elected in November making Breckinridge, at age 35, the youngest Vice President in American history.

Though never a proponent of secession or of extreme state rights views, still Breckinridge felt strong Southern sympathies in the growing sectional crisis. He tried to decline nomination for the Presidency in 1860, but in the end accepted the nomination of the Southern Rights wing of the split Democrats, and came in second to Lincoln in the Electoral vote. Speaking loudly for conciliation and compromise, he had already been elected to a term in the Senate that commenced immediately upon the expiration of his Vice

Presidency, and back on the floor of the Capitol he continued defending Southern rights and opposing war measures to coerce the Southern states into remaining in the Union. By the fall of 1861, though he had committed no overt act of disloyalty, still he and his influence were sufficiently feared that Federal authorities ordered his arrest. Breckinridge was warned, and escaped to the Confederacy, though privately he admitted little faith in the chances of the Lost Cause.

President Davis commissioned him a brigadier general on November 2, 1861, to rank immediately, and assigned him to A. S. Johnston's army then building in Kentucky. In late March 1862 he took command of Johnston's Reserve Corps, and led it at Shiloh in the attacks on the Hornets' Nest. Promoted major general on April 18, 1862, to rank from April 14, he participated in the retreat to Corinth before being ordered to the defenses of Vicksburg. He commanded a division there until August, when he led two small divisions in the attack on Baton Rouge on August 5, after which he occupied Port Hudson and commenced building its soon-to-be-formidable defenses. Bureaucratic wrangling between his superiors prevented him from taking his command to join Bragg in time for the Kentucky Campaign, but Breckinridge did lead his division in some of the war's bloodiest fighting at Stones River at year's end, where his celebrated feud with Bragg had its beginnings.

The next spring Bragg ordered Breckinridge back to Mississippi to link with Joseph E. Johnston's ill-fated attempt to relieve besieged Vicksburg. Breckinridge fought at the Battle of Jackson, but soon thereafter was once more sent back to Bragg, arriving just in time to command the far right of the army at Chickamauga, where his relentless attacks materially influenced the final collapse of the Federal army. He rose briefly to corps command at Chattanooga, and was there commanding the left of the Confederate line on Lookout Mountain and Missionary Ridge when Bragg's army collapsed in the face of Grant's late November attacks. While Breckinridge's performance was not good here, he was not, as Bragg later alleged, drunk, although Bragg spent years trying to build evidence and even soliciting perjured testimony to support his case.

President Davis certainly did not believe it, for he next ordered Breckinridge to an independent command in the Department of Southwest Virginia in February 1864. Here the Kentuckian's most outstanding achievement was mobilizing forces to repel a Federal invasion of the Shenandoah on May 14, 1864,

at the Battle of New Market, perhaps the most important engagement of its size in the war, for it saved the resources of the Valley for vital weeks that kept Lee's army fed east of the Blue Ridge, and protected his vulnerable left flank as he faced Grant at Spotsylvania.

Following New Market, Breckinridge took most of his division east in time to participate in Cold Harbor, where he was badly injured when his horse was killed under him. Still on a litter, he went to Lynchburg to command its defenses against the approach of David Hunter in June, and then led a corps to Jubal Early's small army in the Raid on Washington and the subsequent battles in the Shenandoah through Winchester, after which he returned to his department. In January 1865, needing Breckinridge's popularity in his otherwise discredited cabinet, Davis offered him the portfolio as the sixth and last secretary of war. Breckinridge accepted, being officially appointed on February 6. Credited with working wonders in improving supply for the armies, and weeding out incompetents like Lucius B. Northrop, Breckinridge knew the cause was hopeless, nevertheless, and devoted most of his energies to seeing the Confederacy to an honorable demise. Especially after the fall of Richmond, he used his influence with Davis constantly to press for surrender and reconciliation. After participating in the Sherman-Johnston peace negotiations in North Carolina, he took command of the fleeing Confederate government, and himself effectively disbanded it at Washington, Georgia on May 4, 1865. He made good his own escape to Cuba in a hair-raising adventure that included running gun battles with renegades, piracy, and a voyage in an open boat across the Caribbean in a near-hurricane. There followed three years of exile in Europe and Canada before he finally returned to Kentucky, where he resumed the practice of law, dabbled in insurance and railroading, and spoke out publicly only on behalf of moderation and conciliation. He died May 17, 1875, and is buried in Lexington, one of the most honored men of his time, North or South. His friend Robert E. Lee spoke of him as a "lofty, pure, strong man...a great man."

William C. Davis

William C. Davis, *Breckinridge: Statesman, Soldier, Symbol* Baton Rouge, 1974

Frank Heck, *Proud Kentuckian: John C. Breckinridge* Lexington, 1976

✶ *Theodore Washington Brevard* ✶

Brevard appears here as colonel of the 11th Florida, though the original photo has been heavily retouched, and the uniform is probably an artist's addition. (Virginia Historical Society)

Born in Alabama, August 26, 1835, but raised in Florida, this Tallahassee lawyer, who married former Governor Richard McCall's daughter, was adjutant and inspector general of Florida during the secession crisis.

With civil war erupting, he resigned his staff position and raised the Leon Rifles, which became Company D, 2d Florida Infantry. That regiment entered national service near Jacksonville on July 13, 1861, and left for Virginia on July 15. After staying in the capital two months, it moved to Yorktown on September 17. It participated in the siege there and the Battle of Williamsburg. When his colonel was killed on May 5, Brevard and several others bravely recovered his corpse under fire. Despite his heroism, Company D did not reelect Brevard when the regiment was reorganized six days later.

He returned to Florida as a mustering officer. On October 25, he was made major commanding the 2d Florida Partisan Ranger Battalion, ranking from September 2. The following June 24, the expanded outfit was redesignated the 2d Florida Infantry Battalion. Brevard became its lieutenant colonel commandant on August 12, 1863, ranking from June 24.

His battalion served at St. John's Bluff, which he abandoned without resistance on October 2, 1862. The following March he participated in Brigadier General Joseph Finegan's operations against Jacksonville, which provoked some of the earliest combat with Negro units. Perhaps with Hibernian hyperbole, Finegan lauded Brevard's "promptness, gallantry, and discretion" in advancing skirmishers toward Federal defenses. The situation on Brevard's skirmish line looked different to the inspector general, who notified department headquarters on March 26 that "General Finegan has given up all idea of attacking Jacksonville, and I expect that many of his officers are not anxious for a very bloody fight." Nevertheless, the Yankees abandoned Jacksonville on March 31.

With them gone, Finegan concentrated on patrolling coasts against raiders, gathering men and cattle for the main armies, and hunting deserters and draft dodgers. Brevard, accordingly, mounted an expedition against the Federal foothold at Fort Myers over the winter of 1863–1864. Before he reached the Fort Meade staging area, the Union invasion of east Florida in February prompted his recall. In a forced march of nearly 600 miles, he hastened northward—but arrived half a day too late to participate in Finegan's victory at Olustee.

In ensuing operations against Jacksonville, he commanded a brigade containing his own outfit and the 28th Georgia Heavy Artillery Battalion. Most troops of both sides soon left Florida. Because district headquarters considered Brevard someone "upon whose judgment, skill, and courage reliance could be placed," it gave him temporary command of the 64th Georgia Infantry Regiment on April 24 to resume moving against Fort Myers. However, barely 100 miles out, that unit was ordered to Virginia on April 29. The 28th promptly replaced it. Throughout May, he operated in south Florida against deserters and raiders.

Brevard and the 28th themselves were ordered to Virginia on May 24. His own 2d Battalion had left for Richmond on May 17 in Finegan's Brigade. The reinforcements joined the Florida Brigade, already there, on May 28, under Finegan's overall command. On April 28 and June 8, the War Department ordered Finegan's five fresh battalions reorganized into three infantry regiments. The 9th Florida was formed on June 20, but orders for the other two regiments were evidently misdirected to Charleston. Not until July 22 were the 10th and 11th organized. Most of the 2d Battalion entered the 10th, but Brevard's staff and two companies plus one independent company joined the 4th Battalion to form the 11th Florida. Two companies of the 28th Heavies also served with the 11th.

Whether Brevard arrived in time to command the 2d in its greatest victory, Second Cold Harbor, is doubtful. He was present by month's end, thus presumably heading it at First Reams' Station. As colonel of the 11th, ranking from June 11, he served at Globe Tavern and probably at Hicksford and Second Hatcher's Run.

Over the final winter of war, the brigade composed of the 2d, 5th, 8th, 9th, 10th, and 11th Florida Infantry Regiments wasted away, the new regiments as well as the old. Distance from sources of recruits contributed to this

decline. So did Finegan's laxity. When he finally left the Army of Northern Virginia in March 1865, division commander William Mahone looked to newcomer Brevard: "The condition of this Brigade in *tone*, discipline, and organization demands vigorous attention," wrote the major general on March 10, "and the services of the best man at its head to save it from utter disorganization." Col. T. W. Brevard, 11th Fla., is the only officer in the brigade worthy of the trust of the charge, and I regard him as one of the most promising officers of my knowledge. I would therefore ask and urge his appointment as a brigadier general at once—the sooner, the better."

Brevard was, accordingly, given that rank on March 28, to date from March 22—the last of the 425 Confederate generals duly appointed by the President. The next, day, however, U. S. Grant launched his final offensive. On April 2–3, the government fled southward, and Richmond and Petersburg fell. In the confusion of the Confederate collapse, Brevard did not receive his commission. Senior colonel David Lang remained the brigadier, and Brevard served in the final campaign as a regimental commander.

He did not reach Appomattox, though. At Sayler's Creek, Brevard and the 5th, 8th, and 11th, detached as a skirmish line covering James Longstreet's wagon train, were captured by the Third Cavalry Division. Usually not listed with the eight other generals seized that day—because neither captor nor captives realized he was a general—Brevard was sent to Old Capital Prison and then on April 19 to Johnson's Island. With the war now over, he took the oath of allegiance on July 25—still signing himself as "colonel"—and was discharged the following day. Presumably only after being released did he learn he was a general.

Back in Tallahassee, he resumed practicing law. He was buried there following his death, June 20, 1882.

Brevard seemed a capable but not outstanding commander in battle. Through General Mahone's confidence in Brevard, a cachet of competence is revealed.

Richard J. Sommers

✶ *John Calvin Brown* ✶

Brown's uniform indicates that this portrait was made probably between August and December 1864, when a wound put him out of the war. (Alabama Department of Archives and History, Montgomery)

Brown, son of Duncan and Margaret Smith Brown, was born in Giles County, Tennessee, on January 26, 1827. His older brother, Neill S. Brown, was a one-term governor of Tennessee. He attended county schools and Jackson College, at Columbia, Tennessee, from which he graduated in 1846, spoke Latin and French, read law in the office of his brother Neill, and in 1848 was admitted to the bar in Pulaski. He built a profitable practice which soon extended well beyond Giles County. Brown, like his brother, was a Whig and following the dissolution of that party, he became a Constitutional Unionist serving as an elector for the John Bell-Edward Everett Presidential ticket in 1860. He campaigned vigorously in opposition to both the secessionists and the Republicans.

Brown's health was impaired by hard weeks on the stump. Following Abraham Lincoln's election, he traveled abroad visiting the British Isles, the Continent, Palestine, and Egypt. His return from overseas coincided with the crisis precipitated by the bombardment of Fort Sumter on April 12–13, 1861, and Lincoln's call for 75,000 volunteers. Brown, although he had been opposed to secession, enlisted in the Provisional Army of Tennessee as a private in a company at the Lynnville Camp of Instruction that on May 16 became Company A, 3d Tennessee Volunteer Infantry, with Brown elected captain. Brown was immediately elected colonel and in July the 3d Tennessee was stationed at Camp Cheatham, near Springfield, Tennessee. Colonel Brown's morning report for the last day of the month showed 885 men present, armed with percussion muskets. There was much sickness, many of the soldiers being hospitalized with measles. At Camp Trousdale on August 7, Brown and his regiment were mustered into Confederate service. From there, in mid-September, Brown advanced his regiment to Bowling Green, Kentucky. There, Brown was given command of a three-regiment brigade in Brigadier General Simon B. Buckner's Division.

Within twenty-four hours of the February 6, 1862 surrender of Fort Henry, Brown and his brigade were en route from Bowling Green to Fort Donelson, where General Albert Sidney Johnston was massing forces to oppose the formidable Union thrust up the Tennessee and Cumberland Rivers. Brown led his reinforced brigade in the Confederate February 15 attack designed to cover the evacuation of Donelson. He and his troops had a key role in overwhelming and driving back a reinforced Union division and opening the

road to Nashville. But, with victory in their grasp, they were recalled by their weak-willed generals to resist a Yankee assault on the Confederate right. On February 16, Brown and his troops were unconditionally surrendered. General Buckner, in his report of the battle, cited Brown for his "gallant and able conduct."

Brown, following his capture along with other general and field grade officers, was imprisoned at Fort Warren in Boston Harbor. He was exchanged in August 1862 and on September 30 was promoted to brigadier general, to rank from August 30. Reporting for duty to Braxton Bragg, whose army had advanced from Chattanooga and had thrust deep into Kentucky, Brown was named to lead a brigade of Floridians and Mississippians assigned to Brigadier General Patton Anderson's Division of Hardee's Corps. At the Battle of Perryville on October 8, Brown was severely wounded leading his troops across Doctor's Creek in a savage attack on the Union left.

Brown, because of his wounds, did not return to duty until mid-January 1863, and on doing so he assumed command of a Tennessee brigade then camped in and around Tullahoma, Tennessee. On July 31 Brown and his brigade were assigned to Major General A. P. Stewart's "Little Giants Division," and at Chickamauga on September 19, Brown and his Tennesseans surged across the Lafayette road shattering a Union division and threatening a major breakthrough. First checked and then thrown back by a Union counterattack, Brown was wounded again and his Tennesseans pulled back. Brown rejoined his brigade in time to lead it in the three-day Battle of Chattanooga, November 23–25. Assigned to Major General Carter C. Stevenson's Division, Brown and his people fought Joseph Hooker's column on Lookout Mountain on the 24th and the next day were positioned on Missionary Ridge. In the latter struggle Brown assumed temporary command of the division, and had his horse shot from under him as he sought to rally his troops to oppose the Federals who had stormed up the ridge.

Brown and his brigade went into quarters for the war's third winter at Dalton, Georgia where, in late December 1863, General Joseph E. Johnston assumed command of the Army of Tennessee. On February 20, 1864, Stevenson's Division, to which Brown's Brigade belonged, was transferred from Hardee's Corps to Hood's Corps. Brown and his Tennesseans took the field in late April and during the next two months, fought against Sherman at Rocky Face, Resaca, New Hope Church, Big Shanty, and Kolb's Farm. On July 7,

A very slight variant of the earlier pose, and obviously taken at the same sitting. (Chicago Historical Society)

the day before Sherman's troops crossed the Chattahoochee, Brown assumed temporary command of A. P. Stewart's Division.

The next eight weeks saw Brown in a fire-fighter's role leading divisions for a few days or weeks while their commanders were either disabled or on leave. He led Hindman's Division in the Ezra Church battle, was promoted to major general, to rank immediately on August 4, and commanded Bates' Division at Jonesboro, August 31–September 1. Brown assumed command of the Tennessee Division in mid-September when Benjamin F. Cheatham replaced William J. Hardee as corps commander. An active participant in Hood's Tennessee Campaign, Brown was present at the Spring Hill debacle and was severely wounded at Franklin in terrible fighting that saw three of his brigade commanders killed and the other wounded and captured. Brown rejoined the army in North Carolina on April 2, 1865. He was paroled at Greensboro one month later.

Brown, on returning to Giles County, was disenfranchised by "Parson" Brownlow's Republican administration, but his Whig connections gave him credibility with moderate Unionists, and his combat record was hailed by those Democrats who were permitted to vote. He was elected to the Tennessee legislature in 1867 and the next year served as president of the convention called to write a new state constitution. He was elected governor of Tennessee in 1870, becoming the first Democrat to be elected governor of his state post-bellum, and was reelected in 1872. While governor, he gave priority to restoration of a stable political and economic system. He championed legislation authorizing the consolidation of unprofitable feeder railroads, reorganized the state prisons, established a state system of public schools, and rationalized the chancery courts. He was defeated by former President Andrew Johnson in a race for the U. S. Senate in 1875.

Brown, disappointed in politics, now concentrated his energy on railroads. In 1876 he became vice president of the Texas & Pacific. He established the railroad east to New Orleans and west to El Paso. As an industrialist, he battled Collis P. Huntington and was an ally and partner of Jay Gould. In 1888 he became president of the Texas & Pacific. He died on August 17, 1889, at Red Boiling Springs, Tennessee, where he is buried.

Edwin C. Bearss

✯ *William Montague Browne* ✯

Browne posed for this portrait during the last six months of the war after his November 1864 appointment as a brigadier. (Library of Congress)

Brown was born July 7, 1823, in County Mayo, Ireland. His ancestors had moved to Ireland from England about the time of King James I. Several historians have failed to learn anything conclusive about his early life, but his biographer has written that "he received a highly polished and thorough education somewhere. There can be no doubt that he was widely traveled over Europe...and that he was well versed in international relations and probably held a place in the diplomatic service of England for some years before he came to America." Browne probably moved to the United States in 1851 or 1852 and became naturalized as a citizen in 1857.

About 1855 or 1856, he began working for the editorial department of the *New York Journal of Commerce*, for which paper he commented on "foreign relations and international developments." By 1858, he had become quite influential in the Democratic party in New York. Browne became associate editor of the Washington *Constitution* in May 1859, and he strongly supported the administration of President James Buchanan. During this period, he came to favor secession of the Southern states and was a close friend of Howell Cobb. Browne left the *Constitution* in January 1861 and moved to the South. On February 26, Confederate President Jefferson Davis made him assistant secretary of state under Robert Toombs. The latter apparently allowed Browne to conduct much of the department's business. Browne continued in this position under Robert M. T. Hunter and acted as secretary of state for about one month between Hunter's resignation and the appointment of Judah P. Benjamin. A historian of the cabinet wrote, "Browne was a capable but unimaginative assistant secretary of State and, in the shaping of Confederate policy, his part was a minor one." On the other hand, Browne's biographer claims that he "played a much more important part in the State Department…than has generally been known; and, in fact, it was Browne, who, during the various changes in the Secretaryship, gave continuity to that Department. He was not simply a head clerk to take dictation and write letters."

Browne's foreign birth may have prevented Davis from appointing him to succeed Hunter. Davis did make him an aide-de-camp with the rank of colonel of cavalry on April 19, 1862, and Browne resigned his governmental post three days later. In late November, Davis sent Browne to Georgia to ask Governor Joseph E. Brown's assistance in enrolling conscripts and returning absentees and to inspect the state's conscript camps. Browne's first military experience occurred when Union forces under Major General John A. Dix made an offensive movement up the Peninsula toward Richmond in June 1863. He received command of three companies organized as the 1st Virginia Battalion Cavalry, Local Defense Troops, and called Browne's Reconnaissance Corps or Browne's Cavalry Battalion. The men performed picket duty on some of the roads leading to the capital during the brief campaign. In January 1864, Browne went on another mission to Georgia, but the details of this assignment are unknown. On April 5, Davis assigned him as temporary superintendent of conscription for the state of Georgia. War Department clerk and obvious Anglophobe John B. Jones wrote of this assignment, "It is probable he offended some of the President's family, domestic or military. The *people* had long been offended by his presence and arrogance."

In Georgia, Browne attempted to get men detailed from the Georgia State Line into the regular Confederate armies. He quickly got into a controversy with Governor Brown over the latter's efforts to circumvent the draft act of February 17, 1864. Davis tried to get Browne to return to Richmond in July, saying that his "absence is felt even more than usual." Howell Cobb informed Davis that Browne's continued presence in the state was necessary and said, "Colonel Browne has conducted controversy [with Joe Brown] with great prudence, and baffled every attempt to

entrap him." In late November 1864, General Braxton Bragg ordered Browne to assume command of a 700-man brigade of local troops in August, "a motley group of mechanics, clerks, and convalescents." Browne took his brigade to Savannah to assist Lieutenant General William J. Hardee in defending that city and arrived there on November 30. As part of Brigadier General Hugh W. Mercer's command on the Confederate right wing, the men assisted in the construction of entrenchments near Savannah, and they evacuated the city with the rest of the army on December 20. Davis had nominated Browne as a brigadier general on December 13 to rank from November 11, but the Confederate senate defeated the nomination on February 18, 1865, by a vote of eighteen to two. War Clerk Jones vented his ire over Davis' action in his diary, "Mr. B. knows no more about war than a cat; while many a scarred colonel, native-born, and participants in a hundred fights, sue in vain for promotion."

By mid-January 1865, Browne and his brigade had returned to Augusta. Davis informed Hardee that he did not wish Browne placed in a position where he would come under the command of militia officers. Browne resumed his duties as commander of conscripts when he got back to Augusta, and he continued to command reserve troops in defense of the town as Major General William T. Sherman's armies marched into the Carolinas. By late March, Browne had moved to Athens, which he had made his home. Union troops arrested and paroled him there on May 8, and he signed the oath of allegiance on August 12. Browne attended Lumpkin Law School at Athens, received a law degree, and was admitted to the Georgia bar in February 1866. He also operated a cotton plantation near Athens. For several years, Browne served as correspondent for the *Louisville Daily Courier* and the New York *World*, and he briefly edited the Macon *Daily Journal and Messenger*. He edited a farm journal called *The Southern Farm and Home* from 1869 to 1873. The next year he accepted a position as a professor of history and political science at the University of Georgia. Browne held this position until his death on April 28, 1883. He was buried at Oconee Hill Cemetery in Athens.

Arthur W. Bergeron, Jr.

Jones, *A Rebel War Clerk's Diary*, ed. by Earl Schenck Miers New York, 1958 ;

★ *Goode Bryan* ★

Born in Hancock County, Georgia, about August 31, 1811, attended Mt. Zion Academy there, then entered the United States Military Academy, where his education followed a precarious course. After his second year at West Point, Bryan was "found deficient and turned back, to recommence the studies of [his] respective classes." He eventually ranked twenty-fifth among the thirty-six graduates in the singularly undistinguished class of 1834. In conduct that year, Bryan stood 199th out of 242 cadets in all classes.

Upon graduation, Bryan won the customary commission as brevet 2d lieutenant, but he resigned after just nine months of service with the 5th United States Infantry in the garrison at Augusta Arsenal. Through the rest of the 1830s, the young man employed his training by serving as a civil engineer working on construction of the Augusta & Athens Railroad. In 1839 he removed to Alabama, where he engaged in planting and held rank as a militia colonel; his wealthy father "settled him upon" the plantation. With the onset of the Mexican War, Bryan participated in raising the 1st Alabama Volunteer and received appointment as the regiment's major in June 1846. When the unit disbanded in May 1847, Bryan gave volunteer service as an aide to General John Wool for four more months.

After the Mexican War, Goode Bryan resumed planting in Alabama for a time. He relocated to Jefferson County, Georgia, from 1849 to 1853, and then to Richmond County and Lee County from 1853 to 1861. During much of that time Bryan held the rank of captain in the state militia, and he represented his region in the Georgia Secession Convention—where he voted in favor of separation. At the outset of the war Bryan owned eighty-six slaves and showed the substantial net worth of $110,500.

Bryan began Confederate service with the 16th Georgia Infantry as lieutenant colonel on July 19, 1861, and became its colonel on February 15, 1862. The regiment belonged to Cobb's Brigade of Magruder's Division through the Peninsula Campaign and the Seven Days. Colonel Bryan led the 16th through the summer and fall battles in 1862, and at Chancellorsville and Gettysburg.

During early 1863 the colonel engaged with fervor in the religious revival that swept through the army. In March, a soldier wrote that Bryan was among "100 men begging the forgiveness of their sins" at a Fredericksburg prayer meeting. A member of the 16th

---

The uniform on this portrait of Bryan has been heavily retouched sometime in the past, and may have been painted over a civilian suit. No other uniformed pose has come to light. (U.S. Army Military History Institute, Carlisle, Pa.)

136

Georgia saw religious overtones in the colonel's performance at Gettysburg on July 2 when Bryan "commenced exhorting his regiment and praising them in the same tone of voice he used in his prayers when he closed old preacher Sam Sanders meeting at the camps."

As early as March 1862, Georgia politicians were seeking promotion for Bryan—who then was a freshly minted colonel—to brigadier general's rank. Joseph B. Kershaw, a brigadier in the division in which the 16th Georgia served and later the divisional commander, also recommended Bryan for promotion. While General William T. Wofford remained firmly in charge of Cobb's old brigade, including the 16th Georgia, the other Georgia brigade in the same division needed a general after Paul J. Semmes fell at Gettysburg. Bryan was appointed brigadier general on August 31, 1863, to take rank two days earlier; the Senate confirmed the rank on February 17, 1864. The new general reported to Longstreet on September 7, 1863, to assume command of what had been Semmes' Brigade. Bryan led his new command west with the First Corps almost immediately after joining it. The unit was among those arriving too late to fight at Chickamauga, but General Bryan led it against Fort Sanders of November 29, 1863, in the unhappy climax of Longstreet's failed Knoxville Campaign. In the aftermath, he was one of many who testified in defense of Lafayette McLaws against charges levied by Longstreet.

General Bryan led his brigade through the early 1864 battles in Virginia, but chronic illness that had dogged him for years impaired his performance. In October 1862 Bryan's wife had written, without his knowledge she said, vainly seeking an appointment for him to head the Macon Camp of Instruction because he was too sickly for field campaigning. On February 12, 1863, Bryan submitted a resignation. While nothing came of that, it probably was further indication of ill health. As the Federals closed on Richmond in June 1864, General Bryan was hospitalized for dysentery and general debility. On the 11th, this resulted in a thirty-day furlough home to Augusta. On August 20, 1864, Bryan tendered his resignation on the basis of a surgeon's report citing "gouty diathesis, complicated with great derangement of the kidneys." The next month Richmond accepted the resignation (September 7 or 20). An officer in the brigade, perhaps jaundiced by his perspective as

brother of Bryan's apparent successor, wrote on August 23 of the general's resignation: "I guess it will be accepted as he has never been a very efficient officer...[and] became of very little service....it is none of Old Bryan's business as to who shall succeed him in command. He has not been with the Brigade a sufficient length of time to be a capable judge as to who is competent." Bryan's war ended officially when he was paroled at Albany, Georgia, on May 19, 1865. He apparently survived unwounded, despite one close call from a bullet deflected away from his chest by a silver spectacles case.

For two decades after the war Bryan lived in Augusta, holding positions in that city's government for most of the period. He died in Augusta on August 16, 1885, and is buried in Magnolia Cemetery.

Robert K. Krick

One of the more photographed of Confederate generals, Buckner posed for this portrait in the pleated blouse typical of several generals in the Western Theater, his insignia embroidered on his collar. (United Daughters of the Confederacy Collection, Kentucky Historical Society, Frankfort)

✴ *Simon Boliver Buckner* ✴

Buckner was born in Hart County, Kentucky, on April 1, 1823. Known as Bolivar, he entered a seminary in Munfordville at the age of nine, the Christian County Seminary in Hopkinsville at fifteen, and West Point at seventeen. Finishing eleventh out of twenty-five graduates in 1844 as a brevet 2d lieutenant in the 1st infantry, Buckner began his military career at Sackett's Harbor on Lake Ontario. He next served as an assistant professor of ethics at West Point from August 28, 1845, until May 9, 1846, when he secured a promotion to 2d lieutenant and a transfer to the 6th Infantry in northern Mexico. The 6th joined Major General Winfield Scott's army in January 1847 and participated in the siege of Vera Cruz. On August 20, Buckner sustained a slight wound and earned a brevet 1st lieutenancy at Churubusco. Similar heroics at Molino del Ray on September 8 gained him a brevet captaincy. He also fought at Chapultepec and at the Belen Gate and served as regimental quartermaster from August 8 until December 17. Buckner had the honor of lowering the American flag for the last time in Mexico City before returning to West Point as an assistant instructor of infantry tactics for the 1849–1850 term.

In the fall of 1850, Buckner rejoined his company at Fort Snelling, Minnesota Territory, which relocated to Fort Atkinson, Kansas in September 1851, where he escorted civilians between Forts Leavenworth and Atkinson. Promoted to 1st lieutenant on December 3, 1851, on November 3, 1852, Buckner became a staff captain assigned to the 6th's commissary department in New York City.

Buckner resigned on March 26, 1855, to handle his father-in-law's real estate in Chicago. He became a major in the militia and was Illinois' adjutant general from April 3 until October 1857, when he left Illinois for Nashville before settling in Louisville in February 1858. He also acquired property in Hart County, Kentucky. He was a captain in the militia from 1858 until 1860, when he became Kentucky's inspector general.

A magnificent early war portrait of Buckner in brigadier general's uniform, probably taken in 1862. (William Turner Collection)

At the beginning of the war, Buckner posed in his Kentucky State Guard uniform, before he took sides with the South. (William Turner Collection)

When war came Buckner, who owned no slaves and opposed secession, became responsible for maintaining Kentucky's neutrality. Fearing confiscation of his wife's property in Chicago, he deeded it to his brother-in-law. After discussing Kentucky's neutrality with President Abraham Lincoln in early July, Buckner resigned as inspector general on July 20 because of interference from the pro-Union legislature. On August 17, Lincoln offered him a commission as brigadier general of volunteers but Buckner declined and headed to Richmond, Virginia. In Nashville on September 11, he tendered his services to the Confederacy.

Richmond appointed Buckner a brigadier general on September 14, 1861, to rank from that date, and ordered him to occupy Bowling Green, which Buckner did four days later. While the Confederate government confirmed his appointment, Union officials in Louisville indicted him for treason and seized his property.

On February 16, 1862, after Brigadier Generals John B. Floyd and Gideon J. Pillow had fled, Buckner surrendered the garrison at Fort Donelson to his former West Point classmate and long-time friend Brigadier General Ulysses S. Grant. Buckner wrote poetry during five months of solitary confinement at Fort Warren, Boston Harbor, until his exchange on August 16, 1862, when he was promoted to major general to take rank immediately and ordered to Chattanooga.

Buckner led a division in Major General William Joseph Hardee's Corps during General Braxton Bragg's invasion of Kentucky. Buckner's knowledge of the terrain contributed to the successful investment of Munfordville, where Union Colonel John R. Wilder accepted Buckner's word that he had no recourse but surrender. At Perryville, Buckner's Division cracked the Union line; Hardee reported, "To Major-General Buckner I am indebted for the skillful management of his troops, the judicious use of his artillery, and for the opportune services of himself and the veteran division under his command."

In mid-December Buckner took command of the District of the Gulf, and on May 11, 1863, he assumed command of the Department of East Tennessee. On August 6, his department became a district in Bragg's Department of Tennessee, a consolidation Buckner favored for strategic reasons.

Buckner abandoned Knoxville in late August and joined Bragg in time to lead a corps at Chickamauga. Buckner advocated Bragg's removal following that battle and Bragg retaliated on October 17 by reducing

Buckner to divisional command and two days later Bragg abolished the District of East Tennessee. Bragg then ordered Buckner's Division to east Tennessee, but illness prevented Buckner from accompanying it.

Slow to recover, Buckner spent early 1864 handling bureaucratic matters, including the court martial of Major General Lafayette McLaws. Given command of Major General John Bell Hood's Division in February, Buckner relinquished that position on March 8 to become temporary commander of the reestablished Department of East Tennessee, an assignment that became permanent in April. He assumed departmental command on April 15, but learned on May 2 that he had been ordered to the Trans-Mississippi Department on April 28.

It was early summer before Buckner could report to General Edmund Kirby Smith, and he did not assume command of the District of West Louisiana until August 4. Repeated requests by Kirby Smith secured Buckner's promotion to lieutenant general, to rank from September 20, 1864. On April 19, 1865, Buckner's district was merged into the District of Arkansas, which he commanded. On May 9, he also became Kirby Smith's chief of staff, and it was Buckner who surrendered the Trans-Mississippi Department in New Orleans on May 26.

The U. S. War Department ordered Buckner to remain in Louisiana. He settled in New Orleans and wrote for the *Crescent*, worked as a commission merchant, and served as president of an insurance company. On December 28, 1867, a court returned his property in Kentucky and early in 1868 he was allowed to return to Kentucky. He purchased the Louisville *Courier* and served as its editor for twenty years. Litigation also recovered his wife's real estate in Chicago in 1872.

Turning to politics, Buckner was elected governor in 1887 and was the vice presidential candidate of the "Gold Democrats" in 1896. After 1896, he limited himself to public speaking and died at "Glen Lily," his plantation near Munfordville, on January 8, 1914, and his remains were interred in the State Cemetery at Frankfort. Buckner was the last survivor of the three highest grades in the Confederate Army.

Lawrence L. Hewitt

This carte-de-visite shows Buckner in a brigadier's blouse and was probably made in Mobile in early 1863. (William Turner Collection)

Shown now with the buttons of major general or lieutenant general, Buckner must have sat for this portrait in the early months of 1864 when he visited Richmond. (Cook Collection, Valentine Museum, Richmond)

At the same sitting, he turned for this pose. (Library of Congress)

Buford's considerable bulk is evident in this portrait showing him
sometime after his September 1862 appointment to brigadier general.
(Alabama Department of Archives and History, Montgomery)

⋆ Abraham Buford ⋆

Born on January 18, 1829, in Woodford County, Kentucky, Abraham Buford was tutored privately until he entered Centre College, which he subsequently left in 1837 to attend West Point. In 1841 he graduated fifty-first, next to last in his class, and was breveted a 2d lieutenant in the 1st Dragoons. Buford served on the frontier where he received his commission as 1st lieutenant on December 6, 1846. After he was transferred to northern Mexico, his gallantry at Buena Vista earned him the rank of brevet captain on February 23, 1847. He participated in the 1848 Santa Fe Expedition and eventually received his commission as captain on July 15, 1853.

After resigning from the army on October 22, 1854, he returned to Woodford County and purchased "Bosque Bonita." Following in his father's footsteps, Buford raised Thoroughbred horses and short-horn cattle; he also served as president of the Richmond & Danville Railroad.

Although an extreme advocate of state rights, he opposed secession and supported Kentucky's neutrality in 1861. He remained neutral until Confederate forces entered the Bluegrass in 1862, when he finally cast his lot with the South. Late that year, on November 29, he was appointed brigadier general, to rank from September 2, 1862. Standing over six feet in height and weighing, at times, over 300 pounds, Buford matched his imposing physique with a dominating will and forceful personality. He established a recruiting camp near Lexington and, when the Confederates withdrew from Kentucky that fall,

Buford commanded three new cavalry regiments and led them in a raid on La Vergne, Tennessee, during the Murfreesboro Campaign.

On January 30, 1863, Buford received orders transferring him to Lieutenant General John C. Pemberton's command in Mississippi. Lacking an assignment commensurate with Buford's rank, Pemberton seconded Buford to Major General Franklin Gardner at Port Hudson, Louisiana, and suggested to Gardner that he create for Buford a new brigade comprised of both infantry and cavalry. Gardner regarded the suggestion as ludicrous and organized an infantry brigade for Buford on March 15 by drawing units from his other brigades. Buford commanded the extreme left of Gardner's fortifications.

On April 6, Buford's request to accompany two of his regiments to Jackson, Mississippi, rather than accept assignment under Major General Sterling Price in the Trans-Mississippi, was approved. New orders arrived on the thirteenth instructing Buford to take his entire brigade to Tullahoma, Tennessee, but on the eighteenth, after he had arrived in Selma, Alabama, and his regiments were strung out from Selma to Chattanooga via Atlanta and Mobile, he and his men were ordered back to Jackson in response to the Union Navy's passage of the Vicksburg batteries on the sixteenth.

Initially assigned to Major General William W. Loring's command at Jackson, Buford was detained at

Unpublished view of Buford taken probably late in the war. (Medford Historical Society, Medford, Massachusetts)

Meridian, Mississippi, to oppose Colonel Benjamin Grierson's raiders at Enterprise. Though he was ordered to Vicksburg on May 2, new instructions the following day halted his brigade at Edwards' Depot. As part of Loring's Division, he led his brigade at Champion's Hill, where it, along with most of Loring's Division, was cut off from Pemberton's retreating army. Buford remained in Loring's Division and while serving under General Joseph E. Johnston, he participated in the siege of Jackson; he subsequently served in Mississippi under Lieutenant Generals Hardee and Polk.

Reassigned to Major General Nathan Bedford Forrest on March 2, 1864, and placed in command of a cavalry division five days later, Buford commenced a raid into west Tennessee on the ninth with his new command and participated in numerous engagements, including Fort Pillow, April 12, and Brice's Crossroads, June 10. During the latter engagement Buford pressed the fleeing Federals while Forrest attempted to cut them off. Forrest gave Buford the credit for this victory. Under the direction of Lieutenant General Stephen D. Lee, Buford led his division in a dismounted assault against a fortified enemy on July 14. Returning to Forrest's command, Buford participated in a raid which commenced on September 16 at Verona and covered middle Tennessee and north Alabama.

With one brigade, Buford began another raid in October, moving north from Corinth, Mississippi. After passing through Jackson, Tennessee, he deployed artillery along the Tennessee River near Fort Helman, Kentucky, on the twenty-eighth. The following day, his men captured a steamer and Forrest reported, "Buford, after supplying his own command, turned over to my chief quartermaster about 9,000 pairs of shoes and 1,000 blankets." On the thirtieth, Buford's men captured the gunboat *Undine* and two transports. When Forrest arrived on the thirty-first, he organized a makeshift navy and, accompanied by Buford's men ashore, moved up the Tennessee River to Johnsonville where the Confederates damaged supplies valued at $6,700,000 on November 4. The following day Buford moved south to rejoin the Army of Tennessee.

Buford's troops were the first to encounter the enemy at Spring Hill, Tennessee, on November 29, where his troopers fought on foot. He missed the battles around Nashville, having participated in a raid near Murfreesboro, but he rejoined the Army of Tennessee and covered its retreat. This duty resulted in his being severely wounded at Richland Creek on December 24, 1864. When he returned to active duty on February 18, Forrest placed him in charge of all cavalry in Alabama. Buford held this post until the end of the war, participating in several engagements, including the defense of Selma on April 2, 1865. He surrendered at Gainesville in early May.

After the war, he returned to "Bosque Bonita" and resumed breeding Thoroughbreds. As one of the more prominent turfmen in the state, he included in his stable several acclaimed horses. Having accepted defeat on the battlefield, Buford supported programs that would unite the country during his term in the Kentucky legislature, to which he was elected in 1879. In the early 1880s he suffered a series of severe financial reverses which ultimately cost him his plantation. The pressure of both financial and personal problems caused Buford to commit suicide at Danville, Indiana on June 9, 1884. He was interred alongside his wife and son in Lexington, Kentucky, in accordance with his final request, which was contained in his suicide note. Two of his cousins, John and Napoleon Bonaparte Buford, attained the rank of major general in the Union Army.

Lawrence L. Hewitt

This half profile possibly predates the previous portrait. (National Archives)

☆ *Robert Bullock* ☆

This portrait was probably taken in the late 1860s. (Virginia Historical Society)

Bullock was born on December 8, 1828, in Greenville, North Carolina. He attended the common schools there. In 1844, he moved to Florida, where he lived at Fort King, near present-day Ocala. Bullock taught at the first school established in Sumter County. From 1849 to 1855, he served as clerk for the Marion County Circuit Court. Bullock raised a mounted company for service against the Seminoles in 1856, and he led it as captain until the war ended eighteen months later.

When the Civil War began, he organized a volunteer company in Marion County and was elected its captain. On March 23, 1862 Bullock's and several other companies fought a brief engagement with Federal gunboats at Smyrna, Florida. The enemy planned to land troops and destroy some weapons, ammunition, and other supplies that had come in on blockade runners, but the Confederates drove them off. When the 7th Florida Infantry Regiment was organized in Gainesville in April, Bullock was elected its lieutenant colonel. The regiment received orders to report to Chattanooga in mid-June so that it could assist in the defense of that city. About July 1, the regiment was assigned to the brigade of Colonel William G. M. Davis of Brigadier General Henry Heth's Division, Department of East Tennessee. Bullock's Regiment did some minor skirmishing and picket duty on the Tennessee River as Major General Don Carlos Buell's Union Army neared Chattanooga. Heth's Division left Chattanooga in August to participate in

Major General Edmund Kirby Smith's invasion of Kentucky. While in that state, Davis' Brigade formed part of the garrison of Frankfort, and it withdrew back to eastern Tennessee with Kirby Smith's army after the battle of Perryville.

The brigade saw duty at Cumberland Gap, Strawberry Plains, and Loudon during the winter of 1862–1863 and the spring and summer of 1863. Bullock sometimes commanded the regiment during the absence of its colonel, and he was promoted to colonel on June 3 after the resignation of the regiment's first commander. As part of Colonel Robert C. Trigg's Brigade of Brigadier General William Preston's Division, the 7th Florida accompanied Lieutenant General Simon B. Buckner's army as it moved from eastern Tennessee to reinforce Bragg's army in northern Georgia. Bullock's men did not see any fighting on September 19, the first day of battle at Chickamauga, but were heavily engaged the next day. The regiment captured 150 Union prisoners during the battle.

In the reorganization of the Army of Tennessee after Chickamauga, Bullock's regiment became part of Brigadier General Jesse J. Finley's Brigade of Major General John C. Breckinridge's Division (commanded by Brigadier General William B. Bate). Finley's Brigade occupied trenches at the base of Missionary Ridge when Major General Ulysses S. Grant's Union Army assaulted that position on November 25, 1863. Bullock fell into enemy hands during the fighting. Sent to prison at Johnson's Island, he was released from there in Mach 1864 but did not rejoin his regiment until exchanged in May. Bullock led his men at the Battle of Resaca on May 16 and assumed command of the brigade after Finley received a wound.

Bullock's men next saw action at the Battle of New Hope Church on May 25. Around Kennesaw Mountain in June, the Floridians saw only minor skirmishing. They were heavily engaged in the Battles of Peachtree Creek on July 20 and Atlanta on July 22. Bullock was wounded in fighting at Utoy Creek on August 6. After Finley was severely wounded at Jonesboro on August 31, Bullock succeeded to command of the brigade. He led the brigade into Tennessee and was slightly wounded in the Battle of Franklin on November 30. Bullock was promoted to brigadier general on January 17, 1865, to rank from November 29. Following the Battle of Franklin, Bate's Division was sent to assist Major General Nathan Bedford Forrest's cavalry in a movement against the Union garrison at Stones River. Bate stationed Bullock's Brigade at Overall's Creek to watch the enemy in the town while his other brigades destroyed the nearby railroad. Federal troops attacked Bullock's men late on December 4 and drove the brigade back. Bullock received a severe wound that disabled him for further field service. In his report of the campaign, Bate said of Bullock that he bore himself "with heroic courage both through good and evil fortune, always executing orders with zeal and alacrity" and that he bore himself "in the face of the enemy" as became the reputation that he had "heretofore bravely won."

After the war, Bullock studied law and was admitted to the Florida bar in 1866. From 1866 to 1868, he was judge of the probate court in Marion County. Bullock served as a Democratic party presidential elector in 1876 and was elected to one term in the state house of representatives in 1879. He was clerk of the Marion County Circuit court from 1881 to 1889. From the later date until 1893, Bullock served in the United States House of Representatives. He was again a circuit court judge in Marion County from 1903 until his death. He died on July 27, 1905, in Ocala and was buried there in Evergreen Cemetery.

Arthur W. Bergeron, Jr.

Biographical Directory of the United States Congress, 1774–1989 Washington, D.C., 1989

J. J. Dickinson, "Florida," *Confederate Military History;*

Taken post-September 1863, this portrait shows Butler with a brigadier's collar insignia on his old tunic as colonel of the 2d South Carolina Cavalry. (Museum of the Confederacy, Richmond)

⋆ *Matthew Calbraith Butler* ⋆

He was born on March 8, 1836, in Greenville, South Carolina. His father, Dr. William Butler, was a naval surgeon, U.S. Congressman, and Indian agent; his mother, Jane Perry Butler, was the sister of Commodores Oliver Hazard and Matthew Calbraith Perry. Matthew Butler, the eleventh of sixteen children, attended the male academy in Greenville before accompanying his father to Fort Gibson, where Dr. Butler served as agent for the Cherokees. Following his father's death in 1850, Matthew returned to South Carolina, where he resided with his uncle, Senator Andrew P. Butler, and his grandmother, at Edgefield. He attended Edgefield Academy before entering South Carolina College with junior status in 1856. He withdrew during his senior year and, having studied law with his uncle, was admitted to the bar in 1857. In 1858 he married Maria Calhoun Pickens, daughter of Governor Francis W. Pickens, and the newlyweds established their residence in Edgefield. Elected to the state legislature in 1860 as a secessionist Democrat, Butler resigned to become captain of a cavalry company from Edgefield which formed part of the Hampton Legion. Six of his brothers also fought in the Confederate Army.

Butler was promoted to major following his participation at the First Battle of Manassas. Commended for bravery for his participation in a charge that resulted in a hand-to-hand encounter with enemy cavalry at Williamsburg in May of 1862, he was appointed colonel of the 2d South Carolina Cavalry Regiment in August of 1862. He participated in the Second Manassas Campaign, the invasion of Maryland, which brought him exceptional praise in Brigadier General Wade Hampton's report, in the raid on Chambersburg

Quite probably taken during the same sitting as the previous image, this one shows Butler's drawn features after the loss of his foot at Brandy Station. (U.S. Army Military History Institute, Carlisle, Pa.)

Near the close of the war, though perhaps prior to his September 1864 promotion to major general, Butler sat for this portrait. (*Confederate Veteran*, III, p. 42)

in October, and in the raid on Dumfries and Fairfax Station in December.

Neither the loss of his right foot at the Battle of Brandy Station nor his youthful age of twenty-seven prevented his promotion to brigadier general when he returned to duty on September 1, 1863. Hampton noted in his report on Brandy Station:

"In the list of wounded are Colonel Butler, who has lost his leg, thus depriving the service (for the present only, I trust) of one of the most gallant and able officers it has been my good fortune to command..."

The following year, Butler led his brigade with distinction in the fighting in The Wilderness and around Spotsylvania Court House, at Howe's Shop, Cold Harbor, and especially during the Battle of Trevilian Station. Described as "a striking figure. Handsome, graceful, [and] cool" with "a remarkable memory of names and faces" and a congenial nature. Butler led his men into battle armed only with a silver-mounted riding whip. His men loved him because he was always concerned about their welfare. Promoted to major general on December 7, to rank from September 19, Butler and his division were ordered to South Carolina on January 19, 1865, to oppose the unceasing advance of Major General William T. Sherman's forces. In charge of the rear guard of Lieutenant General Joseph Hardee's army at the evacuation of Columbia and Cheraw, Butler surrendered in April of 1865 and received his parole shortly thereafter.

Bankrupted by the war, Butler returned to Edgefield and resumed his law practice. Elected to the state legislature in 1865, he attempted to fuse the honest elements, both white and black, into a single political party. A delegate at the Union Reform Convention of 1870, Butler submitted the platform and received the nomination for lieutenant governor. He was defeated despite his energetic campaign. During 1870 and 1871 he labored on behalf of the overburdened taxpayers who sought fiscal relief. He was a member of the convention of May of 1871, and he also served on a committee which waited upon President Ulysses S. Grant. His lack of success in the decade following the Civil War finally convinced him that the only salvation for South Carolina lay in the Democratic Party. He renounced his allegiance to any fusion party and actively promoted the Democratic ticket. When the Democratic convention met in August of 1876, it was Butler who nominated his former Confederate commander, Wade Hampton, for governor.

During this early period of association with the Democrats, Butler had been associated with several race riots. One of these violent protests resulted in the burning of his plantation residence, and a more famous incident occurred at Hamburg. Butler testified before a senatorial committee that his presence at Hamburg was the result of his having gone there to represent the local whites in a civil action against a company of black militiamen. Being the preeminent campaigner for Hampton secured his election to the U.S. Senate in December of 1876 without opposition. Initially, this honor seemed meaningless because the Republican legislature, which also claimed to represent the state, declared D. T. Corbin, a conspicuous prosecutor in the Ku Klux Klan cases, to be the winner of the senate seat. The issue remained unsettled until November 30, 1877, when Butler was finally sworn in. One account credits Butler's ultimate triumph to Pennsylvania Senator Donald Cameron, who used his influence because of a favor rendered years before to Simon Cameron by Butler's father. Butler served three terms in the senate and used his position to secure numerous improvements for South Carolina, especially in regard to public buildings and the enlargement of the harbor at Charleston. He was defeated in a bid for a fourth term in 1894 by the populist Ben Tillman, the result of an agrarian revolt coupled with the arrival at the polls of the first post-Civil War generation of voters.

Butler's forced retirement from the senate did not end his service to his country. He practiced law in Washington in 1895 but had returned to Edgefield by 1898 when the outbreak of hostilities with Spain brought about his appointment as a major general of volunteers by President William McKinley. He also served on the commission that supervised the Spanish evacuation of Cuba before returning to Washington. Elected vice president of the Southern History Association in 1903, he turned his attention to business the following year as president of the Hidalgo Placer Mining and Milling Company of Mexico. After living as a widower for several years, Butler remarried in 1906. He was semi-retired when he died on April 14, 1909, in Washington, D.C.; he was interred on his family plantation in Edgefield.

Lawrence L. Hewitt

Brooks, O. R. *Butler and His Cavalry in the War of Secession.* 1909

Probably in the final months, with expanded facial whiskers, Butler stood before the camera for this somewhat retouched half-length portrait. (Miller, *Photographic History*)

Cabell appears to have a general's insignia on his collar in this portrait, which would date it to sometime after January 1863. (Library of Congress)

⋆ William Lewis Cabell ⋆

Known as "Old Tige," Cabell was born in Danville, Virginia, on January 1, 1827. He attended the local public school and as a young man joined a volunteer militia. When the Mexican War began, his friends volunteered. Cabell had been appointed to West Point, and instead of heading for Mexico, he left for New York. After his graduation from the United States Military Academy in 1850, thirty-third out of forty-four, Cabell was assigned to a company of the 7th Infantry Regiment under Captain Braxton Bragg. His first duty was to train and drill new recruits. In April 1851 the 7th Infantry left for the frontier where Cabell saw service at Fort Gibson in the Indian Territory. A few months later he was ordered 400 miles west on the Ouachita River to provide working parties protection from Indians during the construction of Fort Arbuckle. While in Indian Territory he became acting assistant quartermaster and acting assistant commissary of subsistence. In 1855 he was promoted to 1st lieutenant and became acting assistant commissary of subsistence. The next year he married a Fort Smith woman, and this union gave him a permanent tie with the region. After a promotion to captain in 1857, Cabell was part of the expedition sent to relieve Colonel Albert Sidney Johnston in his fight with the Mormons. Cabell took part in rebuilding Fort Kearney, then directed much of the work on Fort Cobb.

When the Civil War began he was on leave from the army moving his family to Fort Smith. As soon as he learned of Virginia's secession, Cabell headed for the Confederate capital, but declined to see President Davis until after Washington had accepted his resignation. Davis, anxious to have Cabell's experience, personally intervened to insure the action was taken. As soon as confirmation of the resignation arrived, Davis on March 16 commissioned Cabell a major, and chief quartermaster and commissary officer for Virginia. In this position he participated at First Manassas. Following the battle, Cabell, P. G. T. Beauregard, and Joseph E. Johnston designed the Confederate battle flag with the St. Andrew's cross to distinguish it from the Stars and Bars. In January 1862 he was assigned to the Trans-Mississippi, and became chief quartermaster on the staff of General Earl Van Dorn. When Union forces under General Samuel R. Curtis threatened Van Dorn's position in Arkansas, Cabell was assigned to active command and took over the troops along the White River; he was to prevent Federal forces from striking the Confederates from the direction of the Mississippi River. During this time Cabell manned the supply depots, and after Van Dorn's defeat at Pea Ridge was able to provide supplies to the army from Arkansas. His experience in logistics proved invaluable, and he demonstrated his ability to manage difficult situations. During this time Davis nominated him for promotion from major to brigadier general, and east of the river Cabell was assigned command of the First Brigade, Second Division, Army of the West. Although Van Dorn's men were too late to participate in the battle at Shiloh, Cabell saw action at Iuka and Corinth, Mississippi. During the attempt to retake Corinth on October 3 and 4, 1862, he was wounded in the foot and observed that the injury "gave me a good deal of pain at the time, but did not disable me." On the 5th, in an engagement at Davis' Bridge across the Hatchie River while withdrawing his men, Cabell's horse fell on him. His thigh and hip were very seriously injured, and his left leg completely paralyzed. This injury kept him out of action for several weeks; on October 16, he was relieved from command of the brigade and ordered to headquarters at Holly Springs where he was reassigned to Little Rock.

He was pleased to be returning to Arkansas, but because his rank as brigadier general had never been confirmed by Richmond, he reverted to a major in the quartermaster department. In November 1862 General

This portrait has been so heavily retouched that it is almost impossible to tell if it was originally a photograph. If so, it does show Cabell as a brigadier. (Warner, *Generals in Gray*)

Theophilus H. Holmes appointed him inspection officer for the quartermaster department of the Trans-Mississippi Department with headquarters at Fort Smith, but his high personal standards for his work did not go unnoticed; by December he was chief quartermaster. On April 23, 1863, Cabell finally received a permanent promotion to brigadier general to rank from January 20, and he returned to active duty. General Edmund Kirby Smith ordered him to "collect absentees from the service" and form a brigade of absentees and regular units in northwest Arkansas.

In April he participated in an unsuccessful attack on Fayetteville, and several fruitless attempts to take Fort Gibson in the Indian Territory. Ordered back to Arkansas as he retreated south, he fought a battle at Devil's Backbone, sixteen miles from Fort Smith, on September 1. The following day he reached Waldron, then moved on to Arkadelphia where he joined General Sterling Price. Early in 1864 he took command of a brigade in Fagan's Cavalry Division, Army of Missouri, and later that year commanded the First (Arkansas) Cavalry Brigade, First (Arkansas) Cavalry Division, Cavalry Corps, in the Trans-Mississippi Department. During the Camden Campaign, Cabell commanded part of Price's cavalry that daily harassed Frederick Steele's army. On April 17 Cabell was detached from Fagan's Division and ordered to report to General John S. Marmaduke for special duty. He commanded his brigade in an attack upon a Union supply train at Poison Spring on April 18. He soon rejoined Fagan's Division, and with Shelby's command, formed a force to operate east of the Ouachita River. On April 23 he commanded a division composed of his own brigade and that of Thomas P. Dockery. At Marks' Mill on April 25, Fagan's troops attacked a wagon train, and later reported: "The killed and wounded of Cabell's Brigade show how stubborn the enemy was and how reluctantly they gave up the train. Men never fought better. They whipped the best infantry regiments that the enemy had (old veterans, as they were called), and then in numbers superior to them."

After Steele withdrew to Little Rock, Cabell moved to Monticello in southeast Arkansas. Cabell took part in General Sterling Price's last raid into Missouri, and in the assault near Fort Davidson at Pilot Knob, had his horse shot from under him. Sterling Price reported, "I must be allowed to call attention to the courage and gallantry of Brigadier General Cabell in leading his men to the assault, having his horse killed under him within forty yards of the fort." Cabell was a "bold, undaunted, skillful officer. Impetuous, yet wary, he commanded his brigade in such a manner as to win praise from all." General John B. Clark recalled: "I hope it will not be considered out of place for me to call attention to the dashing gallantry displayed by General Cabell in leading troops to this terrible assault."

Cabell was captured at Marais des Cygnes, Kansas, on October 25, 1864. He was sent to St. Louis, then Johnson's Island, and in December transferred to George's Island in Boston Harbor. He was not released until July 24, 1865. After the war he returned to Fort Smith, but in 1872 moved to Dallas, Texas. He served as the Democratic mayor of Dallas four times, was a U.S. marshal for four years, and engaged in railroading. He also took part in the Louisiana Lottery and was active in veteran affairs. He was instrumental in obtaining state pensions for ex-Confederates, and worked toward the building of the Confederate Soldiers' Home in Austin. When the Spanish-American War broke out, the seventy-one-year-old Cabell notified the War Department that he was ready to fight. The department thanked him, but declined his offer. Cabell died in Dallas on February 22, 1911, and is buried in Greenwood Cemetery.

Anne Bailey

⁎ *Alexander William Campbell* ⁎

This portrait of Campbell is sufficiently indistinct that it cannot be determined if his uniform is genuine or an artist's addition. If genuine, it shows him as a colonel, probably early in the war. (Virginia Historical Society)

Campbell was born in Nashville, Tennessee, June 4, 1828, and matriculated at West Tennessee College. After attending Lebanon Law School, he entered a partnership with the Nashville firm headed by Howell E. Jackson, a future justice of the United States Supreme Court.

Answering Governor Isham G. Harris' call for volunteers, Campbell enlisted in the Confederate Army as a private, was soon commissioned a colonel and assigned duty as a staff officer to General B. F. Cheatham. On October 18, 1861, he was commissioned colonel of the 33d Tennessee Infantry, then being organized at Union City, Tennessee. Campbell and his unit remained at the camp of instruction in Union City until mid-January 1862, when they were ordered to report to Leonidas Polk at nearby Columbus, Kentucky. Colonel Campbell noted that at the time only a few of his companies were armed, mostly with shotguns and hunting rifles. And that the regiment was not completely armed until a few weeks before the Battle of Shiloh, when they obtained some flint and steel muskets as a loan.

Campbell and his regiment, upon the Confederate March 2 evacuation of Columbus, were ordered to Corinth, Mississippi. As a unit in General Alexander P. Stewart's Brigade, Campbell led his regiment into combat for the first and last time at Shiloh. In the desperate April 6 afternoon fighting north of the Corinth road and west of Tilghman Branch, Campbell commanded two regiments—the 5th Tennessee—as well

158

as the 33d. Corps commander Polk, commenting on Campbell's leadership in the struggle, wrote:

"In advancing [the 5th and 33d] drew the enemy's fire over the heads of the regiments in their front. It was of so fierce a character that they must either advance or fall back. Campbell called the regiments before him to charge. This they declined to do, he then gave orders to his own regiments to charge, and led them in gallant style over the heads of the regiments lying in advance of him, sweeping the enemy before him and putting them completely to rout."

In this charge, Colonel Campbell was severely wounded but remained in command.

On April 7, Campbell and his regiment fought with General J. Patton Anderson's Brigade. Facing heavy reinforcements, the Confederates broke off the battle and returned to Corinth to regroup. While confronting the enemy, the units posted in the Corinth earthworks, in accordance with the "Bounty and Furlough Act," were reorganized. In this May 8 reorganization, Campbell was not reelected but was continued on duty with the army as a supernumerary, and on the retreat from Kentucky in mid-October was in charge of the army's ordnance train.

Campbell, on December 25, 1862, was named assistant adjutant and inspector general on the staff of General Polk, now a lieutenant general and leading a corps in Braxton Bragg's Army of Tennessee. As a member of Polk's "military family," Campbell participated in the Battle of Stones River, December 31, 1861–January 2, 1863. The next service to which he was assigned, in mid-January, with his duty station at Fayetteville, Tennessee, was with Brigadier General Gideon J. Pillow in the Volunteer and Conscript Bureau. On July 29 Campbell was captured, along with two lieutenants, twenty-five privates, and two caissons at Lexington, Tennessee. He had been sent to west Tennessee to oversee elections and to recruit men to organize into a regiment and command. He was confined at the Johnson's Island prison pen for Confederate officers.

Paroled and exchanged in the autumn of 1864, Campbell, on February 18, 1865, was named acting inspector general on the staff of Nathan Bedford Forrest, then headquartered at West Point, Mississippi. By mid-March he was leading Rucker's Brigade in Brigadier General William "Red" Jackson's Division of Forrest's Corps. Though this was Campbell's first duty as a troop commander in nearly

three years, one of Forrest's veterans recalled that he was a gentleman. "He carried his good breeding into camp, and even in the woods there was an air of refinement in all his ways." His brigadier general's commission was dated March 2, 1865, to rank from the previous day, and, although he hammered Croxton's brigade near Scottsville, Alabama, he did not reach Selma in time to participate in that city's defense against James H. Wilson's hard-charging columns. He surrendered and was paroled, along with other members of Forrest's command, at Gainesville, Alabama, on May 11, 1865.

Campbell returned to the bar in the post-war years. Active in politics, in 1860 he was an unsuccessful candidate for the Democratic nomination for governor of his native state. He died in Jackson, Tennessee, on June 13, 1893, and is buried there.

Edwin C. Bearss

✦ *James Cantey* ✦

Cantey sat for this image sometime after his
January 1863 promotion to brigadier general. It is
his only known wartime portrait. (Chicago
Historical Society)

Born on December 30, 1818, in Camden, South Carolina, graduated from South Carolina College, later practiced law, and served two terms in the state legislature before the outbreak of the Mexican War. When the war began in 1846, he enlisted as an officer in the Palmetto Rifles and suffered a wound in one of the battles. In 1849, he relocated to Russell County, Alabama and became a planter.

Cantey was living in his adopted state when the Civil War began in 1861. With his war record and stature in the community, he was elected colonel of the 15th Alabama. The regiment eventually traveled to Virginia, where by the spring of 1862 it was in the brigade of Isaac Trimble. Stationed in the Shenandoah Valley, Cantey's Regiment participated in Stonewall Jackson's storied campaign in the region.

The 15th Alabama's finest day in the campaign came on June 8, at Cross Keys. Trimble assigned Cantey to an advanced skirmish line, and the Alabamans delayed the advance of John Fremont's Federal units for over an hour. When the Yankees attacked, Trimble's brigade repulsed the assault and counterattacked. Cantey's men drove the Federals for a mile before Trimble recalled the troops.

Jackson's army then transferred to the Richmond front and participated in the Seven Days Campaign. Trimble's Brigade saw limited combat in the week long series of battles. At the campaign's conclusion, Confederate authorities returned Cantey to Alabama. He assumed command of a brigade that consisted of the 17th, 21st, and 29th Alabama and the 37th Mississippi. He received his promotion to brigadier general on January 8, 1863 with seniority from that day.

Cantey served throughout 1863 in Alabama, stationed much of the time in Mobile. In August, he received two additional brigades and command of the Eastern Division of the Department of the Gulf. During the winter of 1864, the 1st and 26th Alabama were added to his brigade while the 21st Alabama was transferred to another command. About this time, Cantey's Brigade joined the Army of Tennessee in winter quarters at Dalton, Georgia, and was assigned to the division of Edward C. Walthall in Alexander P. Stewart's Corps.

At the outset of the Atlanta Campaign in May 1864, Cantey commanded a 4,000-man force in the defenses of Resaca, Georgia. The fortifications guarded the mouth of Snake Creek Gap along the Oostanaula River. With the advance of William T. Sherman's Union forces, Resaca became a key point along the line of Confederate General Joseph Johnston's army.

On the afternoon of May 9, the advance elements of James McPherson's Union Army of the Tennessee approached Resaca. When a Confederate cavalry brigade withdrew into the fortifications, Cantey's force manned the works. The Federals opened with artillery fire and advanced skirmishers. The Southerners huddled in the works and repulsed the Federal sorties. As for Cantey, according to a Georgia officer, he remained in a bombproof during the bombardment and combat. The Georgian described the brigadier as "poor Cantey."

Cantey remained with the Confederate Army as it withdrew southward toward Atlanta. By September, Cantey had relinquished command because of an unspecified illness. He returned to duty periodically during the conflict's final months, but his disability kept him from any extended period of duty. His brigade fought in the battles around Atlanta, participated in John B. Hood's Tennessee campaign and served in the Carolinas during the early months of 1865. Cantey returned to his brigade to surrender with them in North Carolina in April.

After the war, Cantey returned to Alabama and farmed. He died in Fort Mitchell on June 30, 1874, and was buried in the family plot. He had served the Confederate cause for four years, but the promise of Cross Keys was never fulfilled. The year of relative inactivity in Alabama in 1863 might have sapped his martial fervor. His conduct at Resaca could be construed as cowardice under fire, or the result of illness. At best, Cantey was a mediocre brigade commander.

Jeffry D. Wert

✶ Ellison Capers ✶

Ellison Capers was born in Charleston, South Carolina, on October 14, 1837, and with the exception of two years in Oxford, Georgia, he spent his early life there, where he attended two private schools and Charleston High School. He also studied at the Conference School in Cokesbury and at Anderson Academy. He entered the South Carolina Military Academy in 1854 and graduated head of his class, finishing in November 1857, thereafter remaining at the school as an instructor of mathematics for one year. During the 1858–1859 academic year he served as the principal of the preparatory department at Mt. Zion College in Winnesboro, and in February of 1859 he married Charlotte Palmer of Cherry Grove Plantation. In the fall of 1859 Capers returned to the military academy with the rank of 2d lieutenant and took a position as assistant professor of mathematics. Before the end of 1860 he had attained the rank of professor. Although an astute attorney, he never practiced law nor did he seek a political career.

Enlisting shortly after the secession of his state in December 1860, Capers was unanimously elected major by the members of a volunteer rifle regiment. Initially stationed at Castle Pinckney, he commanded the light artillery deployed on Sullivan's Island during the bombardment of Fort Sumter. He continued to serve in the Charleston area until November, when he resigned his state commission as lieutenant colonel and his position at the Military Academy in order to work with Clement H. Stevens of Charleston to raise a regiment for Confederate service. Their efforts resulted in the mustering in of the 24th South Carolina Infantry on April 1, 1862, with Stevens as colonel and Capers as lieutenant colonel.

Ordered to Cole's Island on April 4, Capers spent the next year along the Carolina coast. During the bombardment of Cole's Island on May 20, 1862, he commanded Fort Palmetto. Five days later he was transferred to James Island, where his most significant combat in the Carolinas occurred. On June 3, he opened the James Island campaign at the head of four companies. Brigadier General States Rights Gist praised his "gallant bearing and conduct" during a skirmish on the island on June 3, 1862.

On the 16th, Capers fought with distinction in the Battle of Secessionville. Stevens praised him for "gallant conduct in defending advanced battery of 24-pounder guns." Brigadier General Nathan G. Evans reported that Stevens, seeing that the 24-pounder battery near Clarke's house was not being fired, directed Lieutenant Colonel Capers, of his regiment, to take command of his battery and to fire on the enemy. With

The only genuine uniformed wartime portrait of Capers to come to light is this small image, probably showing him as lieutenant colonel of the 24th South Carolina Infantry sometime prior to the summer of 1864. (*Confederate Veteran*, VII, p. 260)

which, though one piece was dismounted, he did gallant and effective service, firing constantly into the flank of the enemy. On the third assault of the enemy Lieutenant Colonel Capers was very successful with his piece, piercing the columns of the enemy eleven times.

On March 15, 1863, Capers was placed in charge of all troops stationed between the Combahee and Ashepoo Rivers, including the heavy batteries at Combahee Ferry and on the Ashepoo.

Finally, in May 1863, the 24th reached the front, joining General Joseph E. Johnston at Jackson, Mississippi, in his fruitless efforts to relieve Vicksburg. Capers quickly learned the consequences of war. He commanded the regiment in the fighting about Jackson on May 14. During that engagement he sustained a wound while acting, according to Gist, in a particularly distinguished manner. Following the Battle of Chickamauga, Georgia, in September, Gist reported that "the intrepid Capers" had sustained a severe wound during that engagement.

Capers was promoted to colonel shortly before the opening of the Atlanta Campaign in May 1864. His regiment saw action at Dalton, Calhoun, New Hope, Kennesaw and Pine Mountains, Smyrna, and along the banks of the Chattahoochee River. Reportedly in command of the brigade on August 31, he only exercised regimental command during the Battle of Jonesborough the following day. On September 12 his regiment was ordered to constitute the provost guard for the post of Jonesborough. When the Confederate Army marched northward from Palmetto, Georgia on the 29th, Capers once more held temporary command of Gist's Brigade.

During General John Bell Hood's invasion of Tennessee, Capers sustained his third wound during the Battle of Franklin in November. Upon Gist's death in that same engagement, Capers assumed command of the brigade, a position that was made permanent when he was promoted to brigadier general on March 2, 1865, to rank from the previous day. He surrendered at Bentonville, North Carolina, in April of 1865 and reached his home in Charleston the following month.

In 1866, South Carolina Governor James L. Orr appointed him secretary of state. Capers accepted the post but having been deeply moved by the horrors he had experienced during the war, he entered the ministry. Although his father had been a Methodist, the younger Capers selected the Episcopal church of his more remote ancestors. His first assignment was Christ Church in Greenville in 1867 and the following year he resigned his position as secretary of state. He served in Selma, Alabama, in 1875, but returned to Greenville after an absence of only one year. In 1886 he declined the position of bishop of the Easton, Maryland diocese to which he had been elected. The following year he was called to the Trinity Church of Columbia, and on July 20, 1983, he was consecrated assistant bishop of South Carolina. He was elected chancellor of the University of the South at Sewanee, Tennessee, in 1904. A stroke resulted in his paralysis and finally in his death, which occurred at his home in Columbia, South Carolina, on April 22, 1908.

Bishop Capers' activities and interests went beyond his strictly ecclesiastical duties. He served as Chaplain-general of the Confederate Veterans, was a member of the Southern Historical Association, and wrote extensively. His works appeared in several periodicals and included numerous articles dealing with his military experiences as well as book reviews. He wrote *South Carolina*, Volume V of Clement A. Evans' *Confederate Military History*, which was published in 1899. The bishop also extolled the benefits of higher education, an area that he believed to be the concern of the church as well as the state government. Quick to speak out against the decline of society because of lawlessness, Capers' most positive accomplishment following the war was probably the contribution he made through personal contacts and public addresses to the reuniting of the once-divided nation.

Lawrence L. Hewitt

Capers, Walter B. *The Soldier-Bishop*, 1912.

✮ *William Henry Carroll* ✮

No photograph of Carroll has appeared, much less anything in uniform from his brief service as a general. This drawing is all that seems to survive of him. (Virginia Historical Society)

The eldest son of a six-time Tennessee governor, William Carroll was born in Nashville, probably in 1810. The elder Carroll was a close friend of Andrew Jackson, who once served as his second in a duel with Jesse Benton, uncle to Confederate general Samuel Benton. William Henry Carroll's early career was varied. He first ran a plantation in Panola County, Mississippi, but moved to Memphis in 1848 where he served as postmaster for a number of years. During the secession crisis in 1861, Carroll had enough political influence to be appointed brigadier general in the Tennessee provisional army. Later, when Tennessee actually joined the Confederacy, he again probably used his political connections to get appointed colonel of the 37th Tennessee Infantry.

In September 1861 Major General Leonidas Polk, commander of the Tennessee region, sent Carroll from Memphis into the mountains of east Tennessee to raise troops for the Confederacy. Colonel Carroll did well and was able to organize the 7th, 8th, and 9th East Tennessee Provisional Regiments. Perhaps in recognition of this feat, or through political influence, Carroll was promoted to brigadier general on October 26, 1861, to rank from that date.

Although only one of Carroll's Regiments was armed, in November he was sent with two of his regiments to Knoxville via Chattanooga. Entering Chattanooga in mid-November, Carroll had 1,600 men, but only 800 muskets. This difficulty in securing weapons vexed Carroll unendingly and he constantly complained of his inability to arm his men. In Chattanooga, where he stopped to disperse some local Unionists, Carroll was observed by Colonel S. A. M. Wood of the 7th Alabama. Wood was not impressed. To Major General Braxton Bragg, Wood wrote, "[Carroll] has been drunk not less than five years. He is stupid, but easily controlled. He knows nothing, and I believe I can do with him pretty much as I please."

Leaving Chattanooga after a brief stay, Carroll continued to Knoxville and took command of that post by late November. There he assembled a force of approximately 5,000 men to control eastern Tennessee and sent out numerous patrols to chase Unionist bridge burners. But Carroll was still plagued by a lack of weapons, most of his armed men having only squirrel rifles, flintlocks, and shotguns. To maintain control over Knoxville's large hostile population, Carroll declared martial law, arrested approximately 200 Unionists, and hanged at least one bridge burner. But his excuses for failing to arm his men finally fell on tired ears. On December 17th an exasperated Secretary of War Judah P. Benjamin reminded Carroll that he had had plenty of time to secure weapons and that his soldiers' twelve months enlistments were about to expire. Carroll was given until January 10, 1862 to complete arming the units or all unarmed companies and regiments were to be disbanded. Benjamin later backed down from his ultimatum, but evidence indicates that Carroll still failed to arm all his men. In justice to him, however, it should be pointed out that a chronic shortage of weapons plagued all Confederate commanders in Tennessee at that time.

In January 1862 Carroll was ordered to Kentucky by Albert S. Johnston to support Brigadier General Felix Zollicoffer. Under a command of Major General George B. Crittenden, Carroll and Zollicoffer attacked a Union force at Mill Springs on January 19. In the fight, Zollicoffer was killed and Carroll withdrew after losing 103 men. Crittenden noted that Carroll "in his dispositions and conduct during the engagement, manifested both military skill and personal valor." But not all were impressed with Carroll or Crittenden. On January 27, Colonel Landon C. Haynes wrote President Jefferson Davis that the Confederate Army in Kentucky was totally demoralized and that both the soldiers and civilians had lost confidence. Haynes asserted, "It must be restored. I am confident it cannot be done under Generals Crittenden and Carroll."

Carroll remained in command of a brigade of Tennessee infantry, however. Then at Iuka, Mississippi, Major General William J. Hardee investigated reports of Crittenden's and Carroll's incompetence. On April 1, 1862, Hardee reported, "I found sufficient evidence against them to require their arrest." The night before Carroll had been arrested on charges of drunkenness, incompetence, and neglect of his command. Crittenden was arrested on April 1 for drunkenness. A court martial was scheduled but Carroll continued to serve in the meantime. On August 9, 1862, Braxton Bragg listed Carroll among a number of officers he felt were unfit for duty. Then on November 22, Bragg wired Adjutant General Samuel Cooper that Carroll and another brigadier "are not safe men to intrust with any command." Under this relentless pressure, Carroll resigned his commission on February 1, 1863.

Carroll then traveled to Canada to join his family, which had sought refuge there after the fall of Memphis. He died in Montreal on May 3, 1868. Carroll was buried there, but in 1869 his body was exhumed and reburied in Memphis' Elmwood Cemetery. Oddly, his tombstone cites both an incorrect date of birth and death.

Terry Jones

⋆ *John Carpenter Carter* ⋆

No uniformed portrait of Carter has been found. This civilian view probably dates from 1860-61, and has been retouched. (Museum of the Confederacy, Richmond)

Carter was born on December 19, 1837, in Waynesboro, Georgia. From 1854 to 1856, he attended the University of Virginia. He then studied law at Cumberland University in Lebanon, Tennessee. He taught law there after he graduated and was admitted to the state bar. Carter moved to Memphis in 1860 and opened a law practice there.

At the beginning of the Civil War, he raised a volunteer company that became part of the 38th Tennessee Infantry Regiment. That regiment served in Colonel Preston Pond's 3d Brigade, Brigadier General Daniel Ruggles' 1st Division, II Corps, Army of Mississippi, in the Battle of Shiloh, April 6–7, 1862. The men saw heavy fighting there, particularly on the first day, being stationed on the army's left flank. Colonel R. F. Looney of the 38th Tennessee wrote in his official report, "Capt. John C. Carter deserves the highest praise for his great coolness and high courage displayed throughout the entire engagement. At one time he took the flag, and urging his men forward, rendered me great assistance in moving forward through the entire regiment."

Carter received promotions through the ranks of major and lieutenant colonel, and by the time of General Braxton Bragg's invasion of Kentucky, he was colonel of his regiment. The 38th Tennessee was assigned to Brigadier General Daniel S. Donelson's Brigade of Major General Benjamin F. Cheatham's Division during that campaign and saw fairly heavy fighting at the Battle of Perryville on October 8. Carter again received praise from his superiors for his conduct in the action. Donelson's Brigade participated in the Confederate attack on the Federal position known as the Round Forest at the Battle of Stones River on December 31. As it moved forward, the 38th Tennessee delivered a "murderous fire" on a Union regiment advancing against it and caused the enemy soldiers to fall back quickly. Though Carter's regiment numbered fewer than 300 men, it captured seven enemy cannons and more than 500 prisoners in the assault. One of Cheatham's staff officers wrote after the war that Carter led his men "with his accustomed skill and courage."

Brigadier General Marcus J. Wright succeeded Donelson in command of the brigade, and the 38th Tennessee served under Wright during the various campaigns of 1863. Carter exercised brigade command briefly during absences by Wright. During the Battle of Chickamauga, September 19–20, Carter had a Tennessee infantry battalion under his command in addition to his own regiment. The men fought for about three hours on September 19 but were only lightly engaged the next day. When the army marched against Chattanooga, Wright's Brigade was detached to garrison Charleston, Tennessee, northeast of Chattanooga. Wright took the brigade back to the army on November 23 but left Carter in command of the post at Charleston. Carter had under him: his regiment, four companies of engineers, and a small cavalry force. A Federal cavalry brigade attempted to cross the Hiwassee River, but Carter's men drove it back.

On November 30, a strong Union force advanced towards Carter's position. He reluctantly ordered a retreat toward Knoxville after having his men destroy all the bridges at Charleston and Loudon. His men soon joined Lieutenant General James Longstreet's army near Knoxville. In his report of this action, Wright wrote that Carter "maintained his position under the severest test to which a soldier can be subjected with the highest constancy, gallantry, and firmness,...The zeal, ability, and courage with which he conducted his isolated command out of the difficulties which environed him cannot be too highly commended."

Carter and his regiment remained in east Tennessee for several months. They did guard duty and helped repair bridges in the area. Carter commanded Wright's Brigade during all of the battles of the Atlanta Campaign and performed most competently. Wright and several other Tennessee and Georgia politicians recommended him for promotion to brigadier general. One supporter argued for Carter's advancement by citing his educational attainments, and added, "His habits are unsurpassed in the army for sobriety and morality." Carter received the promotion on July 8, effective July 7, 1864. Carter's and another brigade led the attack of Cheatham's Division in the Battle of Peachtree Creek on July 20, and they suffered heavy casualties. Details of the division's role in the Battle of Atlanta on July 22 remain sketchy, but the men apparently did not engage the enemy until very late in the afternoon. Still in "brutally violent" fighting, they drove back the Federal force on their front until darkness stopped the action.

Carter's Brigade remained in reserve during the Battle of Jonesboro on August 31. When Brigadier General George Maney was relieved of command of Cheatham's Division late that day, Carter succeeded to that position and held it for a few days. Cheatham replaced Lieutenant General William J. Hardee as corps commander in late September, and some reorganization of Cheatham's old division, now under Major General John C. Brown, occurred. Carter's Brigade was broken up, and he took over Maney's old brigade. Carter led his new command into Tennessee with the army in November. At the Battle of Franklin on November 30, Carter's Brigade was in the second line of Brown's Division as it attacked the Union center. He led his men forward to reinforce the brigade of Brigadier General States Rights Gist once that officer's assault had broken down.

While leading an attack, Carter received a mortal wound. He died in a private home on December 10, 1864. Carter is buried in Rose Hill Cemetery at Columbia, Tennessee. A former member of Cheatham's staff characterized Carter after the war as having "a wonderful gentleness of manner, coupled with a dauntless courage."

Arthur W. Bergeron, Jr.

James D. Porter, "Tennessee," *Confederate Military History*; Christopher Losson, *Tennessee's Forgotten Warriors: Frank Cheatham and his Confederate Division* (Knoxville, 1989);

☆ James Ronald Chalmers ☆

While Chalmers' buttons are arranged for a colonel, the four rows of braid on his sleeves and the hint of a wreath around the stars on his collar show that this image was made after his February 1862 promotion to brigadier. (Goulet-Buncombe Collection,Southern Historical Collection, University of North Carolina, Chapel Hill)

Chalmers was born on January 11, 1831, in Halifax County, Virginia, but his family moved to Holly Springs, Mississippi. After graduating from the South Carolina College in 1851, Chalmers returned to Holly Springs, became a lawyer, and in 1858 was elected district attorney. As a delegate to the state's secession convention in 1861, he chaired the committee on military affairs and readily voted for secession.

Chalmers' prominence won him a colonel's commission and command of the 9th Mississippi Infantry. Dispatched to Pensacola, Florida, he joined Braxton Bragg's force and participated in a raid against the Federal garrison on Santa Rosa Island on the night of October 8, 1861. Chalmers' actions earned Bragg's admiration and Bragg consistently praised Chalmers throughout the war. Upon a recommendation from Bragg, Chalmers was promoted to brigadier general on February 13, 1862, to rank immediately.

With a brigade of Mississippi and Tennessee infantry, Chalmers fought well in Bragg's Corps at Shiloh. Placed on the extreme right of the army, Chalmers led his men in numerous assaults that overran two Federal camps on the first day. On April 7, when his brigade was heavily pressured by the Union counterattack, Chalmers seized the colors of the 9th Mississippi and personally led the attack that drove the Federals back. Such bravery inspired divisional commander J. M. Withers to describe him as "the gallant and impetuous Chalmers." Bragg's report flowed with praise. Chalmers, he wrote, "filled—he could not have excelled—the measure of my expectations."

After Shiloh, Chalmers was temporarily given command of all the cavalry screening the army in north Mississippi. He performed this duty well until poor health forced him to return to his brigade in August. During Bragg's Kentucky invasion in the late summer of 1862, his aggressiveness temporarily soured Bragg's admiration. Chalmers was in advance of the army and on September 14 took it upon himself to attack a large Federal garrison protecting an important railroad crossing on the Green River, near Munfordville. Fighting from impenetrable blockhouses, the Yankees riddled Chalmers' attacking troops. He withdrew only after losing 288 men to the Yankees' 72. Chastened, Chalmers informed Bragg of his failure and glumly noted his actions might bring censure from headquarters. Bragg was outraged and labeled Chalmers' attack as being "unauthorized and injudicious."

After the failed Kentucky campaign, Chalmers' Brigade fell back to Murfreesboro, Tennessee, with Bragg's army. On December 31, 1862, his unit was on the extreme right of Leonidas K. Polk's Corps. When Polk attacked, Chalmers led his men into the slaughterhouse fronting the Round Forest. Immediately, Chalmers was struck down by an exploding shell. Withers wrote that Chalmers was "borne senseless from the field," and noted that with the loss of the "fearless energy of this gallant officer," the brigade quickly lost all order. Murfreesboro cost the brigade 548 casualties and ended Chalmers' infantry career.

In March 1862 Chalmers was given command of the Fifth Military District, comprising the northernmost counties of Mississippi. There is some evidence that he was reluctant to leave his infantry brigade and had to be persuaded to accept the new assignment. But with characteristic zeal, Chalmers took to his new job. Organizing a cavalry brigade, he kept the Yankees off balance in his district through raids and skirmishes until he was relieved in November. Well-liked, Chalmers was affectionately called "little 'un" by the men in his cavalry command.

In February 1864 Chalmers' Brigade was assigned to Nathan Bedford Forrest's command. Chalmers was a proud officer and sometimes expressed disappointment at being transferred to other commands rather than being promoted. Nonetheless, he served Forrest well for the rest of the war, despite occasional disagreements. For instance, in March Chalmers was

relieved of his command when he wrote a "disrespectful" letter complaining that Forrest had taken away his only tent for the use of Forrest's brother. But this matter blew over and Chalmers was leading Forrest's 1st Division by month's end.

In late March, Chalmers threatened Memphis while Forrest launched a raid into Tennessee and Kentucky. On April 12 both converged on Fort Pillow, Tennessee, an earthen fort on the Mississippi River with a large Negro garrison. When the Federals refused to surrender, the Confederates attacked and captured the fort, killing and wounding almost half the command. Because most of the black troops were killed and very few taken prisoner, the Confederates were accused of massacring the black soldiers. Several Yankees who survived the battle presented vague and hearsay testimony that implicated Chalmers in the slaughter. The only Federal who personally spoke to Chalmers asked him if the blacks were killed after the fort fell. Chalmers reportedly replied that he believed they had been because of the intense hatred the Rebels had for black soldiers. The Yankee added, however, that Chalmers stated that Forrest did not order the killings and that "both Forrest and he stopped the massacre as soon as they were able to do so." Chalmers made no mention of a massacre in his report, but maintained "the enemy made no attempt to surrender…Many of them were killed while fighting, and many more in the attempt to escape."

After the fall of Fort Pillow, Chalmers' Division returned to north Mississippi. In July he and Forrest engaged A. J. Smith's raiders near Tupelo in a bitter but unsuccessful fight. The autumn of 1864 proved more successful, when the cavalry raided into Tennessee. Chalmers blockaded the Tennessee River and on October 30 his command assisted in the shelling and capture of two Union gunboats. On November 3, the raiders attacked Johnsonville, Tennessee, and destroyed numerous Union gunboats and millions of dollars worth of supplies. In his report Forrest praised Chalmers' "skill, coolness, and undaunted courage" during the raid.

After the Johnsonville raid Forrest's cavalry was ordered to lead John Bell Hood's movement into Tennessee. Chalmers was in numerous skirmishes as the Rebels raced northward. At the Battle of Franklin on November 30, his division guarded Hood's left flank and engaged in heavy skirmishing throughout the day. After Franklin, Chalmers was separated temporarily

For this later portrait, Chalmers has changed his uniform buttons to match his rank. (Miller, *Photographic History*)

from Forrest and operated more independently with Hood's army. At Nashville, his division again was on the extreme left. In the Union attack of December 15, Chalmers' men were overwhelmed and forced back. On the 16th, Hood put Chalmers in command of his left wing and Chalmers briefly held back the Yankees. The next day Hood placed him over all of his cavalry and ordered Chalmers to protect the rear while the wrecked army retreated. Chalmers led the cavalry until Forrest rejoined the army on December 19 and resumed command.

After the disastrous campaign Forrest and Chalmers returned to north Mississippi and endured near-starvation through early 1865. On February 13, 1865, Chalmers was given command of all the Mississippi Cavalry in the department. He later accompanied Forrest into Alabama and surrendered with him in May 1865.

After the war, Chalmers became a leading politician in Mississippi. During Reconstruction he led a group of whites against a Negro riot near his home in Friar's Point and drove their leader, the mulatto sheriff, out of the county. He was elected to the state senate in 1875 and 1876, and was involved in six hotly disputed Congressional elections. He won three times—in 1876, 1878, and 1882—with each election being marred by contested election returns. At times he ran with the support of the Republican Party. Chalmers retired from politics in 1888 and moved to Memphis to resume his law practice. He died on April 9, 1898, and was buried there.

Terry Jones

Foote, Shelby. *The Civil War: A Narrative.* New York, 1963, 1974.

Henry, Robert Selph. *"First With the Most: Forrest."* New York, 1944.

Wyeth, John Allan. *That Devil Forrest: Life of General Nathan Bedford Forrest.* Baton Rouge, 1989.

✶ John Randolph Chambliss, Jr. ✶

Taken between his promotion in December 1863, and his death in August 1864, this portrait is the only one known showing Chambliss as a brigadier general. (Museum of the Confederacy, Richmond)

Chambliss was born on January 13, 1833, at Hicksford in Greenville County, Virginia. He entered the United States Military Academy in 1849 and graduated in 1853, thirty-first in a class of fifty-two. At West Point, he was a classmate of James B. McPherson, John Bell Hood, and Phil Sheridan. Chambliss was breveted a 2d lieutenant in the mounted rifles and received an assignment to the cavalry school at Carlisle Barracks, Pennsylvania. He resigned from the army on March 4, 1854, and returned home. There he operated a plantation. From 1856 to 1861, he served as an aide-de-camp, with the rank of major, to Governors Henry A. Wise and John Letcher. Chambliss commanded a militia regiment as colonel from 1858 to 1861 and was for two years a brigade inspector. In July 1861 he was commissioned colonel of the 41st Virginia Infantry Regiment.

There are no details outlining Chambliss' service in this capacity. He became colonel of the 13th Virginia Cavalry Regiment in late July 1862. The regiment served under Major General Daniel H. Hill on the south side of the James River. When Hill conducted operations against Union shipping on the river on July 23–31, he sent Chambliss on an expedition toward Suffolk. Chambliss took his regiment to the vicinity of the Rappahannock River when the Army of Northern Virginia invaded Maryland. He assumed command of the forces watching the enemy north of that river and near Manassas. At various times, he had as many as four regiments under his command. Chambliss' regiment joined Brigadier General William H. F. "Rooney" Lee's cavalry brigade in mid-November. During the Battle of Fredericksburg on December 13, Chambliss' men helped watch the crossings over the Rappahannock River to the south of the Confederate Army's main position. The regiment remained in winter camps near Fredericksburg, and on at least one occasion, a Confederate general commanding in southeastern Virginia requested the service of the regiment there, the area in which it had been raised.

As Major General Joseph Hooker began his operations against the Army of Northern Virginia in April 1863, Chambliss and his troopers helped guard various fords on the Rappahannock and Rapidan. The regiment fought in skirmishes at Kelly's Ford and Beverly Ford on April 14–15. Chambliss and fifty of his men drove back two Federal squadrons in the latter engagement, and both Rooney Lee and Jeb Stuart praised them for their victory. The brigade assisted in opposing the Union cavalry raid of Major General George Stoneman toward Richmond from April 29 to May 7. Chambliss and his men played an important role in the Battle of Brandy Station on June 9. In the early part of the fighting, Chambliss led dismounted sharpshooters opposing the Union cavalry's advance. Rooney Lee received a severe wound, and since the brigade's next senior colonel had been killed, Chambliss assumed command of the brigade.

He continued leading the unit during subsequent engagements at Aldie and Middleburg on June 17. The brigade virtually destroyed the 1st Rhode Island Cavalry in the latter engagement. Stuart took the brigade with him on his ride around the Union Army into Pennsylvania. On June 30, Chambliss attacked Brigadier General Judson Kilpatrick's brigade at Hanover, drove it back, and captured a small number of prisoners. Chambliss and his men fought well in the fierce cavalry battle near Gettysburg on July 3. His brigade helped to protect the army's wagon trains during the retreat back to Virginia. Chambliss became quite ill but, according to Stuart, "with that commendable spirit which has always distinguished him, remained at the head of his brigade."

When Stuart reorganized his cavalry in early September, Rooney Lee's brigade, still under Chambliss, received assignment to Major General Fitzhugh Lee's division. He led his brigade in an engagement at Brandy Station on October 11, and Stuart praised his gallantry and "fearless bearing in the charge." Federal forces drove the brigade back toward Bristoe from Bull Run Creek on October 17. Two days later, Chambliss and his men did not reach the field of the famous "Buckland Races" engagement until the fighting had practically ended, and they could only assist in gathering up Union prisoners.

Chambliss' Brigade saw no real action in the Mine Run Campaign in late November, doing mostly picket duty at various fords. In mid-December, Chambliss received orders to take his brigade to the Shenandoah Valley to help resist an enemy raid against Staunton. The men had returned to the main army by the middle of January 1864. Chambliss was promoted to brigadier general on January 27, to rank from December 19, 1863. Rooney Lee returned to duty in April with a promotion to major general and was given a new division consisting of Chambliss' and Brigadier General James B. Gordon's Brigades. Chambliss' men remained with the main army during the Battles of The Wilderness and Spotsylvania and the retreat toward Richmond.

On June 23, the brigade attacked a Federal force at Forge Bridges near Charles City Court House and drove it back. The next day, during an engagement at Nance's Shop, or Samaria Church, Chambliss' troops attacked the flank of a Union cavalry division and helped push it back. Several days later, Chambliss was with Lieutenant General Wade Hampton trying to intercept a Union cavalry raid toward the Weldon Railroad south of the James River. On June 28 near Sappony Creek, Chambliss attacked and defeated a portion of the enemy force. Hampton wrote after the campaign, "General Chambliss, by his gallantry, great zeal, and his knowledge of the country, contributed largely to the success we gained." In August, Rooney Lee's Division rode north of the James River to reinforce troops threatened by a Federal advance toward Richmond. Union Brigadier General David M. Gregg's cavalry division began an attack up the Charles City Road on August 16. Early in the action, Chambliss rode toward the front near White's Tavern with his staff and was killed. General Robert E. Lee commented on his death with these words: "The loss sustained by the cavalry in the fall of General Chambliss will be felt throughout the army, in which, by his courage, energy, and skill, he had won for himself an honorable name." Chambliss is buried in Emporia, Virginia.

Arthur W. Bergeron, Jr.

Jedediah Hotchkiss, "Virginia," *Confederate Military History*, ed. by Clement A. Evans, reprint ed.; Wilmington, N.C., 1987 , Emory M. Thomas, *Bold Dragoon: The Life of J. E. B. Stuart* New York, 1986 ;

★ Benjamin Franklin Cheatham ★

One of the more photographed generals, Cheatham sat for his finest portrait probably in 1864, as a major general. (National Archives)

Cheatham, the son of Leonard Pope and Elizabeth Cheatham, was born in Nashville, Tennessee, October 20, 1820. He volunteered for service in the war with Mexico and fought in the Battle of Monterrey as a captain in the 1st Tennessee Regiment and, as a colonel, led the 3d Tennessee in Major General Winfield Scott's celebrated campaign from, Veracruz to Mexico City. He participated in the 1849 California Gold Rush. Returning to Tennessee in 1853, he became a planter and was named a major general in the state militia. A pro-secession Democrat, Cheatham was appointed, by Governor Isham Harris, a brigadier general in the Tennessee Provisional Army on May 9, 1861, and by President Jefferson Davis to the same rank in the Confederate States Army, July 9, 1861, to rank from that date.

A hard drinking individualist, known for his colorful but forceful language, Cheatham was popular with his junior officers and the rank and file. He was a good administrator, understanding the art of looking after the welfare of his troops whether on the march or in camp. Associated with the units that were to constitute the Army of the Mississippi (redesignated the Army of Tennessee in November 1862), Cheatham first saw Civil War combat at Belmont, Missouri, on November 7, 1861. Shuttled across the Mississippi River, with three Tennessee regiments, he gained the enemy's rear, and had a major role in defeating Union troops led by U.S. Grant.

Cheatham was promoted major general March 14,

This early uniformed image of Cheatham is possibly from early 1861 when he served as commanding general of Tennessee state troops before his July 1861 appointment as a Confederate brigadier. (Alabama Department of Archives and History, Montgomery)

Sometime between July 1861 and March 1862, Cheatham sat for a series of portraits, possibly in Nashville. (Library of Congress)

Yet another pose from the 1861-62 sitting. (Alabama Department of Archives and History, Montgomery)

Following his promotion to major general, Cheatham posed once more for another series of portraits, probably in 1863. (Alabama Department of Archives and History, Montgomery)

Another pose from the same sitting. (William Turner Collection)

1862, to rank from March 10, one week after he and his troops had evacuated Columbus, Kentucky. At "Bloody Shiloh", he commanded one of the two divisions constituting Leonidas Polk's Corps, and, besides being slightly wounded, had three horses shot from under him. Calling attention to Cheatham's leadership, Polk noted, "those of the troops who acted under the immediate orders of General Cheatham bore themselves with conspicuous gallantry." He led a division during the Kentucky Campaign and, at Perryville, on October 8, a slashing onslaught spearheaded by Cheatham and three brigades wrecked an enemy division, killed two Union generals, and enabled the badly outnumbered Confederates to gain the bulge on Alexander D. McCook's corp. While watching the Tennesseans' surge, General Polk saw Cheatham riding forward shouting, "Give'em hell boys!" Polk, cognizant of his status as an Episcopal bishop, called out, "Give it to 'em boys, give 'em what General Cheatham says!"

At Stones River, on December 31, Cheatham's attacks were dilatory, his brigades going into action individually rather than simultaneously—and he was drunk. Because of Cheatham's popularity with his Tennessee troops, his statewide influence, and previous distinguished combat record, Braxton Bragg did not order Cheatham before a court of inquiry. Bragg, while failing to censure Cheatham, did not commend him in his report of the battle. Cheatham returned Bragg's contempt, joining the growing number of Army of Tennessee generals who championed Bragg's ouster. Cheatham and his Tennesseans participated in the Tullahoma Campaign, and were further disenchanted as Bragg's army was outmaneuvered and compelled to abandon the rest of middle Tennessee. At Chickamauga, Cheatham and his five-brigade division battered the Federals, on September 19-20, "sustaining the reputation" as headlong fighters gained wherever they attacked. The Confederate victory did not put a damper on Bragg's critics. A visit to the army by President Jefferson Davis sustained Bragg, and Cheatham saw his division of twenty-two Tennessee regiments reorganized, and General Polk transferred. At Missionary Ridge, on November 25, Cheatham and his reorganized division, when the Confederate center collapsed, engaged the onrushing Federals and delayed them until darkness put a stop to the fighting and enabled Bragg's shattered army to escape to Dalton, Georgia.

General Joseph E. Johnston replaced Bragg as the army's leader and during the winter of 1863-64, reorganized the army and restored its morale. Cheatham again commanded his four brigades of Tennesseans, one of the four divisions constituting William J. Hardee's Corps, as the Federals opened the Atlanta Campaign, on May 7, 1864. Cheatham and his Tennesseans met the enemy at Resaca on May 15; skirmished with the foe at Adairsville on the 17th; held rifle-pits along the New Hope Church-Dallas line from May 25 to June 4, and confronted the Federals from the Pine Mountain, Lost Mountain and Mud Creek line earthworks, from June 5-19, as rain beat down and turned the area into an ocean of mud. At Kennesaw Mountain, on June 27, Cheatham and his people shattered all-out Union attacks in the "Dead Angle," on a ridge that has since been known as Cheatham Hill.

On July 18, when General John B. Hood replaced Johnston as army commander, Cheatham assumed command of Hood's Corps, and led it in the battle of Atlanta, in which his troops initially gained some success, capturing five cannon and six stands of color. Upon the arrival of S.D. Lee, recently promoted to lieutenant general, on July 26, Cheatham resumed command of the Tennessee Division, which he led at Jonesboro, August 31-September 1, and on the retreat from Atlanta to and beyond Lovejoy's Station. In mid-September, General Hardee was detached from the Army of Tennessee and Cheatham assumed command of Hardee's Corps and led it during Hood's ill-fated Middle Tennessee Campaign. At Spring Hill, on November 29, Hood, having outmaneuvered General John M. Schofield, was in a favorable position to overwhelm the Army of the Ohio. Hood's failure to do so, and the question of who was responsible, led to bitter controversy between Hood and Cheatham and their partisans that is still debated by historians. Each general, in detailing what occurred, contradicted the other. Hood stated that he showed Cheatham the enemy columns marching up the Franklin road, pointed out where he was to post his three-division corps, and repeatedly urged him to attack. Hood recalled that Cheatham ignored these orders until the opportunity to rout Schofield was lost and also stated that Cheatham subsequently, "confessed the great error of which he was guilty." Cheatham countered that, at the time referenced by Hook, "only a mirage would have made possible the vision" of the Yankees on the road;

One pose from this sitting survives only in a poor tiny copy. (*Confederate Veteran*, XXI, p. 208)

Probably made at the same sitting, this portrait makes the hardened old fighter look almost gentle. (Museum of the Confederacy, Richmond)

he had deployed his troops as ordered; to his surprise Hood then told him to delay his attack until daybreak; and a confession such as Hood recalled was imagination on Hood's part. In any case, it is clear that, while Hood slept, and Cheatham, it was said, dallied with Mrs. Jessie Peters, Schofield's army passed.

At Franklin, on November 30, Cheatham, in response to Hood's orders, hurled his corps against a strongly fortified position held by Union soldiers and saw two of his three divisions shattered. At Nashville, on December 15, Cheatham held his ground, but the next day his troops were routed from Shy's Hill and sent scurrying southward on a terrible and heart-wrenching retreat across the Tennessee River and on into Mississippi. Cheatham and the survivors of his once-proud corps then made the round-about trip from Mississippi to North Carolina, where they reported to General Joseph E. Johnston. Cheatham led troops into battle for the last time at Bentonville on March 19-20, 1865, and was embraced in the surrender agreement signed by William Tecumseh Sherman and Johnston on April 26 at Durham Station. On May 1, Cheatham was paroled at Greensboro.

He headed back to Tennessee, returned to the family farm, and, in 1866, married Anna Bell Robertson, a daughter of A.B. Robertson. He ran unsuccessfully for the U.S. House of Representatives as a Democrat in 1872; declined an appointment in the Federal government proffered by President U.S. Grant, his erstwhile foe; and was for four years superintendent of the Tennessee State Prison. In 1885 he was named by President Grover Cleveland to be postmaster of Nashville, a position that he held until his death, September 4, 1886. The love and esteem in which Cheatham was held, by veterans, as well as the public at large, was underscored by "the vast attendance upon his funeral, which was declared... to be the most imposing ever held in Nashville." He is buried in Nashville's Mount Olivet Cemetery.

Edwin C. Bearss

★ James Chesnut, Jr. ★

James Chesnut, Jr., was born on January 18, 1815, in Camden, Kershaw County, South Carolina, where his family had been prominent since the French and Indian War. The youngest of thirteen children and the first cousin of future Confederate Brigadier General Zacharia C. Deas, James graduated with honors from Princeton in 1835. He read law in Charleston under the renowned James Louis Petigru, joined the bar in 1837, and began his practice in Camden. He married Mary Boykin Miller, the daughter of a former governor of the state, on April 23, 1840.

A state's rights Democrat, Chesnut represented the Kershaw District in the lower house of the South Carolina General Assembly from 1840–1846 and 1850–1852; he served in the upper house from 1854 to 1858, the latter two years as president. He represented his state at the Nashville Convention in 1850, where he advocated secession. Following the death of Senator Josiah J. Evans in 1858, Chesnut became a U.S. Senator. His abilities as an orator quickly made him a conspicuous member of that chamber, as did his defense of slavery: "commerce, civilization, and Christianity go hand in hand, and their conjoint efforts receive their chief earthly impulse from this reviled institution."

With the secession of his native state imminent, Chesnut resigned from the Senate on November 10, 1860. Representing the Kershaw District at the South Carolina convention, he served on the committee that drafted the Ordinance of Secession. As a member of the Provisional Congress of the Confederate States in 1861, he served on the committee that drafted that nation's permanent constitution and he tried to have the slave trade reopened. He served on the Committees on Naval Affairs and the Territories and supported the Davis Administration.

His initial military service began in Charleston, where he served as an aide on Brigadier General P. G. T. Beauregard's staff with the rank of colonel in April 1861. Along with Captain Stephen D. Lee, Chesnut delivered messages from Beauregard to Major Robert Anderson demanding the surrender of Fort Sumter. The two zealous Confederates have been charged with the responsibility of bringing about the firing on the fort; however, this accusation is unfounded.

Chesnut continued to serve on Beauregard's staff following the general's transfer to Virginia. Beauregard gave Chesnut the honor of presenting his plan of cooperating with General Joseph E. Johnston

No Certainly genuine uniformed portrait of Chesnut has been found. This has been artistically retouched, so it is probable that the uniform is entirely imaginary, but the portrait probably dates from the war years. (Museum of the Confederacy, Richmond)

in July of 1861 to President Jefferson Davis and, consequently, Chesnut became the key witness in the dispute between Davis and Beauregard following the First Battle of Manassas.

Chesnut left Confederate service early in 1862 to accept an appointment by South Carolina's governor to serve as chief of militia on the state's executive council, a position he resigned from in November to become an aide to Davis with the rank of colonel of cavalry. As a ranking member of Davis' staff, Chesnut faced extensive, demanding, and varied duties, a natural outgrowth of Davis' confidence in the judgment of this "cool, quiet, self-poised colonel." In September 1863, Chesnut met with Governors Joseph E. Brown of Georgia and John G. Shorter of Alabama on behalf of Davis to urge them to send reinforcements to northwestern Georgia. Following General Braxton Bragg's victory at Chickamauga, Chesnut inspected Bragg's forces encircling Chattanooga. He notified Davis on October 5: "Your immediate presence in this army is urgently demanded." Davis hastened west, but left it to Chesnut to solve the personal animosities between Bragg and his subordinates. Although Chesnut repeatedly notified Davis that no reconciliation seemed possible between the aggrieved parties and urged the President to reassign Bragg to Richmond, Davis adamantly refused. Chesnut departed Bragg's command in October but Davis, at Bragg's request, ordered him to return on November 1 to ascertain the facts regarding the intensification of the resentment between Bragg and his officers.

Chesnut, apparently dissatisfied with his staff assignments in late 1863, requested a field command. Davis appointed him a brigadier general on April 23, 1864, to rank immediately, and seven days later assigned him to command all the reserve forces in South Carolina, a position he held until the end of the war.

During the summer of 1864, Major General Samuel Jones, commander of the Department of South Carolina, Georgia, and Florida, repeatedly criticized Chesnut for failing to support Jones' Confederate regulars with his reserves. As Union Major General William T. Sherman's forces swept across Georgia and threatened to enter South Carolina, Chesnut received authorization to take an unspecified number of his South Carolina reservists into Georgia; he had reached Augusta by November 23. Six days later he departed Augusta and returned to South Carolina with 1,000 men.

When Chesnut arrived at Grahamville, South

Carolina, early on the morning of September 1, one day too late to participate in the Confederate victory there, his command numbered no more than 350 effective soldiers. By December 26, that number had increased to 1,600 men, who were deployed between Honey Hill, Bee's Creek, and Dawson's Bluff. Ordered to assist in the defense of Coosawhatchie, Chesnut directed his troops from Grahamville until the end of December. Still Chesnut's superior despite his demotion from head of the department to command of the District of South Carolina, Jones continued his criticism of Chesnut, reporting the latter's failure to promptly forward troops to Coosawhatchie. On January 2, 1865, Chesnut received orders to move his command, now numbering 1,200 effective reservists, to Adams' Run, in the Fourth Sub-District of the District of South Carolina.

On March 7, 1865, Chesnut was transferred to General Joseph E. Johnston's command in Charlotte, North Carolina. The following day Chesnut received orders to leave there and return to South Carolina without his reserves; they would remain with Johnston. On April 21, he was in Chester, South Carolina.

When the fighting ended, Chesnut returned to his law practice in Camden. Although disfranchised because of the positions he had held in the Confederacy, Chesnut labored to end Reconstruction in South Carolina as quickly as possible. He presided over a convention in 1867 that protested the continued military occupation of his state. In 1868 he served as a delegate to the Democratic National Convention and two years later as a delegate to the state democratic convention. In 1871 and 1874 he chaired the executive committee of the taxpayers' conventions and during the presidential campaign of 1876 he chaired the Kershaw County Democratic convention.

Chesnut died at Saarsfield, the family plantation near Camden, on February 1, 1885. His wife wrote the illustrious Diary from Dixie, which has appeared in several editions, the most reliable of which is that edited by C. Vann Woodward in 1981.

Lawrence L. Hewitt

Faust, Patricia L., ed., *Historical Times Illustrated Encyclopedia of the Civil War*. New York, 1986.

Woodward, C. Vann, *Mary Chestnut's, Civil War*, New Haven, Conn, 1981

✶ Robert Hall Chilton ✶

Chilton was born in Loudoun County, Virginia, on February 25, 1815. His career at the United States Military Academy followed a curve descending so steeply that it suggests Chilton would not have successfully completed his education had he attended during the school's five-year era. From a lower-middle ranking during his first year, Chilton slipped steadily to finish as forty-eighth out of fifty graduates in the class of 1837. Classmates who became familiar Civil War figures included Bragg, Early, Hooker, Pemberton, Sedgwick, and W. H. T. Walker. Cadet Chilton stood 143d of 211 students in the Academy in conduct during his final year; his rowdy comrade Jubal A. Early ranked in the bottom twenty on the same list.

Second Lieutenant Chilton's initial assignment in 1837 was to the 1st United States Dragoons. On February 21, 1842, Chilton received promotion to 1st lieutenant in the same regiment. During the years before the Mexican War, the lieutenant served at Fort Leavenworth, Kansas; in the Choctaw country of the Indian Territory; and in Texas on the expedition to the Falls of the Brazos. Chilton accepted staff duties as an assistant quartermaster in May 1846 that carried with them promotion to captain. That December the captain moved back to a line assignment at that rank, still with the 1st Dragoons. During the hard-fought American victory at Buena Vista in 1847, Captain Chilton exhibited "gallant and meritorious conduct" that won him a major's brevet.

After a postwar stretch back on the frontier, Chilton transferred in July 1854 to staff duty as paymaster with permanent rank as major. In that capacity he received postings to Washington, New York, Detroit, and San Antonio. His Regular Army roles in Texas brought Chilton into acquaintance with R. E. Lee, who would be the primary influence on his Confederate career.

The United States Army accepted Chilton's resignation on April 29, 1861, a few days after his native state seceded. The new Confederate government appointed him lieutenant colonel on May 20, to take rank from March 16, and assigned him to the Adjutant & Inspector General's Office. A document ordering Chilton to Ashland, Virginia as colonel of cavalry to relieve R. S. Ewell in command of the cavalry camp there apparently was cancelled.

While serving with the A&IGO in Richmond, Chilton issued an order on the last day of 1861—whether on his own initiative or not is unclear—directing general officers to secure "a complete history of each regiment, battalion and independent command in your Department." The initiative was not fruitful, unfortunately, though Chilton thoughtfully forwarded forms to hold the information.

On June 4, 1862, Lieutenant Colonel Chilton was ordered to report to R. E. Lee for duty as his chief of staff. Language in a letter written later by Lee intimates that Chilton was selected for that duty by the

Despite serving in or near Richmond for most of the war, Chilton seems not to have made many visits to a photographer. This small portrait is the only one in uniform known. (Virginia Historical Society)

A&IGO in response to a non-specific request from Lee. On October 28, 1862, Lee announced Chilton as inspector general of the army, in addition to his duty as chief of staff. Beginning that same month the question of Chilton's rank came under discussion. His appointment as brigadier general was dated October 20, and he accepted it four days later—but the Confederate Senate rejected the nomination on April 11, 1863. In the aftermath, Chilton was promoted colonel on April 11, to take rank all the way back to October 13, 1862.

In response to those events, Chilton engaged in a flurry of activity to bolster his case. He solicited from Lee, by means of a long set of questions, a testimonial statement that he had always "been zealous and active in the discharge of...official duties." Lee also wrote to the secretary of war on behalf of his staff officer, wondering why the Senate had rejected Chilton and touting the colonel's "fidelity, honesty, and intelligence." In a phrase that sounds decidedly neutral, Lee declared moderately that he "desired no change" in the post of chief of staff.

Chilton also ascertained that his trouble in the Senate came from supporters of General John B. Magruder, and demanded a court of inquiry to examine the incident that offended them. A few weeks after Chilton's appointment in June 1862, he had written to A&IGO Samuel Cooper about Magruder's demeanor during the Seven Days, reporting that Magruder had behaved with a degree of "excitement at Malvern Hill which impaired his capability." Chilton introduced evidence to support his statement, and proved that he had sent a copy to Magruder to avoid any inference that he was dealing clandestinely. In May 1863 the court adjudged Chilton's actions honorable.

At the height of the twin complications of Senate rejection and the Magruder court, Chilton discharged his duty during the Chancellorsville Campaign in a substandard fashion. When sent to General Early's rearguard detachment on May 2, 1863, Chilton garbled a reiteration of Early's discretionary retreat orders and insisted that they were preemptory. This gaffe caused considerable difficulty and nearly a disaster.

Bob Chilton (as everybody called him, almost always using both names, according to Lafayette McLaws) finally did receive a general's wreath on February 16, 1864, to take rank from December 21, 1863. He resigned the rank on April 1, 1864, however,

knowing it was intended for Lee's chief of staff, and having meanwhile been reassigned to the A&IGO in Richmond. This voluntary downgrade, Chilton remarked aptly, was "an unusual circumstance in [Military] life." The general-cum-colonel finished the war "in charge of the Bureau of Inspection," paying special attention to "incompetent officers, bad cooking," in hospitals around Richmond. He was paroled at Greensboro about May 1, 1865.

After the war Chilton administered a manufacturing company in Columbus, Georgia, and died in that town on February 18, 1879. He is one of many Confederate generals buried in Richmond's Hollywood Cemetery.

Robert K. Krick

⋆ *Thomas James Churchill* ⋆

This obviously postwar portrait of Churchill is the only one that has come to light, and probably dates from his years as governor of Arkansas in the 1880s. (Virginia Historical Society)

Churchill was born on his father's farm near Louisville in Jefferson County, Kentucky, on March 10, 1824. He was one of seven children; his sister Julia married Dr. Luke P. Blackburn, governor of Kentucky. He graduated from St. Mary's College at Bardstown in 1844, and studied law at Transylvania University in Lexington. When the war with Mexico began, Churchill joined the 1st Kentucky Mounted Riflemen. On the way to Mexico his regiment stopped briefly in Little Rock, where he met the woman who would later become his wife. In January 1847 he was captured by Mexican cavalry, and held prisoner in Mexico City. When General Winfield Scott's army advanced on the city, Lieutenant Churchill was moved to Toluca and not exchanged until just before the war's end. At the close of hostilities he returned to Arkansas, married, and began farming a plantation near Little Rock.

At the outbreak of the Civil War he was postmaster at Little Rock. Churchill tried to raise a cavalry regiment in the counties around Fort Smith, but had difficulty in obtaining volunteers because the men refused to join for three years. The War Department, however, authorized him to receive twelve-months men, and by June he had a full regiment. The recruits elected Churchill colonel, and the regiment joined General Ben McCulloch's command at Fort Smith. Churchill participated in the battle at Wilson's Creek, Missouri, where he had two horses shot from under him. He also fought in the Battle of Pea Ridge, Arkansas. On

March 6, 1862, he was promoted to brigadier general to rank from March 4; he commanded the Second Brigade in the Army of the West. Churchill crossed the Mississippi River with General Van Dorn, and at Corinth in May reported 2,332 troops. He joined General E. Kirby Smith in the Kentucky Campaign, and fought at Richmond, where he earned the praise of the commanding general. But on December 10, 1862, he was reassigned to the Trans-Mississippi Department and reported back to Little Rock.

General Theophilus H. Holmes sent him to command the Confederate fortification of Fort Hindman on the lower Arkansas River at Arkansas Post. Early in January 1863 General John A. McClernand's army, along with Admiral David D. Porter's fleet, assaulted the unfinished fort. Churchill, whose orders were "to hold out till help arrived or all dead," asked General Holmes for reinforcements but unfortunately, when help did not arrive in time, he was forced to surrender after a white flag mysteriously appeared over the Confederate line. Churchill commented that when he saw the flag appear in the midst of a Texas regiment, "I was forced to the humiliating necessity of surrendering the balance of my command." Taken captive on January 11, he was imprisoned for three months at Camp Chase, Ohio, before being exchanged and assigned to the Army of Tennessee. Churchill was not able to live down the embarrassment of being the man who had surrendered Arkansas Post. In May, Secretary of War James Seddon recommended removing Churchill from the surrendered men and holding a court of inquiry. In the summer after the Arkansas Post prisoners had joined Braxton Bragg's army, he was replaced by James Deshler, and on December 10, 1863, assigned to the Trans-Mississippi Department and ordered to return back to Little Rock.

In Arkansas he was given command of a brigade of Texas cavalry, but the men refused to serve under him because of the bitterness still surrounding his surrender of Arkansas Post. Instead, he assumed command of a division of Arkansas infantry which included the brigades of James C. Tappan, Alexander T. Hawthorn, and Lucien C. Gause. He took part in the Red River Campaign in 1864 where at Pleasant Hill a Confederate victory depended upon Churchill flanking the Federal left. But Churchill did not move far enough south and instead of rolling up the enemy, he crossed in front of the Federal position. When General A. J. Smith realized this, he lashed into the Confederate line and Churchill had to fall back. General Richard Taylor recalled: "Churchill came to report the result of his attack, and seemed much depressed...A worthy, gallant gentleman, General Churchill, but not fortunate in war." Furthermore, Taylor believed: "Instead of intrusting the important attack by my right to a subordinate, I should have conducted it myself." On April 14, Churchill's Division headed for Arkansas to reinforce the Confederates facing General Frederick Steele in the Camden Campaign. Churchill participated in the battle at Jenkins' Ferry, April 30. After being reinforced by John G. Walker's Texans, Churchill reported that the enemy fled, "leaving us the proud victors of the battlefield." In August he assumed temporary command of the District of Arkansas, and in September was in command of the troops in southern Arkansas in the absence of General John A. Wharton. Promoted major general on March 18, 1865, to rank from the previous day, he surrendered in Texas.

After the war he returned to Arkansas, and when the Democrats regained control of the state government, he was elected state treasurer, and reelected in 1876 and 1878. In 1880 he was elected governor over a Greenback opponent. Charges of discrepancies in the state treasury for the years from 1874 until 1880 emerged while Churchill was governor, and his enemies used this as a means to discredit both the governor and the Democratic Party. Churchill's one term in office was marred by the treasury scandal as well as the way he handled a crisis in Perry County. When his term ended, he retired to his farm in 1883, and did not seek public office again. In his later life he was active in the United Confederate Veterans and served as commanding major general of the Confederate Veterans of Arkansas. After a long illness, he died on May 14, 1905, at his daughter's home in Little Rock, and was buried at Mt. Holly Cemetery.

Anne Bailey

Robert Kerby, *Kirby Smiths' Confederacy* New York, 1974

This portrait of Clanton could have been taken at any time after November 1863, though it may have been taken by a Mobile photographer near the end of the war. (Alabama Department of Archives and History, Montgomery)

⭒ *James Holt Clanton* ⭒

Clanton was born in Columbia County, Georgia, on January 8, 1827. His family moved to Macon County, Alabama, in 1835. Clanton attended public schools in that county and the University of Alabama. He volunteered as a private in the Mexican War, serving at the end of that conflict in the famous Palmetto Regiment of South Carolina. Clanton studied law in Tuskegee, was admitted to the Alabama bar in 1850, and opened a practice in Montgomery. In 1855, as a Democrat, he was elected to represent Montgomery County in the state legislature. He opposed secession and was an elector for the John Bell ticket in the presidential election of 1860.

When the Civil War started, Clanton raised a cavalry company and was elected its captain. His unit saw duty on the Florida coast. In November 1861, Clanton became colonel of the 1st Alabama Cavalry Regiment, which was organized at Montgomery. His regiment received orders to report to Corinth, Mississippi, the following spring. Clanton and his men skirmished with Union troops at Monterey and Pittsburg Landing, Tennessee, a few days before the Battle of Shiloh. Major General Braxton Bragg pronounced Clanton "gallant to rashness" in these skirmishes. At Shiloh, his men helped open the fighting and then served on the army's right flank. Brigadier General James R. Chalmers wrote that Clanton "remained almost all the time with my brigade and, though constantly exposed to the most dangerous fire, exhibited the most fearless and exemplary courage, cheering on those who seemed inclined to falter or grow weary." In his battle report, Chalmers' Division commander, Major General Jones M. Withers, called Clanton "indefatigable." During the subsequent siege of Corinth, Clanton led his regiment and was sometimes temporarily in command of a small brigade. His men helped cover the army's retreat when it evacuated that town in late May 1862.

Clanton later resigned as commander of the 1st Alabama Cavalry, perhaps because of some kind of dis-agreement with General Bragg. He returned to Alabama to help raise more troops for Confederate armies. As a special aide-de-camp to Governor John G. Shorter, he received orders in December 1862 to go to Coffee County to repel an enemy raid up the Choctawhatchie River, aimed at destroying some salt works. Shorter authorized Clanton to recruit a force for thirty days to assist in that work. In the spring of 1863, Clanton received authority from the War Department to recruit another regiment for use in defending the coastline of Alabama and western Florida. He established his headquarters at Montgomery and eventually raised one infantry and three cavalry regiments and a field artillery battery. On May 1, 1863, Clanton received orders to take his command to Pollard, where it would become part of the District of the Gulf. From time to time, he commanded what was called the Eastern Division of that district. He received a commission as brigadier general on November 18, 1863, to rank from November 16. On December 25, some of Clanton's men laid down their arms and threatened to desert. An investigation revealed a secret peace society at work in his brigade and cleared Clanton of any blame for allowing the situation to develop. Clanton did act zealously in prosecuting the ringleaders in this affair. As a result of this unrest, however, Clanton and his brigade were ordered to northern Alabama in early 1864. This would take Clanton's troops away from their homes and, hopefully, from the temptation to be disloyal.

He established his headquarters at Gadsden and assumed responsibility for protection of the iron and coal industries of that area. Lieutenant General Leonidas Polk, then commanding the Department of Alabama, Mississippi, and East Louisiana, called Clanton "an experienced cavalry officer, very efficient and enterprising." General Joseph E. Johnston, however, thought Clanton was incompetent and refused to allow Clanton's Brigade to join his army in April. Clanton's troops fought in several skirmishes in the Decatur and

Probably an earlier image of Clanton, taken during 1864. (Virginia Historical Society)

Danville area with the Federals during the succeeding months. Clanton's men opposed Major General Lovell H. Rousseau's raid into northern Alabama, July 10–22, 1864, and Clanton lost his entire staff in a fight at Ten Islands near Greensport on the Coosa River on July 14.

Clanton's Brigade was assigned to the District of Central and Northern Alabama during the late summer of 1864. In October, the brigade harassed the railroad lines that supplied Major General William T. Sherman's army at Atlanta, and at one time Clanton exercised command of his own and another cavalry brigade. Clanton and his brigade moved to Meridian, Mississippi, in December 1864 in response to an enemy raid from Baton Rouge, Louisiana toward Mobile, Alabama. Though unsuccessful in stopping this Federal force, Clanton again received orders to assume command at Pollard. His men did repulse an enemy raid from Pensacola in mid-December.

On March 25, 1865, Clanton was seriously wounded in a skirmish with Union forces at Bluff Spring, Florida. The Federals ordered him to surrender, but he refused. He fired on and wounded a Union officer and then tried to ride away. An enemy ball hit him in the small of his back, passed through his intestines before exiting, and knocked him from his horse. The wound was thought to be lethal, and Clanton had his chief of staff, who was captured with him, write out his will. He was paroled by the Federals the next day, told to report at Barrancas if he recovered, and left under the care of a surgeon at a civilian's house. By April 22, Clanton was at Pollard and sent a dispatch to the Union commander at Barrancas that he could travel and was on his way to that point. He reached Barrancas five days later. Clanton resumed his law practice after the war and assumed a leading role in the state's Democratic party. He acted as state's attorney for a railroad case in the late 1860s. David M. Nelson, a former Union Army officer, shot and killed Clanton on a street in Knoxville, Tennessee, on September 26, 1871. Clanton was buried in Montgomery, Alabama.

Arthur W. Bergeron, Jr.

Thomas M. Owen, *History of Alabama and Dictionary of Alabama Biography*, Spartanburg, S.C. 1978 , Joseph Wheeler, "Alabama," *Confederate Military History*, ed. by Clement A. Evans, reprint ed.; Wilmington, N.C., 1987 , Ephraim Brown Papers, Ohio Historical Society;

⋆ *Charles Clark* ⋆

Clark only served a little more than a year in uniform, and may not have had a portrait taken during that time. This civilian image almost certainly dates from after the war. (Virginia Historical Society)

Clark was born May 25, 1810 in Lebanon, Ohio. After graduating from Augusta College in Kentucky, he moved to Natchez, Mississippi, in 1831 to teach school. An epidemic closed the school and he was forced to relocate to Benton, where he continued to teach and to study law as well. After gaining the friendship of influential General Thomas Hinds, Clark advanced rapidly. As a Whig, he served in the Mississippi legislature from 1838 to 1839 and from 1842 to 1843. He entered the Mexican War as a captain in the 2d Mississippi Infantry and was elected colonel of the regiment when his predecessor resigned; however, Clark never engaged in combat.

At the Mississippi secessionist convention of 1851, he supported the Unionists, and that same year as a member of the constitutional convention, he denounced the doctrine. But his politics were about to change along with his lifestyle. In 1852, he moved to Bolivar County and became a successful planter. By 1860 his assets included 3,000 acres and fifty-three slaves and were valued at $170,000. In 1856 he was elected to the state legislature and then reelected to serve from 1859 to 1861. In 1857 he made an unsuccessful bid for election as the Whig candidate for Congress. His loss undoubtedly influenced him to change his politics, because he immediately became a secessionist Democrat. At the Democratic conventions in Charleston and Baltimore in 1860, he supported John C. Breckinridge for the Presidency. In 1861, he lost out to a cooperationist in his attempt to win a seat at the Mississippi secessionist convention.

Appointed a brigadier general of state troops following Mississippi's secession, he was soon promoted to major general. Always supportive of Governor John Pettus' preparations for war, he alienated the "Home

Guards" of Natchez by characterizing them as "occupying positions that women with broom handles could succeed in." He commanded state troops at Pensacola, until the acceptance of the Mississippi regiments into Confederate service, following which action he was appointed a brigadier general of volunteers in the Confederate Army on May 22, 1861, to rank immediately.

Subsequent to his service in Kentucky and Virginia, he led a division at Shiloh, where he was wounded in his right shoulder. When he returned to active duty and was assigned to Major General John C. Breckinridge, Clark commanded an understrength division in the attack against Baton Rouge. During a charge that he led against the 6th Michigan, a bullet shattered his right thigh bone. His wound, which crippled him for life, forced him to be left on the battlefield, where he was captured. Unfit for further military service, Clark was paroled and allowed to return home in February of 1863. He resigned from the army on October 31, 1863.

Clark, ignoring the fact that he required crutches, returned to politics. In November 1863 he was elected governor of Mississippi over opposition from eleven weak candidates, garnering seventy percent of the vote; his victory marked a shift from the adventurous days of secession to a more conservative trend. William Howard Russell described him at his inauguration on November 16 as a man who "spoke with sense and firmness of the present troubles, and dealt with the political difficulties in a tone of moderation which bespoke a gentleman and a man of education and thought" who had not "the smallest disposition" to surrender or "to consent to a reunion with the United States." "Reconstruction" would be "the climax of infamy," Clark concluded, and asked the citizens of Mississippi, "like the remnant of the heroic Pascagoulas when their braves were slain, [to] join hands together, march into the sea, and perish beneath its waters."

During his tenure, Clark urged state residents to support the war effort. He was quoted as saying Mississippians should "repel raids, not make them," and he practiced this philosophy by striving to improve the mounted militia units. But he faced a multitude of problems, including a continuous battle with the Confederate government to retain militia forces.

He achieved only limited success in punishing state officials who not only failed to perform their duties but also profited from speculation and consorted with ardent Unionists, in repealing exemptions from conscription granted to too many state officials, and in preventing lawlessness. The later was due largely to military desertion, a problem so bad that on November 16, 1864, he agreed to grant amnesty to deserters who promised to join the militia and to hunt down other deserters.

In an effort to bolster Confederate ranks, Clark joined other governors in October 1864 in urging the use of Negroes in the army as teamsters, laborers, or in any other effective manner, thus paving the way for the national government to pass a bill the following March that provided for the enlistment of slaves as soldiers. Clark publicly supported the bill, although he opposed granting the slaves their freedom in exchange.

The state's ravaged economy also commanded his attention, and he encouraged home industry and domestic use of Mississippi's agricultural products. He upheld the right of civil authorities to issue writs of replevin, which allowed considerable trade with the enemy.

As the end of the conflict drew near, Clark encouraged reconciliation. Upon learning of the surrender of Lieutenant General Richard Taylor, who commanded the Department of Alabama, Mississippi, and East Louisiana, Clark notified Union authorities on May 22: "I will not attempt to resist the Armed force of the United States in taking possession of the premises." He also addressed a special session of the legislature on May 18, where he spoke of his "profound sentiment of detestation" over the murder of President Abraham Lincoln and of his concern for Mississippi's future. Clark surrendered two days later and was confined in Fort Pulaski, near Savannah, Georgia, until he was allowed to sign an oath of allegiance on September 2, 1865, and shortly afterward was paroled. After his release he returned to "Doro," his plantation in Bolivar County, and successfully resumed his activities as a planter and as a lawyer. He urged conciliation but avoided politics because of the fact that he was "still a prisoner of state and on parole." He was appointed chancellor of the fourth district in 1876 and served as a trustee of the University of Mississippi until his death on December 18, 1877. He died and was buried at "Doro."

Lawrence L. Hewitt

✴ *John Bullock Clark, Jr.* ✴

Despite four straight years of active service, Clark did not leave behind a uniformed portrait that has yet been discovered. This postwar image probably dates from the 1870s or later. (Virginia Historical Society)

Clark was born January 14, 1831, in Fayette, Missouri. His father, John B. Clark, Sr., was a prewar congressman, brigadier general in the Missouri State Guard, and a Confederate congressman. John B. Clark, Jr., attended Fayette Academy and the Missouri University (later the University of Missouri). After finishing his schooling he spent two years in California before returning east to attend Harvard Law School. He was a lawyer in Fayette when the war began.

In the divided state of Missouri, Clark decided to side with the Confederacy. He became a lieutenant in the Missouri infantry, then captain of a company in the 6th Missouri Infantry. He served as a major in the Battle of Carthage in July, at Wilson's Creek in August, and at Springfield in October. When Colonel J. Q. Burbridge was wounded during the Battle of Wilson's Creek, Clark assumed command of the men in the 1st Missouri Infantry. He fought in an "efficient and intrepid manner" in spite of a slight wound to himself and his horse. By the time of the Battle of Pea Ridge in March 1862 he was a colonel, and commanded the Third Division, Missouri State Guard. This division consisted of six skeleton regiments, making in the aggregate about 500 men. On November 16, 1862, Clark's regiment of Missouri infantry was mustered into Confederate service, and on January 31, 1863, the regiment formed part of Frost's brigade, Trans-Mississippi Army, Major General Thomas C. Hindman commanding.

By May 1863 Clark commanded the first brigade in Frost's Division (Defenses of Lower Arkansas). In

June, Clark's regiment was ordered to operate against the Federal transports going down the Mississippi, and his men proved a menace to Union shipping. He took part in the Battle of Little Rock in September 1863, and following the loss of the capital, moved with the army to Arkadelphia. In January 1864 Colonel Clark commanded Thomas F. Drayton's Brigade, Price's Division, in the District of Arkansas, which included the 8th and 6th Missouri and a Missouri Battery. On March 29, fellow Missourian and Colonel Solomon G. Kitchen of the 7th Missouri Cavalry complained to General Marmaduke: "Colonel Clark has come here with orders from the War Department which has caused a great deal of confusion; he is telling all of my men that he has been confirmed as colonel of my regiment, and that he has orders to take command of them wherever he finds them. What shall I do with him...If Clark was out of here and no conflict with my orders I could very soon get up a good command, one strong enough to capture all the Yankees north of Arkansas River."

There is some confusion about Clark's appointment as brigadier general. On April 13, 1864, General E. Kirby Smith appointed him, to rank from January 1. However, Smith's appointments were not sanctioned or confirmed by the Senate and were, therefore, technically invalid. Nevertheless, at some later date President Davis apparently nominated Clark, to rank from March 6, and it was as such that he took part in the Camden Expedition; he led the First Brigade at the Battle of Jenkin's Ferry in April; his brigade formed part of the Missouri division under Brigadier General Mosby M. Parsons. By August, however, Clark had been transferred to the cavalry, in Major General Sterling Price's Cavalry Corps, First Missouri Cavalry Division under acting Major General John S. Marmaduke. He had assumed command of Marmaduke's Brigade when Marmaduke took command of the division. The command consisted of the Second Missouri Cavalry Brigade which included the 3d, 4th, 7th, 8th, and 10th Missouri. Clark participated in General Price's last invasion of Missouri where he led around 1,200 men, and took command of Marmaduke's Division after Marmaduke's capture. General Sterling Price reported that Clark, "true to his past fame, bore himself with undaunted courage and bravery, as well as skill and prudence. His brigade was most skillfully handled."

After the war he was elected to Congress, where he served from 1873 until 1883. In 1883 he became clerk of the House of Representatives, and from 1889 until his death he was a lawyer in Washington D.C. He died September 7, 1903, and is buried in Washington D.C. His father, John B. Clark, Sr., served as a U.S.Congressman from 1857 until 1861. When the war began he became a brigadier general in the Missouri State Guard, and remained in the position until he was named to the Confederate Congress. But he had frequent disagreements with other politicians; he antagonized President Davis by criticizing the government, and angered the Confederate governor of Missouri, Thomas Reynolds. After the war he resumed the practice of law, and died in Missouri in 1885.

Anne Bailey

☆ Henry DeLamar Clayton ☆

Though Clayton served in uniform through the entire war, no portrait in military costume has come to light. This photograph was taken several years after the war. (Medford Historical Society, Medford, Massachuetts)

Clayton was born in Pulaski County, Georgia, on March 7, 1827. His family moved to Lee County, Alabama, in the 1830s. Clayton attended Vineville Academy near Macon, Georgia, and received a degree from Emory and Henry College in Virginia in 1848. He studied law under future Alabama governor John Gill Shorter in Eufaula, Alabama, and opened a practice in Clayton after being admitted to the bar in 1849. Clayton entered the Alabama legislature as representative from Barbour County in 1857 and was reelected two years later. He formed a militia company called the Clayton Guards and became its captain in 1860. Governor Andrew B. Moore appointed Clayton colonel of the 3d Regiment, Alabama Volunteer Corps, in August 1860.

As troops began volunteering for service at Pensacola, Florida, in January 1861, Clayton tried unsuccessfully to get his regiment accepted for duty at that place. He resigned his commission and was mustered in as a private in his old company in an effort to get into active service. Governor Moore then made him a colonel on February 6 and placed him in charge of all the state's troops at Pensacola. When the 1st Alabama Infantry Regiment was formed on March 28, Clayton became its colonel. The regiment helped fortify the area of Fort Barrancas, trained as heavy artillerists, and participated in the bombardment of Fort Pickens on November 22–23. Clayton became ill with a fever in August and also was absent from his regiment for several months on court martial duty. He resigned his commission in January 1862.

Returning home, he organized the 39th Alabama Infantry Regiment and received a commission as its colonel when it was mustered in on May 15, 1862. The regiment was ordered soon afterwards to Tupelo, Mississippi, where it became part of Brigadier General Franklin Gardner's Brigade of Major General Jones M. Withers' Division. Clayton and his men accompanied the army on its invasion of Kentucky. They were present at but saw little fighting in the Battle of Perryville on October 8. At the Battle of Murfreesboro, the 39th Alabama formed part of Brigadier General Zachariah C. Deas' Brigade in Withers' division. Clayton received a severe wound during the fighting, necessitating a leave of about thirty days. General Braxton Bragg recommended Clayton for promotion to brigadier general for his performance at Murfreesboro. When he returned to duty, he commanded the consolidated 26th and 39th Alabama regiments. His unit camped at the fairgrounds and helped construct fortifications for Shelbyville, Tennessee. Clayton received his promotion to brigadier on April 15, 1863, dating from April 23, and assumed command of Alexander P. Stewart's old brigade of five Alabama regiments. The brigade joined Stewart's Division when it was formed on June 6.

Clayton first led his men in action at the Battle of Chickamauga, September 19–20. Clayton received a wound during one charge, and his brigade lost about 400 men in one hour. Two cannons and more than 600 prisoners fell into the brigade's hands. Stewart commended Clayton and his men, saying "they moved forward...with great spirit and alacrity, and in admirable order." The brigade was again heavily engaged at Chattanooga on November 25. The men were sent to prevent a Federal flanking movement near the Craven House; they were nearly surrounded and cut off at one point. When the army retreated to Dalton, Georgia, the brigade went with it. The men saw some action at Rocky Face Ridge, or Crow's Valley, in February 1864 when Union forces made a reconnaissance toward Dalton. On February 25 in a half hour engagement, Clayton's brigade defeated an attack by a Union brigade twice its strength. Clayton led his men in the various marches and fights of the Atlanta Campaign. On July 8, 1864, he was promoted to major general to rank from the previous day, and assumed command of Stewart's old division of four brigades. His division fought at Ezra Church on July 28 and Jonesboro on August 31. In the latter battle, Clayton had three horses killed under him.

Clayton led his division during General John B. Hood's campaign into Tennessee. His men captured Florence, Alabama, on October 30, securing the crossings of the Tennessee River at that place and enabling the army to get across the stream unmolested. The division operated south of Columbia, Tennessee, trying to draw the enemy's attention away from Hood's flanking movement at Spring Hill. Thus, the men arrived too late to participate in the bloody Battle of Franklin on November 30.

In the Battle of Nashville, December 15–16, Clayton's division repulsed all attacks on the first day and withdrew from the field on the second day only after the army's left had been crushed. Clayton commanded the rear guard as the army retreated toward Mississippi and helped prevent the Federal pursuit from completely destroying the army. He received praise from Hood and his corps commander, Lieutenant General Stephen D. Lee, for his conduct during the retreat. Lee wrote that he had "never seen excelled the personal gallantry he displayed," and Hood commented on Clayton's "admirable coolness and courage in the discharge of his duties." At Tupelo, Clayton's division was reduced to two brigades. He led the remnants of the division into North Carolina to join General Joe Johnston's forces. The men fought in the Battle of Bentonville, March 19–21, 1865. Clayton voluntarily retired in April 1865 "because of a surplus of senior officers and the great mental and physical strain of which he had been complaining since Atlanta."

After the war, Clayton resumed his law practice and operated a farm. He was elected a judge of the Eighth (later Third) Judicial Circuit Court in May 1866, was removed in 1868 by the Reconstruction government, and was reelected in 1874 and 1880. Clayton ran unsuccessfully for governor of Alabama in 1886, having resigned his judgeship. In June 1886, Clayton became president of the University of Alabama. He died in Tuscaloosa on October 3, 1889, and is buried in Eufaula.

Arthur W. Bergeron, Jr.

Holman D. Jordan, "The Military Career of Henry D. Clayton," *The Alabama Review*, XIII (1960), 127–34; Thomas M. Owen, *History of Alabama and Dictionary of Alabama Biography*, (Spartanburg, S.C., 1978), Joseph Wheeler, "Alabama," *Confederate Military History*, ed. by Clement A. Evans, (reprint ed.; Wilmington, N.C., 1987),

Cleburne posed for Ben Oppenheimer in Mobile for this portrait, while visiting for the wedding of General William J. Hardee. (Alabama Department of Archives and History, Montgomery)

✯ *Patrick Ronayne Cleburne* ✯

Patrick Ronayne Cleburne was born on March 17, 1828, in Bridgepark Cottage on the River Bridge, in County Cork, Ireland. His early education was derived from private tutors and as a student in a private school near Ballincoilig. At the age of 18 he became a druggist's apprentice. His deficiencies in Greek, Latin, and French prevented him from passing the examination administered in the Apothecaries' Hall Trinity College, Dublin. Humiliated by this failure, Cleburne enlisted as a private in the 41st Infantry Regiment. An inheritance he received on his twenty-first birthday enabled him, now a corporal, to purchase his discharge from the army. Accompanied by an older brother and sister and a younger half-brother, he sought his fortune in the United States.

Cleburne was 21 when he arrived in New Orleans. He continued to Cincinnati, where he worked as a druggist 's clerk for six months. Relocating to Helena, Arkansas, in May 1850 he took a similar position which resulted in his becoming a full partner on January 1, 1852. In 1855 a yellow fever epidemic struck the town: while most of the citizens fled to the countryside, he and two others, including future Confederate Major General Thomas C. Hindman, stayed and nursed the sick.

Cleburne had studied law in his spare time in Helena and was admitted to the bar on January 22, 1856. Although he was an ardent Whig, the replacement of that party by the anti-foreign know-nothings in the South compelled Cleburne to become a Democrat. This political upheaval resulted in an assailant shooting Cleburne in the back that summer.

In 1880 he assisted in the organization of a military company known as the Yell Rifles in which he enlisted as a private and whose members elected him captain. In February 1861, he led the company to Little Rock to seize the U.S. Arsenal—prior to the secession of the state. Arkansas secession on May 8 was followed on the fourteenth by Cleburne's election to the colonelcy

of the 1st Arkansas Infantry, a unit which later became one of three regiments to share the distinction of being known as the 16th Arkansas Infantry. Cleburne and his regiment occupied various garrisons along the Mississippi River until July, when it joined Brigadier General William J. Hardee in north central Arkansas for an invasion of Missouri. Cleburne accompanied Hardee to Bowling Green, Kentucky, that fall and when Hardee's command was increased to a division, he gave Cleburne command of one of his brigades.

Cleburne's abilities as an organizer during the Confederate withdrawal from Kentucky earned him a brigadier general's commission on March 6 to rank from March 4, 1862. Hardee praised his performance at Shiloh: "No repulse discouraged him; but after many bloody struggles he assembled the remnant of his brigade and was conspicuous for his gallantry to the end of the battle." By early August, Cleburne had been transferred from Tupelo, Mississippi, to Knoxville, Tennessee, and on the fourteenth he found himself commanding the vanguard of the Confederate invasion at Kentucky. Among the Confederates, Cleburne is most deserving of the credit for the decisive victory at Richmond on the thirtieth, where a minie ball struck him in the left jaw and mouth while he led his two-brigade division in a charge. Cleburne was one of four officers specifically mentioned in the joint resolution of the Confederate Congress that thanked the participants for the "signal victory achieved" at Richmond. Cleburne, who managed to return to duty by September 25, was reduced to brigade command on October 5. Three days later, while leading the brigade in a charge near Perryville that pierced the center of the Federal line, his horse was killed and he was painfully wounded near the ankle. Hardee reported that Cleburne "led his brigade with his usual courage and judgement, was wounded, but remained in command until the close of the day." Promoted to major general on December 20 to rank

Apparently, Cleburne took his old brigadier's uniform along with him, for this image, too, was made during the winter 1863-64 visit to Mobile. (*Confederate Veteran*, IX, p. 62)

By the time he sat for Oppenheimer, however, Cleburne was a major general, as shown in this very slight variant of an earlier pose. (Herb Peck, Jr. Collection)

from the thirteenth, Cleburne earned further prominence for his performance at Stones River.

In 1863, Cleburne distinguished himself at Chickamauga and Chattanooga. In the latter engagement, his division successfully held the northern end of Missionary Ridge. When the Confederate center and left gave way, Cleburne was assigned to cover their escape. General Braxton Bragg wrote: "...Cleburne, whose command defeated the enemy in every assault on the 25th, and who eventually charged and routed him on that day, capturing several stand of colors and several hundred prisoners, and who afterward brought up our rear with great success, again charging and routing the pursuing column at Ringgold on the 27th, is commended to the special notice of the Government."

Cleburne's resistance at Ringgold Gap earned him the thanks of the Confederate Congress: "Cleburne, and the officers and men under his command, for the victory obtained by them over superior forces of the enemy at Ringgold Gap..., by which the advance of the enemy was impeded, our wagon train and most of our artillery saved, and a large number of the enemy killed and wounded."

But many who praised him for his performance on the battlefield soon denounced him as a traitor when they learned of his proposal for restoring his diminished units to their appropriate strength. The steady depletion of the Confederate ranks prompted Cleburne to carefully prepare a paper that urged the Confederate government to arm slaves who were willing to fight in the Confederate army. Although thirteen other officers signed the proposal which was presented on January 2, 1864, General Joseph E. Johnston refused to forward it to the authorities in Richmond on the grounds that it dealt with an issue of a more political than military character. Another officer, however, saw to it that it got into the hands of President Jefferson Davis. Davis returned it with the request that it be suppressed because of the impact it would have on the general public. Had Cleburne never written the document, he, rather than Alexander P. Stewart, would undoubtedly have succeeded Lieutenant General Leonidas Polk to corps command. It is even possible that Cleburne instead of John Bell Hood would have moved up from corps command ro replace Johnston at Atlanta.

Cleburne continued to serve with the Army of Tennessee as a major general during 1864. He partici-pated in Johnston's withdrawl to the outskirts of Atlanta and in Hood's aggressive defense of that city. He accompanied Hood into Tennessee where, on November 30, he died on the battlefield of Franklin. Initially buried near Franklin, his remains were reinterred in Helena.

Known as the "Stonewall Jackson of the West," Cleburne rivaled the Virginian as a disciplinarian who managed to retain the love and confidence of his men. Although not as demonstratively religious as Jackson, Cleburne was a devoted Episcopalian. Unlike Jackson, he never married. Cleburne was one of only two foreigners to attain the rank of major general in the Confederate army.

Lawrence L. Hewitt

Buck, Irving A. *Cleburne and his Command* (Jackson, Tenn., 1959)

Purdue, Howell and Elizabeth. *Pat Cleburne. Confederate General: A Biography* (Tuscaloosa, Alabama, 1973)

As evidence of the informality of generals' observance of uniform regulations, this portrait shows Clingman with a major general's buttons, though he never rose above brigadier. (National Archives)

✶ *Thomas Lanier Clingman* ✶

Born in Huntersville, North Carolina, July 27, 1812, he served as U.S. Representative and Senator, 1843-1845 and 1847-1861, changing from unionist Whig to secessionist Democrat. Even after Abraham Lincoln's inauguration, he attended Senate sessions, withdrawing March 28 without resigning; the body expelled him, July 11.

By July, he was aide to General Joseph E. Johnston in Virginia. Previously he had witnessed Fort Sumter's fall and served as North Carolina's emissary to the Confederacy. In September, however, the Raleigh legislature did not elect him Confederate senator.

Clingman fared better with the 25th North Carolina Infantry Regiment, whose officers elected him colonel, August 13, 1861. The 25th entered national service at Wilmington, September 29. It transferred to South Carolina, November 8, and returned to Kinston just after New Berne fell. In the April reorganization, Clingman was reelected colonel.

Although he lacked military experience and education, his political prominence and Tarheel ties brought him a brigadier-generalcy, May 17, 1862, to rank from that date. His brigade in the Army of Pamlico contained the 54th and 55th North Carolina Infantry Regiments. When most troops of that army moved to Virginia for the Seven Days Battles, the disabled Clingman remained in charge of the District of Pamlico and Cape Fear. On August 18, his command was restricted to Wilmington; he was superseded there about September 3 by General Gabriel J. Rains.

Clingman then took leave. He aspired to command L. O'Bryan Branch's old brigade, but R.E. Lee politely prohibited such assignment by observing that "I think it better that General Clingman should remain in North Carolina, where he could probably be of more service than here." He was, accordingly, given the new brigade of North Carolina Infantry regiments at Wilmington, November 20. This outfit initially contained the 51st, 56th, and 61st. The 56th, however,

seemed "too good a regiment...to spare," so the "indifferent" 31st replaced it, along with the 8th, whose discipline, reported the inspector, "has been sadly neglected...; the fault is entirely with the officers." The latter two units had been captured at Roanoke Island. That disaster, plus Clingman's inexperience, tarnished the brigade throughout the war.

Its initial fight, against General John G. Foster's expedition to Goldsboro, December 17, did not enhance its reputation. Although an observer called the battleline brigadier himself "absolutely without fear," Confederate engineer Walter H. Stevens sarcastically reported finding "General Clingman's command falling back, one regiment double-quicking...from the railroad bridge to the county bridge...General Clingman...said his men would not stay at the railroad bridge, and asked me if I thought he had better cross the bridge. I thought if the men would not stand they had better cross, and told him so."

The following spring, General D.H. Hill considered that "Clingman's troops have been much demoralized, and...can only be trusted behind earthworks" as at Wilmington. The prospect of receiving them, however, made Wilmington commander Chase Whiting complain that "the importance of this place and the very limited number of troops at my command indicate that those few should be the best possible, not the worst...However, I will go to work on Clingman's Brigade and get it into shape. If it were not for some of the officers...there would be but little difference (from John R. Cooke's splendid brigade)."

Clingman spent 1863 and early 1864 traversing the tidewater between Petersburg and Savannah to counter real or rumored dangers. The 31st and 51st won glory helping repulse the assault on Battery Wagner, July 18, and all his regiments served in that redoubt during the Charleston siege. He himself commanded Wagner, July 29-August 1, but usually he superintended significant but less threatened sectors:

An early war portrait, with uniform retouched and quite possibly added entirely by an artist, this would have been taken prior to May 1862 if genuine. (Department of Archives and Manuscripts, Louisiana State University, Baton Rouge)

western James Island and especially Sullivan's Island.

Back in Virginia by 1864, he and the 51st were the only veterans to reach Petersburg before the Yankees occupied nearby Bermuda Hundred, May 5. After skirmishing north and east of town, his men joined General Robert F. Hoke's Division, May 10, and remained with it until war's end. Finally in the main war zone, Clingman was heavily engaged for the next 100 days: unsuccessfully at Second Drewry's Bluff and Second Cold Harbor, successfully at Second Ware Bottom Church, Petersburg (June 16-18), and the Crater. Cavalry drove him from Old Cold Harbor, May 31, and infantry pierced his line there, June 1, jeopardizing Lee's whole position. Though his entire staff was killed or wounded, Clingman—armed with only a fence rail—rallied his men to contain the breakthrough.

The war for Thomas Clingman virtually ended at Globe Tavern, August 19, when he was severely wounded in the leg and disabled for over seven months. Although fellow politicians urged his promotion to major general and Jefferson Davis actually considered him to succeed the slain Dodson Ramseur, Clingman was too injured even to rejoin his own brigade until after Bentonville. In hopes of commanding the post of honor in the Raleigh rearguard, the Carolinian urged army commander Johnston to "make this a Thermopylae." "I am not in the Thermopylae business," replied the senior officer, who instead retreated one last time and then capitulated. The Durham surrender included Clingman.

The U.S. Senate rejected his attempt to reclaim his seat. He thereafter practiced law, explored North Carolina's mountains, and discovered their mineral resources. Death came, November 3, 1897; he is buried in Asheville, North Carolia.

The historian of his home county called Clingman "an intrepid man of most arrogant and aggressive character, greatest self-confidence, unlimited assurance, prodigious conceit, stupendous aspiration, immense claims, more than common ability, no considerable attainments or culture, great boastfulness, and much curiosity." Yet to his adjutant, the general was a "brave, patriotic man of extraordinary mental endowments, great learning, boundless ambition; who gave up the goal of his life...to take up arms in defense of his state." Clingman unquestionably was a brave battler for Southern rights. Although his arena was the legislature, not the battlefield. An inept leader of an ineffective brigade, he never succeeded in forging a fierce fighting force. Its mixed record and his inexperience explain the reservations many of his superiors had about him. His acknowledged courage and eventual sacrifice simply could not offset his lack of military aptitude.

Richard J. Sommers

"The Career of T.L. Clingman," *Southern Historical Society Papers*, XXIV: (1896) 303-308.

Clark, Walter, *Histories of the Several Regiments and Battalions from North Carolina*, Goldsboro, 1901.

Gilbart, Clarence N., *The Public Career of Thomas L. Clingman*, M.A. thesis, University of North Carolina, 1946.

Sondley, F.A., *A History of Buncombe County*, Asheville, 1936.

A variant of an earlier pose made at the same sitting. (Medford Historical Society, Medford, Massachusetts)

Taken in 1862 at the same time and place as a photograph of his brother, General Thomas R.R. Cobb, this image shows Howell Cobb as a brigadier. (University of Georgia Library, Athens)

⋆ *Howell Cobb* ⋆

Perhaps the most famous of the Confederacy's political generals, Cobb was born on September 7, 1815, in Cherry Hill, Jefferson County, Georgia. His family stood among the state's cultural and economic elite and had played a significant role in Georgia politics for more than three decades. Educated at the University of Georgia, Cobb subsequently read law and was admitted to the bar in 1836. Marriage to Mary Ann Lamar in 1834 enhanced his already favorable position in society. Generally free from financial worry, he concentrated on politics and quickly manifested considerable ability in that field. Chosen by the legislature in 1837 to be solicitor general of Georgia's western circuit, he later served several terms as a Democrat in the United States House of Representatives and was elected speaker of that body in 1849. His support for the Compromise of 1850 cost him favor among state rights elements in Georgia, and he won the state's governorship in 1851 as the Union Party candidate. Defeated in a race for United States senator in 1854, he realized that his future depended upon reconciliation with the Democrats. He proclaimed his devotion to southern Democratic principles, won reelection to the House in 1855, and supported James Buchanan's candidacy for the Presidency in 1856. Buchanan named him secretary of the treasury in 1857, an office he held until December 10, 1860, when the growing sectional crisis prompted him to resign.

Cobb called for immediate secession, served as president of the convention that met in Montgomery, Alabama, in January 1861 to form the Southern Confederacy, and administered the oath of office to President Jefferson Davis on February 18, 1861. The Montgomery Convention functioned as the Provisional Confederate Congress for a year, and Cobb remained an influential member, however, he also sought a military position that would enable him to play an active part in the defense of the new nation. Another motive also prompted his interest in a commission: "I had three sons in the army and they were privates," he explained. "I believed I could provide for and protect them better by being in the army myself." He helped raise the 16th Georgia Infantry in the early summer of 1861 and was commissioned its colonel on July 15. The regiment reached Richmond in mid-August, shortly after the southern victory at First Manassas and while Congress remained in session. Cobb joined the 16th after Congress adjourned on August 31, placing two of his sons on his staff (a third son would soon join Cobb's Legion, commanded by Howell's brother T.R.R. Cobb). Cobb and the 16th reinforced the small army of John Bankhead Magruder at Yorktown in late October 1861.

During the balance of the year Cobb divided his time between the army and Congress and studied military manuals. Conscious of President Davis' predilection for West Pointers, he brided at criticism of what one newspaper called "Warrior Statesmen." The specter of politicians in uniform offended many veteran officers, among them Georgian Lafayette McLaws, who wrote his wife in September 1861 that "The Cobbs are coming over to the Peninsula....And (the) report says Howell will come as a Brigadier General. I do not wish to be under any politician, nor will I if it can be helped." The twin demands of military and governmental duties occupied Cobb until February 22, 1862, when legislators elected in November 1861 took over for the Provisional Congress and freed him to devote full attention to his regiment.

Cobb received promotion to brigadier general on February 13, 1862, with assignment to command the 2d Brigade of Magruder's force. Deployed for a time at Suffolk, Virginia, and Goldsboro, North Carolina, the brigade was back on the Peninsula in time to participate in the engagement at Lee's Mill (also known as Burnt Chimneys and Dam No. 1) on April 16, 1862. Magruder's report on Lee's Mill spoke of how, at a crucial juncture, Cobb "in person rallied the troops under terrific fire, and by his voice and his example entirely re-established their steadiness." Cobb himself viewed the action as proof that "political generals" could fight effectively, a belief that made all the more irritating a subsequent rumor that he had not even been on the field. Cobb's next test came on July 1 at Malvern Hill. There his brigade participated in Magruder's late-afternoon assaults and suffered about 33 per cent casualties. After the battle, Cobb saw his name linked with Magruder's in damning gossip. Mrs. Cobb informed him on July 13 of a story that he and Magruder "were *drunk* upon the battlefield." Newspapers in Macon and Milledgeville, Georgia, repeated this charge, which was without foundation but caused Cobb great anguish.

Cobb's last service with the Army of Northern Virginia came in the fall of 1862. Attached to McLaws' Division, his brigade missed Second Manassas but crossed the Potomac as part of Lee's raid into Maryland in September. Accompanying Stonewall Jackson's wing to Harpers Ferry, Cobb received orders from McLaws on September 14 to hasten to Crampton's Gap in the South Mountain range and "Hold the Gap, if it costs the life of every man in (your) command." Cobb reached South Mountain to find Federals pressing heavily against Confederate defenders. Before long, his men broke and fled down the western slope of the mountain. McLaws and Jeb Stuart arrived to find Cobb seemingly helpless amid the chaos. Heros Von Borcke, Stuart's Prussian aide and a man sometimes given to hyperbole, later reconstructed Cobb's frantic greeting: "Dismount, gentlemen, dismount, if your lives are dear to you! The enemy is within fifty yards of us, I am expecting their attack every minute. Oh, my dear Stuart, that I should live to experience such a disaster. What can be done? What can save us?" McLaws and others criticized Cobb for his conduct at South Mountain (McLaws

eventually withdrew his harsher words). Cobb himself, sensing that Crampton's Gap foreclosed opportunities for advancement within Lee's army and worried about his family and property, asked for transfer to some theater closer to Georgia.

In truth, Cobb was illsuited for hard campaigning. Nearing fifty years old and far overweight (one newspaper described him as "fat, pussy, round-faced, jolly looking fellow"), he suffered from the rigors of the field. He also failed to inspire confidence and respect among his men, one of whom, E.H. Sutton of the 24th Georgia, called him a "whipped cur" full of "incompetency." Lee made no attempt to retain Cobb, and on November 11, 1862, he was named head of the Military District of Middle Florida. Thus began a career as a military administrator for which Cobb was well suited, and which would extend to the end of the war. With headquarters at Quincy, Florida, Cobb oversaw efforts to block Federal penetration of the Apalachicola River and to protect Confederate salt works at St. Marks.

Promoted to major general on September 19, 1863, to rank from September 9, he reluctantly accepted a transfer to Atlanta to organize a force known first as the State Troops and later as the Georgia State Guard. The goal was to create units for use strictly in the defense of the state, then threatened by William S. Rosecrans' Army of the Cumberland near Chattanooga. Five unhappy months ensued, during which Cobb and Governor Joseph E. Brown frequently clashed, before the Guard was abolished in February 1864. Two months of inactivity ended on April 5, when Cobb was ordered to Macon to establish headquarters for the new Georgia Reserve Force. Designed to act as a "minute man" corps to cope with local emergencies, the Reserve Force was created by legislation Cobb had helped to draft. Cobb and Governor Brown quarreled almost immediately over the question of whether recruiting for the Reserve Force should take precedence over that for the state militia. Against this background of bureaucratic wrangling, Cobb did his best to harass W.T. Sherman's invading army. A high point came on July 30, 1864, when a mixed force of militia and reserves won a skirmish with raiders under Federal General George Stoneman near Macon. Cobb surrendered to James H. Wilson at Macon on April 20, 1865.

Arrested shortly after his surrender, Cobb received a parole from President Andrew Johnson while on his way to prison. In the fall of 1865 he opened a law practice in Macon; income from that venture, together with profit from his remaining agricultural holdings, kept him financially solvent. An adamant opponent of Republican Reconstruction, he survived until October 9, 1868, when, in the presence of his wife and one daughter, he fell dead in the lobby of the Fifth Avenue Hotel in New York. His remains were shipped to Athens, Georgia, for burial in Oconee Hill Cemetery.

Gary W. Gallagher.